AF424566

STEEL DECKS AND GLASS CEILINGS

STEEL DECKS
AND
GLASS CEILINGS

A NAVY OFFICER'S MEMOIR

JIM JEWELL

JRJ Publisher

Steel Decks and Glass Ceilings: A Navy Officer's Memoir
2022 © Jim Jewell

All rights reserved. No part of this book may be reproduced or transmitted in any form or by any means, electronic or mechanical, including photocopying, recording, or any information storage and retrieval system, without permission in writing from the publisher.

Design by Rudy Ramos

ISBN: 979-8-9860897-0-6 (trade paper)
ISBN: 979-8-9860897-1-3 (ebook)

Printed in the United States of America

Table of Contents

Dedication

Lieutenant George Sitton

One guy who was a critical part to making the deployment a success was First Lieutenant George Sitton. He was an old salt, the epitome of the old Navy on the deck plates.

George was an officer, but he remained a "bosun" at heart. He handled cranes, davits, rigging, line handling, excelling at every facet of deck seamanship with incredible talent. He also could tell sea stories with the best of sea dogs, primarily because he lived them.

He became a good friend. He provided me with an escape to our shared world of old Navy. During this deployment and throughout our tours aboard Yosemite, George and I shared deck, boat, crane, and amphibious stories from our time at sea, especially on the West Coast. We knew many mutual shipmates from the past in deck departments and Boat Master Units. Our shared experience of being first lieutenants gave us a common ground for a break from the rigors we faced.

George and I kept in touch long after we left the ship. George passed away in 2006 in Tyler, Texas at age 59, way too early.

I thought it was only proper to dedicate this book to George.

Yosemite's Track during 1983-1984 Deployment to Indian Ocean

The following charts show Yosemite's track overall and on each of the seas she sailed.

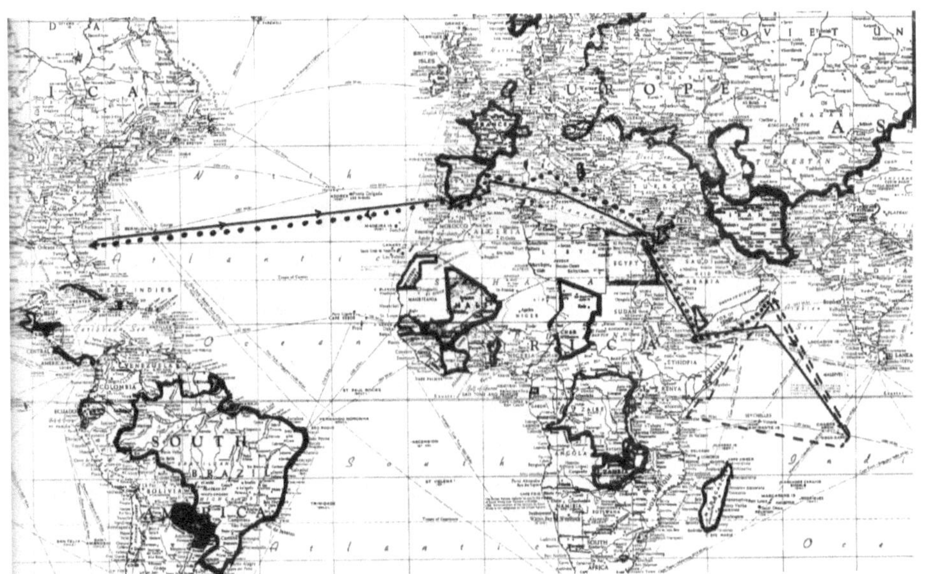

Chart with *Yosemite's* track from the ship's cruise book.

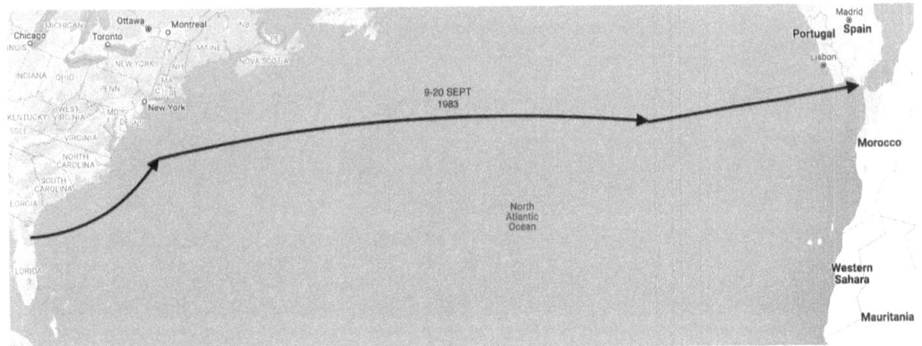

Chart with *Yosemite's* track east from Mayport, Florida to Rota, Spain, and west on return trip from Rota to Mayport.

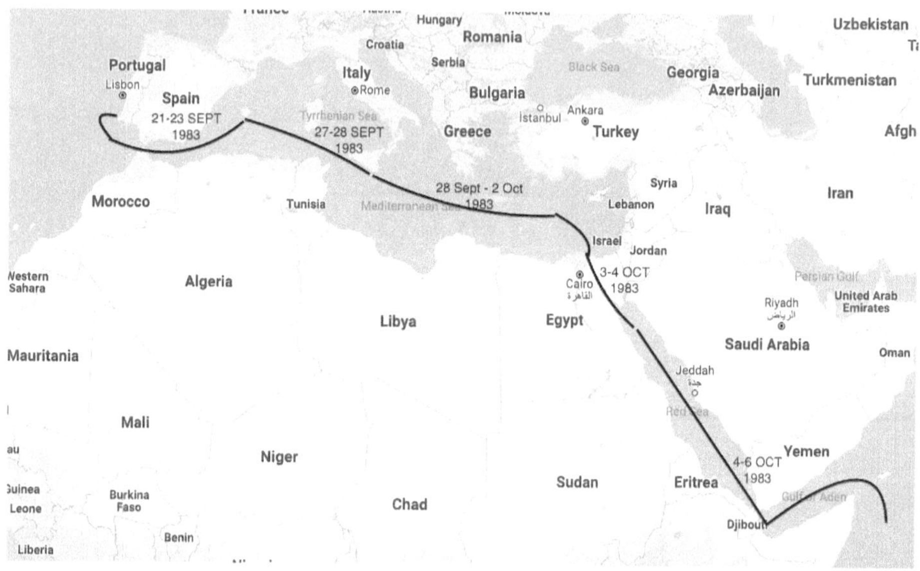

Chart with Yosemite's track east from Rota, Spain to the Gulf of Aden with stops at Palma de Majorca, Naval Air Station Sigonella, Sicily, and Port Said, Egypt.

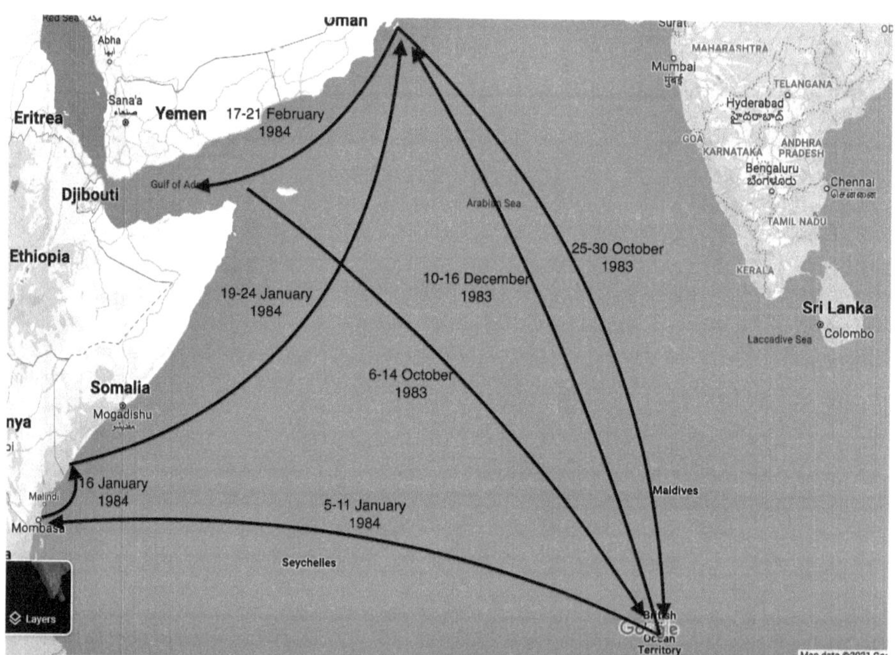

Chart with Yosemite's track east from Gulf of Aden to Diego Garcia, on to Masirah, Oman, return to Diego Garcia, to Mombasa, Kenya, Chismayo, Somalia, return to Masirah, and eastward bound to Gulf of Aden while on journey home.

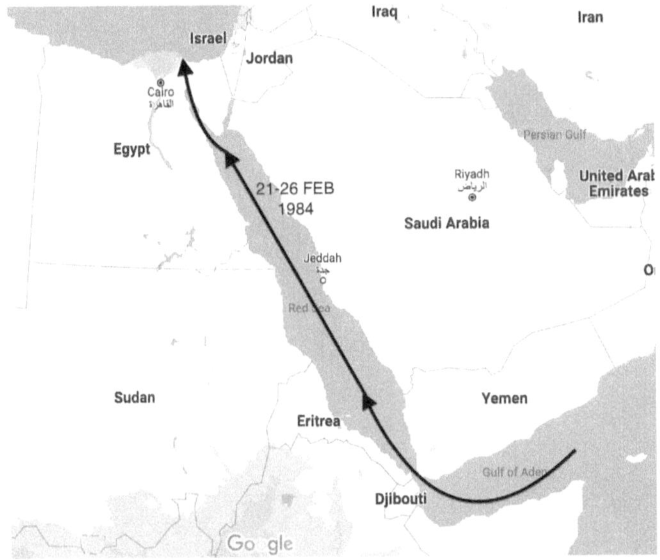

Chart with *Yosemite's* track east Gulf of Aden to Naples, Italy, and Rota, Spain.

Western track from Port Said, Egypt, to Naples, Italy, to Rota, Spain, 26 February to 8 March 1984

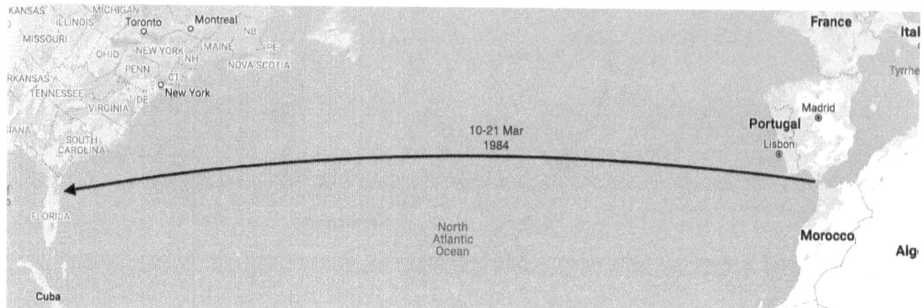

Western track from Rota, Spain to Mayport. FL, 9-21 March 1984

Prologue

"Our will is to keep the torch of freedom burning for all. To this solemn purpose, we call upon the young, the brave, the strong, and the free. Heed my call. Come to the sea. Come sail with me."
RearAdmiral John Paul Jones (1747-1792)

This is a sea story,

A sea story is a recollection of a mariner. The Naval Air and the Submarine forces, part of the Navy, also call their narrations sea stories, but that is a misnomer. Their tales should be called air stories or underwater stories, but those who don't drive ships like to identify themselves with the Navy, hence: sea stories.

Sea stories can even be about landlubbers but told by a seafarer. The Army has war stories. I am not sure what the Air Force call their stories (air stories?) The Marines have to be confused as to what they call their stories since they long ago expanded from their mission of extending military force from ships at sea.

A sea story contains a lot of truth and a bit of fiction. All sea stories can be preceded by the statement, "This is no bullshit!"

A sea story is a tale told to other seamen usually with drinks at a bar.

This sea story is written by an old sea dog. That old sea dog is me.

• • •

Women now have been integrated into the Surface Navy. They are on those steel decks in full force. When this sea story occurred, integrating women into the complement of Navy ships was just beginning. The female officers and enlisted aboard the ship on which I was the executive officer were the first to spend extended out of port time at sea as part of the ship's complement. They proved they belonged. Those women are the real heroes…er, heroines, in this sea story.

This sea story is told from my perspective as the executive officer of the *USS Yosemite (AD 19)*.

Women have long been a part of US Navy history. But the move toward equality and full opportunity for women in all facets of our Navy began after I was commissioned in 1968. The Navy and the world were changing.

In 1972, the pilot program for assignment of officers and enlisted women to ships was initiated on board *USS Sanctuary* (AH 17).

In 1976, 81 women became midshipmen at the United States Naval Academy.

In 1978, Congress approved a change to Title 10 USC Section 6015 to permit the Navy to assign women to sea duty billets on support and noncombatant ships. The Surface Warfare community was opened to women that year as well. In 1979, the first woman obtained her Surface Warfare Officer (SWO) qualification.

Also in 1979, officers and enlisted women began to be assigned to Navy ships. The ships were mostly tenders or repair ships, which had limited time at sea. That year, Ensign (ENS) Deborah A. Loewer who had been at the top of her class at the Navy's Surface Warfare Officer School after receiving her commission from Officer Candidate School (OCS) in Newport, R.I. was one of the first women to report aboard the *USS Yosemite (AD 19)*. She later earned her two stars and served as Vice Commander, Military Sealift Command.

In 1980, 54 female midshipmen in that first class graduated and were commissioned from the Naval Academy.

The women and men aboard *Yosemite* during her 1983-1984 deployment led the way proving women belonged at sea.

My story includes my unfulfilled quest for command at sea and how I dealt with my challenges.

To paraphrase my longtime friend and shipmate JD Waits from our time on the *USS Okinawa* (LPH 3):

"This is my story, and I'm sticking to it."

Chapter 1: Last Chance

August 1983: San Diego, Tennessee, and Florida

It was Tuesday, August 9, 1983.

After my marriage and ten-day honeymoon, followed by a flight from San Diego to Nashville, I picked up my car at my parents' home in Lebanon, Tennessee and drove to Chattanooga to spend the night with my sister and her family on Signal Mountain. The next morning, I threw my suitcase into the back, hugged my sister, Martha Duff, good-bye and settled into the driver's seat of my Mazda Rx7.

It was a 500-plus mile trip from Signal Mountain, Tennessee to Jacksonville, Florida and Naval Station, Mayport. With a lunch break, the drive would take nine, maybe ten hours. I hoped to make it in time to get a haircut at the Naval base barber shop. I had not had a haircut since leaving Newport, Rhode Island in mid-June. It would not be good form for an executive officer (XO) to report aboard his new ship looking shaggy. I wanted to make a good first impression, especially to the commanding officer (CO).

I was looking forward to the drive. It would be the first time since late May that I had the time to put in serious thought about my new job.

It was not a job I particularly wanted.

As I pulled out of the driveway and maneuvered down the switchbacks of Tennessee 127, I calculated lunch time and place. If all went well through Atlanta, I could make Cordele, Georgia for lunch. That would make it tight for getting a haircut. I wished I had called to see when the Navy Exchange barber shop closed. I guessed 1600 or 1700.

It was a long, mostly flat and straight stretch once I reached I-75 on the south side of Chattanooga, straight south through Georgia with only Atlanta traffic being a possible delay, and straight east to Jacksonville on

I-10. I reached over and grabbed the cassette rack from the shotgun seat. I found one of my favorites, Dave Loggins' "Apprentice" album.

I put the cassette in the stereo player in the center of the console and kicked the speed up to 75. I figured that speed was the maximum to keep me from being stopped by the highway patrol.

• • •

I mused while listening and driving. I remained dubious about my orders. I had hoped to be the XO of a large amphibious ship or less likely, a cruiser. They were commander billets and most attractive for advancement. Even more to my liking, I would be going to sea.

When I was accepted for returning to active duty back in 1972, my goal was to spend all my tours on a ship and to become a commanding officer. That was a naïve idea, impossible in today's Navy where promotion requires obtaining non-at-sea skills ashore. Receiving a promotion can be a bureaucratic, and sometimes political thing. I wanted to be a mariner at sea, possibly for the rest of my life. Even though I was selected for commander after being passed over once, I was shocked when my detailer told me I had not been selected to be an executive officer.

I was the Weapons Officer, a.k.a. First Lieutenant, on board the *USS Okinawa (LPH 3)* and would be rotating to a new assignment within the next six months, which I hoped would be as an XO, a requirement to be screened for command at sea. Not knowing what to do, I placed a call to Captain (CAPT) Ted Fenno, the head of Surface Warfare Officer (SWO) detailing branch (where "detailers" assign officers to their next tours). Ted had been the XO of the *USS Stephen B. Luce (DLG 7)* when I had returned to active duty in 1972 after two years as the sports editor of *The Watertown (NY) Daily Times*. The

Weapons Officer on the
USS Okinawa

Luce XO and CO, Commandeer (CDR) Richard Butts, had appreciated my leadership as Anti-Submarine Warfare (ASW) officer and my ship-driving ability. I became the sea detail, general quarters, and refueling Officer of the Deck (OOD) before I left for the Department Head course at Destroyer School.

My call was transferred to CAPT Fenno.

"Congratulations, XO," Fenno greeted me.

Confused, I responded, "But Captain, my detailer just told me I hadn't been selected for exec. I was calling you to find out what you recommend I do next."

There were a few seconds of quiet. Then Fenno said, "Jim, hang on to the phone. I need to do some checking on this."

The phone went silent for over ten minutes. CAPT Fenno came back on line.

"Jim, I apologize. There has been some confusion here. You have been selected for XO. Your detailer will call you in the next few days to tell you what ship and when you will report."

More than grateful, I signed off with, "Thanks, Captain."

As I pulled onto the interstate, I reviewed the possibilities. Either Fenno or the detailer had read the selection notice wrong. I hoped and believed it was the detailer who was wrong. CAPT Fenno would have been involved with the selection process. I couldn't figure out how the detailer could have screwed up so badly.

Regardless, I didn't think it was a good omen.

My suspicions were confirmed two weeks later when I received the next call from my detailer. "Congratulations. You have been assigned as XO of the *USS Yosemite.*"

"You're kidding," I almost shouted, "A tender? Is there any chance we could change it to a cruiser or amphib?"

"No," the detailer replied, "All the assignments are locked in."

• • •

Destroyer and submarine tenders were repair ships built to provide repair and maintenance services to combatants near the area of operations. They were part of the service force, which also included oilers, ammunition ships, cargo ships, and a combination of the latter three. Up to my *Yosemite* assignment, I had served on five destroyers and five amphibious ships, all combatants. As the XO of a Navy unit, I also had ridden two USNS ships that carried Korean troops to Vietnam and back. I appreciated the services of tenders, but I did not want to be assigned to one, especially as XO. I am not disappointed I was not on a carrier.

• • •

All the possible options rushed into my mind. I had never considered what I might do if I wasn't selected or didn't get a combatant ship. I had roughly six years left before I would complete my active duty service and be eligible for a retirement pension. I wanted to achieve my goal to be a CO. I had qualified for command at sea. But the XO tour was a critical and necessary step for selection. Being on a destroyer tender that stayed pier side in its homeport was not going to help.

Perplexed, I asked the detailer to speak to CAPT Fenno once more.

"Captain, my detailer told me I have been assigned as the *Yosemite* XO. I don't really want to spend my last sea tour tied up to a pier. I came back in the Navy to spend all of my career on ships at sea. A tender by a pier wasn't what I had in mind."

"I understand, Jim," the captain replied, "but that's the only assignment we have for you. And tenders now deploy." He hesitated and continued, "The *Yosemite* is the best tender on the East Coast. Before you make any decisions, why don't you call up Admiral Butts? He'll give you his honest opinion."

Of all the CO's I had served under, Admiral Butts was one of the best. When he was a commander and CO of the *Luce,* we became friends. I called, and Admiral Butts was enthusiastic about the *Yosemite.* He even said the tender would deploy in the fall.

• • •

After the two calls, I reconsidered. Even though she was a tender, *Yosemite* had always had a great reputation. I remembered when I was on ships homeported in Newport, I would find ways to take our work to *Yosemite,* the Cruiser Destroyer Force, Atlantic Fleet (CRUDESLANT) flagship at the time, rather than our "parent tender." *Yosemite's* repair work was far superior.

If I declined, I would have to spend the next six years in shore tours. I had never liked the shore establishment. My Navy was at sea. If I was lucky, I would have a good tour on *Yosemite* and get selected for command. That would get me close to the retirement requirement of twenty years of active duty. It wasn't likely, but I knew this was my last and only chance.

I confirmed with my detailer that I accepted the assignment to *Yosemite.* Soon, I found out the deployment would be in September, almost seven months to the Indian Ocean shortly after I would report aboard.

It wasn't until a couple of weeks later, in February, I began to think about the prospect of having women as part of the crew. In the previous fall in San Diego, the married XO of the *Prairie* was relieved for cause after having an affair with his female operations officer. When I heard the news, I thought the *Prairie* XO was just plain stupid. Even though the assignment would have no effect on whether I married Maureen or not – after all, I believed I had found the woman I wanted to be with for the rest of my life – I was glad I would marry 12 days before reporting aboard the tender.

It was going to be tough enough to be XO with women officers and crew. Being single would be like having a target on my back. I had learned from my detailer that the guy who would be CO almost didn't accept me for XO. CAPT Francis J. Boyle was rightfully concerned about the problems a single commander would have as executive officer. He relented and accepted me for the job when he learned I was getting married before reporting aboard.

I also had extremely limited experience with women in the navy. While on the *Anchorage* in San Diego, I once saw a female deck seaman working on a tugboat as the tug escorted us as we stood out of the channel. My only thought about that seaman was that she was different.

When I was the senior Naval officer in the Texas A&M Naval Reserve Officer Training (NROTC) Unit, I worked with Lieutenant (LT) Carolyn Prevatte who was there primarily to act as the coordinator for women in our program as the Aggie Corps of Cadets had just allowed women into the corps. Carolyn was intelligent, professional, and dedicated. It was a pleasure to work with her.

On a Saturday in 1979 when I stayed at the Admiral Kidd Naval base Bachelor Officer's Quarters (BOQ) while attending the Tactical Action Officer (TAO) course in San Diego, I went out to the pool in the central area to relax and take in some rays. I overheard two women junior officers nearby discussing some new policy. I was glad they were dealing with that bureaucratic kind of stuff, which I disliked doing myself.

That's it. I had been around only four women in the Navy in my 15 years of service and had only substantive time with one of them.

I was sailing into unknown waters.

• • •

As I was leaving the USS *Okinawa (LPH 3)* in May 1983 for Prospective Executive Officer (PXO) Training course in Newport, Rhode Island, I went to the captain's cabin to say farewell to CAPT Roger Newman. He had been one of the better COs in my career. We had become good friends as well as golfing partners. After shaking hands and thanking each other for working together through a successful major overhaul and the follow-on operations, Roger turned serious.

"Jim, you know XO is different from all of the other billets you've had," Roger began.

I had been XO as a Lieutenant Junior Grade (LTJG) on a transport unit overseeing Korean troops being transported to and from Vietnam on Military Sealift Command (MSC) ships, and I had been the emergency XO of the *USS Cayuga (LST 1186)* for almost three months, a most successful and challenging tour, albeit short. I had been given a great amount of advice on being a full tour executive officer and had been told many sea stories. I thought I understood what my role would entail. Roger made it crystal clear.

"You know when you become XO, your most important job is to support the captain," he explained, "It doesn't matter what you think about his decisions, if you don't like his actions, or even if you don't like him. Your job is to support him, to do anything to make him successful, to be his voice, his mirror reflection. That is your primary job."

It was rather sobering. I had been thinking about Roger's admonition off and on since I began this journey to *Yosemite*. I think I adhered well to Roger's advice with the exception of one instance.

• • •

My extremely limited experience with women in the Navy, enlisted or officer, produced a great deal of concern for me while I was assigned to the one-month Prospective Executive Officer (PXO) Course at Destroyer School in Newport, Rhode Island.

When I discovered there was no training for being responsible for women on ships, I asked to be sent to Temporary Additional Duty (TAD) in the last week of that training to Washington, D.C. and Norfolk to learn from those in charge of the Women In Ships program and from standing XOs on ships with women on board. The last week of the XO program was for specific types of ships to which the PXOs would be assigned.

There was no specific training for tenders. I was supposed to attend the week of training for service force ships, unrelated to being the XO of a repair ship almost forty years old, and certainly no training for dealing with women as part of the crew.

When the Destroyer School command refused to send me TAD, I was granted a week's leave so I could find out what I could on my own nickel. After arriving in Norfolk, I was unable to schedule an appointment with the Women In Ship's coordinator in D.C. Finally, in a telephone conversation, she and I discussed what I should expect. She told me to read the regulations. Duh! There was no real revealing information.

I was able to meet with one XO, CAPT Livingston on the *USS Yellowstone (AD 41)*, a submarine tender. I left that hour's discussion disillusioned. In my opinion, CAPT Livingston was treating the women in his crew like second-class citizens.

All I knew about women at sea wouldn't fill up a thimble. My only thoughts were to never put myself in a difficult situation, intended or not, and to treat the women in my command as equally as possible.

I just hoped my new commanding officer felt the same and would be able to give me guidance.

As I drove, I thought of an irony. While in Officer Candidate School (OCS), I completed my preference card for my first assignment to be Combat Information Center (CIC) Officer on a destroyer homeported in Mayport, Florida. I had received orders for exactly that, but on Thursday, January 31, 1968, two days before I was to be commissioned, I received new orders to report to ASW School in Key West and report to the *USS Hawkins (DD 873)* homeported in Newport, Rhode Island. At least my desire to be stationed in Mayport had been granted, only 16 years later.

The traffic through Atlanta had been slow. I decided to skip lunch and just refuel with the hope of arriving in Mayport in time for that haircut. As I turned off I-75 onto I-10 East, I quit thinking about anything except driving and directions.

I made it to the base in good time, but the exchange was closed. Not wanting to report aboard and deal with meeting folks that night, I checked into the Bachelor Officers Quarters (BOQ) to get some sleep and hopefully get a haircut before reporting aboard the next morning.

When I awoke the next morning, the front desk told me the exchange barbershop did not open until ten. So around 0830, knowing morning quarters and officer's call would be completed, I checked out of the BOQ, drove to *Yosemite's* berth and reported aboard.

My adventure was about to begin. I knew it would be my last chance to stay at sea.

USS Yosemite

Chapter 2: Relieving the Watch

I was saluted when I crossed the brow and reported aboard to the quarterdeck watch. As the Officer on Deck (OOD) called the XO and the captain, the messenger of the watch immediately escorted me up to the 01 Level, starboard side, just aft of the wardroom to the Executive Officer's office and stateroom. Commander (CDR) Brian Sheffield rose to meet me. Brian was an affable, slightly chubby man with thinning red hair.

Earlier, I had learned Brian and the previous CO, CAPT Tim Roberts were Training and Administration of Reserves officers (TAR's). A TAR officer was primarily responsible for being active duty administrators of reserve programs. Their duty stations alternated between reserve commands and non-reserve assignments, occasionally on at-sea duty.

In 1972 when I had requested return to active duty while I was the sports editor of the *Watertown (NY) Daily Times,* my Bureau of Personnel (BUPERS) liaison had recommended I go TAR. Such a decision would almost guarantee my acceptance.

I wanted to go back to sea, not administer reserves. I wasn't all that fond of the Naval Reserve. Getting accepted for returning to active duty as a surface warfare officer was a much tougher proposition. In large part because CAPT Max Lasell, the CO of my first ship, *USS Hawkins (DD 873),* made a special presentation on my behalf before the acceptance board, I was one of six accepted to return to active duty as a SWO.

Having spent a year in reserves after flunking out of Vanderbilt and losing my NROTC scholarship, and almost two years as an officer in the Watertown, New York Reserve Unit, I was not overly enthusiastic about the TAR program. I realized that was a prejudice I had to overcome. Regardless, I was genuinely relieved when I learned CAPT Boyle was not a TAR, and in fact, a successful surface warfare officer who had been the Senior Examiner of the Atlantic's Propulsion Examining Board (PEB), and before reporting to *Yosemite*, had been the chief staff officer for Commander, Destroyer Squadron Two.

Brian laid out the relieving process schedule for me. It would be short. Brian needed to take off for leave and his new duty station by the following Tuesday, giving us only two working days to complete the relieving process. Since we were in our homeport, he gave me the stateroom forward, an extension of the XO's cabin. Brian would be coming to the ship from his home for the duration of his time on board.

I was fine with the short relief process. I hated long reliefs, which many relieving XO's, or any officer for any billet, used to cover their act and to validate anything wrong that had happened on the previous watch. I preferred a short meeting with subordinates and an inspection of spaces. If there was anything wrong, unless it was egregious or possibly criminal, I was inclined to fix it later rather than shift the blame back to the previous regime. This time, I had two full working days and the weekend to be briefed by seven department heads and five others in charge of special programs.

First, I had to meet the CO and afterwards spend most of that first working day with Brian getting the lowdown on the state of the ship.

Brian escorted me up the flight of "stairs" to the captain's cabin. They were located on "Times Square," an immaculately clean and polished landing area just outside my new office. Even though all stairs were called "ladders" in the Navy, this "ladder" going up to the 02 level and the captain's cabin were "stairs" in the truest sense of the word, immaculate and polished to the Nth degree.

Brian introduced me to CAPT Boyle and left us alone. The ten minutes were polite, exploratory, and a bit guarded on both sides I thought. I assured the captain my primary function was to support and echo the policies and philosophy of my commanding officer. Leaving, I sensed CAPT Boyle had been guardedly succinct. He struck me as old school Navy and a stickler for protocol. I was fine with that. In fact, I preferred it.

CAPT Boyle's primary concern was getting the ship ready for the deployment. That jived with what I considered most important. The question of women on board did not come up in that first short meeting.

At least he accepted my explanation for needing a haircut. Immediately after that meeting, I went to the ship's barbershop and got a Navy regulation haircut. I felt better.

The briefings from department heads, special programs, and the command master chief were short. I initially was pleased with the professionalism of the department head officers.

The deck and engineering department heads were Limited Duty Officers (LDOs). I had the greatest respect for these former-enlisted officers. I came to rely upon both LT George Sitton, the First Lieutenant, and LT Ken Clausen, the Chief Engineer (CHENG), especially when it came to ship operations.

CDR Tim Allega was obviously a very capable Supply Department head. I assessed his ability to run a good supply department as superb. CDR Ed Wicklander, Repair Department head, was an Engineer Duty Officer (EDO). Ed was excellent at leading a repair organization.

The Supply and Repair departments were almost separate fiefdoms that did not exist on a combatant ship. These two departments were headed by commanders who were senior to me, but not of the line, i.e., authorized to command a ship. I recognized they would be pretty much independent except when I would have to demonstrate who was in charge. Repair certainly was different from my previous experience. Ed had a straight line to the captain, bypassing the XO. I wondered how that would work, particularly while on deployment.

LT Steve Strzemienski, a TAR, ran the Weapons Department. He struck me as a superb choice. Although a TAR, he had qualified as a SWO, and our interview revealed he was more than just competent.

Admin was run by another but more junior LDO, Ensign (ENS) Mike Jackson. This department was the right hand of any XO. Mike and his lead yeoman, Yeoman Chief Petty Officer (YNC), Lucy Gwinner, made me comfortable knowing they would have a personal as well as professional positive relationship with me.

As Operations Officer, LT Kathy Rondeau, was the only female department head. Operations were not as complicated as on a combatant but still a challenge. I was not overly concerned. Kathy demonstrated she had a good grasp of her department and was a sharp, responsible officer.

Master Chief Joe Weaver was an old salt and the Command Master Chief. He was the captain and exec's link to the enlisted. With Master

Chief Weaver being an old boatswain's mate, I understood the "Navy way" would be at the heart of his unique position between the crew and the command.

The Dental Department was run by CDR Bruce Janek. I got a quick medical department briefing from the Corpsman Chief Petty Officer (HMC) Charlie Benda. The new medical officer, LT Frank Kerrigan had reported aboard a day or two before me. These two departments also were fairly independent. I knew I would have to pay attention to their military responsibilities, but otherwise their departments were running smoothly.

I spent Saturday and Sunday settling into my XO cabin, the office and the adjoining stateroom forward. The office was roughly 15 feet in depth and width. There was a couch on the after bulkhead and a side chair next to my large desk on the exterior bulkhead, which had a small porthole above the chair. Behind my desk was a floor-to-overhead built-in bookcase. The entrance door was off the large area called "Times Square" with that ladder leading up to the next level and the captain's in-port cabin. The top half of the door had a windowpane with blinds that I don't remember ever being open.

Forward of the office was a small head. The door to the shower was inboard and forward of my desk. The other entrance was straight forward into my cabin. The toilet was next to the outboard bulkhead, and the shower was on the inboard bulkhead. Inboard of the door to my cabin was the small sink with a mirrored medicine cabinet, which one could see from the office if the after door was open.

The stateroom was narrow, perhaps eight feet wide due to the closet and cabinets for my clothes. The single bunk was against the exterior bulkhead with a porthole. For Navy ship berthing, it was luxurious.

• • •

In addition to determining what I needed in office and personal supplies, I researched other aspects of becoming the XO, like checking instructions and ensuring I understood the Surface Forces, Atlantic Fleet (SURFLANT) policy on substance abuse. I also began a rudimentary "command tickler" where I would have a list of all important command functions and requirements well in advance of when they would occur.

• • •

Saturday evening, the wardroom held a traditional "Hail and Farewell" party at CDR Janek's home. I met Frank and Jan Kerrigan for the first time. Both doctors had recently received their medical degrees from the University of Chicago. While Frank was taking over the Medical Department, Jan was assigned to the base clinic.

Sunday evening, I dined with the captain, his wife Mary Ellen, and their young son, Sean.

Monday continued with briefs from all of the special programs. Tuesday was nearly all about relieving CDR Sheffield. The two of us signed an endless pile of papers transferring duties and responsibilities from the old XO to the new one. The two of us had little discussion about the women aboard. Brian briefed me on some special rules such as any enlisted woman becoming pregnant was to be immediately transferred to a shore command on TAD.

We took the papers to CAPT Boyle who made it all official by signing his agreement to the transfer of responsibility. CDR Sheffield departed the ship at 1500.

I was officially the executive officer of the *USS Yosemite (AD 19)*.

Chapter 3: Preparing for Getting Underway

August, September 1983: Mayport, Florida

Once in the saddle, I began to get a better picture of what was facing me.

CAPT Boyle and I talked at length to come to an understanding as to how I was going to support him.

I have a yellow sheet of lined paper where I listed my goals and concerns for being the ship's XO, which I used as my talking paper for my discussions with CAPT Boyle:

Clear with the CO:

Schedule meetings for AOM (in the military, AOM is the acronym for All Officers Meeting), *Chiefs, First Class Petty Officers, Junior Officers, Divisions*

Meeting content: my dislike of meetings, will hold to absolute minimum, expect maximum attendance.

Other important points/goals:

1. *Critical exception for meetings: PB4T* (Planning Board for Training) *- make it meaningful.*
2. *Briefings, a necessary evil, each major evolution, especially seamanship; some of the best are informal.*
3. *Quarters, 8 O'clock Reports: keep them brief, inspections (ensure all hands know they are responsible).*
4. *Personal meetings: open door policy.*
5. *Accusations: accuser must accompany accused.*
6. *Closed door or sign on door with locator notice of where I am.*
7. *Messing and Berthing Inspections: do not fail to hold them daily.*
8. *Zone Material Inspections*

My important points and MO:
1. *Cleanliness*
2. *Safety*
3. *Paint*
4. *Liberty*
5. *At sea hours*
6. *Females*
7. *Source documents*
8. *Leave*
9. *Notes*
10. *Memos*

The opening discussions between the CO and me were pretty easy. I made sure to see the captain at least three if not four times a day, not counting his afternoon departure. Except for unusual circumstances, I did not leave the ship before the CO departed: bad form for an exec to do otherwise. We shared our ideas on the approach to running a ship. It was old Navy, correct and by the book. We both believed in good order and discipline as paramount for a ship to run well. Early on, we agreed the women on board should, as much as possible, be treated just like the male sailors.

Problems began to arise, but not just because the women were there. *Yosemite* normally had 760 enlisted, 65 chief petty officers (CPO's), and 44 officers. The ship was deploying with over 900 on board. Instead of 65 CPO's, there were 90. In addition, two of these chiefs were female. A separate and private compartment adjacent to the chief quarters had to be constructed. The 106 female enlisted were berthed in one separate compartment off of the main deck, port side. There appeared to be no problems with the berthing except I was not pleased with the sanitation of the heads and the overall cleanliness and neatness of the compartment. That also was true of most of the ship's berthing areas and heads.

I called BUPERS to voice my complaint of too many personnel aboard compared to the documented "ship's complement" numbers. I was informed the Navy was very strict about adhering to the ship's complement for combatants, a congressional requirement, but frequently "hid" extra personnel, especially in critical ratings aboard tenders to have a ready supply of those personnel in an emergency manning requirement for a combatant. I did not like varying from the rules but recognized I was stuck with the problem of too many sailors and would have to live with it.

• • •

It became apparent there was another problem as serious as having women on board. The problem was having a large percentage of the crew with no deployment experience.

Of the 90 chiefs, only 13 previously had been on a deployment. Before the new approach of sending the tenders to forward areas of operation like the Mediterranean and Indian Oceans, the tenders sat at their homeport piers, getting underway for one day each year and coming back to their pier but swapping which side (port or starboard) faced the pier for the next year. Therefore, repair personnel usually shuffled tours of duty from Ship Intermediate Maintenance Activity (SIMA) to the tender in that particular port. Tenders were considered "Class B" sea duty, which meant repair personnel would get credit for sea duty without ever actually going to sea. It was not much more than shore duty.

But not now. These 77 repair chiefs were really going to sea along with the remaining chiefs who were there for the ship's operation and had deployed before. At that time, *Yosemite* and other tenders were designated "Class B" sea duty and ship's company did not draw "Sea Pay" for when the ship was actually at sea. For example, I would have received $260/month for those six-and-a-half months deployed, but because my ship was "Class B" sea duty, I received nothing extra.

Many of the chiefs and their wives panicked. The chiefs did not know what they were going to do being away from their families. The wives (none of the female CPOs on the ship were married) were even more alarmed. They had no clue as to how to deal with the Navy, how to set up the family finances, or take on the family tasks that had been the bailiwick of the husband. Many of the wives were raising hell about their husbands being away on a ship with women in the crew.

One chief had organized a group to establish a short-wave radio station so the chiefs' mess could communicate frequently with their wives. This, of course, was a major threat to classified information, especially the location of the tender. Shortly after we got underway, we cut that off as soon as we discovered the chief's operation.

There were financial arrangements to consider as well, especially for the majority of the crew who had never deployed before. Dina Weaver, the ship's Ombudsman, informed me of Melody, the wife of a chief, who had told Dina the chief had not set up any allotments to go to Melody. That meant all the chief's pay would come to him on the ship. None would go to pay any bills, and Melody and the family would have no income except for what the chief mailed her. (Mail from a Navy ship deployed to the Indian Ocean can take weeks). I called Chaplain Poe who contacted Navy Relief and the Disbursing Officer. Through the effort of everyone involved, an allotment would be coming out of the chief's pay to cover Melody's financial needs through the deployment.

Of course, all such problems were channeled to the XO, me. The old seaman in me kept relying on common sense to handle most of these problems I had not confronted previously. There were no textbook answers. Confronting these problems coincided with running a ship of 900 personnel and getting the ship ready to leave home port for more than half a year.

I was sailing into unknown seas once more.

For many years, I had said getting underway for deployment was great because when the command to "let go all lines" was executed, it meant that all phone lines, along with shore power, steam lines, and of course, mooring lines, would no longer be available for telephone calls (with the technological advancement of satellites and mobile phones, this is no longer true).

The new Navy had many ways to try and help out dependent spouses. When I became a part of the Navy in the 60's, there was a tried-and-true refrain "If the Navy had wanted you to have a wife, they would have issued you one with your seabag." This no longer rang true. Navy Relief was a source for aid and financial assistance for wives (or husbands) left behind on deployment. The Ombudsman Program was created to improve communication between ship crewmembers and dependents. Both worked well, especially with Dina Weaver, our unflappable and outspoken ombudsman. Dina was helped immensely with this task by Chaplain Ernest Poe.

As expected, there were problems with men and women on board the same ship. It was even more of a problem for earlier CO and XO regimes. The duo before CAPT Boyle and myself had a doozy. While underway before CAPT Boyle relieved CAPT Roberts, a female lieutenant was attacked in her stateroom. During the attack she was hit on the head and injured. When *Yosemite* returned to Mayport, she was transferred off the ship. CAPT Roberts and CDR Sheffield, with no real guidance and concerned about the safety of the women officers, set up a security watch in officers' country from taps to reveille. Several of the women officers were embarrassed about the watch. Later, one of the women officers told me, "I personally was embarrassed that some poor enlisted sailor had to sit out there in the passageway all night and babysit us." When CAPT Boyle and I learned of the watch, we discontinued it.

Other problems arose. A female LTJG came to me in private and told me she believed someone was watching her and other women officers when they took showers in the women officers' head. She was concerned there was a crack in the overhead where male crewmembers could become peeping toms. We had our ship fitters thoroughly check the bulkheads. Although the shipfitters didn't find any crack possibly manufactured by a peeping Tom, the work crew sealed up any holes where light might come through or a more-determined peeping Tom might expand and use. The effort insured privacy in the women officer's head.

• • •

The Ombudsman Program mentioned above had been initiated in 1970 in the Zumwalt Chief of Naval Operations (CNO) era. The Navy family ombudsman provides support and guidance as well as acting as an official liaison between the command and its families. Dina Weaver, who was also the wife of the command master chief, was the *Yosemite's* Ombudsman. She came aboard to meet the new XO and have lunch in the captain's mess with the CO and me. I was particularly pleased when Dina saw the framed large photo portrait of Maureen I had hung on the office wall so I could look at her from my desk. Dina saw the photo and told me, "She looks just like Susan Lucci," the soap opera star from "All My Children." I thanked Dina for the compliment but was thinking "Maureen's prettier."

A chaplain was part of the wardroom (commissioned officers' mess) in only one previous command where I served. When I was XO of the MSC transport unit for the year of 1970, a chaplain was one of five officers in the unit. The CO was a Lieutenant Commander (LCDR) billet, the XO billet was for a LT, but I, a LTJG at the time, went through the whole year carrying Republic of Korea (ROK) troops to and from Vietnam and Pusan, Korea unaware I could have applied for a spot promotion. Therefore, I remained a LTJG, rather than becoming a LT, something that might have helped my future career.

The MSC units were formed for being the Navy liaison on ships run by the United States Merchant Marine carrying US military personnel and dependents to various ports around the world. By 1970, the "troop" ships were down to three: the *USNS Barrett (T-AP 196),* the *USNS Upshur (T-AP 197),* and the *USNS Geiger (T-AP 198).* The three rotated with two carrying the ROK troops to Vietnam and back while the other went through upkeep. There was no real need for a Navy chaplain for Korean troops. The chaplain billet was dispensed with about three-quarters into my 1970 tour, and our chaplain was reassigned.

The *Yosemite's* chaplain was a different matter. This billet was to provide religious services and support for the ship's crew and also to other ships in *Yosemite's* area of operation. CAPT Boyle and I viewed our chaplain, LT Poe, as a vital resource in handling morale and personal problems, especially for the women in the crew.

Just prior to my taking the XO position, LT Poe was counseling a second-class petty officer and his wife in the chaplain's office. The wife became very distraught and pulled a handgun out of her purse. The petty officer grabbed at the firearm and the wife shot herself in the leg. LT Poe proved his mettle in that incident. The CO and I had great confidence in our chaplain.

• • •

With the deployment looming, preparation in all aspects accelerated. "I" Division was called that for indoctrinating new crew coming on board. The new personnel went through an indoctrination period on every aspect of shipboard life aboard *Yosemite.* The week-long training concluded with briefs by me and the CO. The indoctrinations increased in frequency as the days moved toward the deployment.

An evolution quite more significant than my becoming *Yosemite's* XO was occurring on Naval Station Mayport. Rear Admiral (RADM) Donnell would relieve the standing admiral as Commander, Cruiser Destroyer Group Twelve. As part of his relieving process, the admiral was scheduled to come aboard Wednesday after I took over on Tuesday, for a 1000-1200 briefing and ship tour followed by a noon mess in the captain's cabin. I was included in the lunch. The *Yosemite* was the repair facility for the ships in the group and therefore was considered part of Group 12.

Admiral Donnell was a tall, large man and as he was touring the ship, his party with CAPT Boyle escorting, passed the ship's motor whale boat in its davits. The admiral peered down into the boat, said nothing, and the tour continued. As is the custom of good CO's (and XO's), the tour route had been carefully combed over several times before the admiral came on board, but the captain had not thought of checking the interior of the boats. CAPT Boyle, a bit concerned about what the admiral might have seen and being unable to look with him because of the height difference returned to the davits after the Admiral Donnell departed. He climbed up to where he could look into the inside of the motor whale boat. He was most pleased and relieved the whale boat's interior was shipshape.

Admiral Donnell's visit created a conflict for me. The XO's Messing and Berthing Inspection normally began at 1000. But on Wednesday, the Planning Board for Training (PBFT or PB4T) was always scheduled at 1000. In a normal work week, I planned to move the inspection to the afternoon and hold the weekly board meeting in the morning. Admiral Donnell's arrival was scheduled to occur at 1000 also.

I had learned from my experience the value of the XO's messing and berthing inspections occurring daily during the work week without fail. Three years earlier I had become the emergency XO of the *USS Cayuga (LST 1186)* after the sitting XO had to be taken off the ship. I was told he was in a straitjacket. Regardless, he had suffered a mental breakdown of some sort.

On my first workday as *Cayuga's* new XO, I discovered messing and berthing inspections had not been conducted for six months. The living quarters for the crew were revolting, unkempt, and dirty. The heads were even worse, and the mess decks and galleys were completely unsanitary. I held messing and berthing inspections at 1000 without fail even when underway and on the weekends for the next two months. The spaces did a complete turnaround, and the crew's morale significantly improved.

I also knew the importance of the PBFT meeting. We moved the board meeting up to 0800 and I held the messing and berthing inspection at 1400.

While my first messing and berthing inspection was not as bad as it had been on *Cayuga*, it did not meet up to my standards. I particularly was displeased with the cleanliness, or lack thereof, in the heads and the poor sanitary conditions in the messes and galleys. I vowed to stick to my plan to not miss any such inspections for the rest of my tour.

With the admiral showing up soon, my first PBFT was very short. We met early, went over the scheduled topics quickly, made sure the next week had no major surprises, and closed the meeting.

From my exposure to Admiral Donnell during the brief tour and lunch, I assessed him to be a realistic and effective leader. After the admiral had departed, CAPT Boyle concurred and praised the flag officer for his leadership.

My second PBFT, occurring a week later, proved unsatisfactory.

As mentioned above, most Navy ships conducted a "Planning Board for Training" every Wednesday at 1000. *Yosemite* was no exception. This is when all department heads and everyone responsible for special programs like drug abuse and welfare and recreation attend. Not only training, but the ship's schedule, any inspections or other evolutions involving the ship would be discussed and an action plan established for the following week including specifics for each of those events. Like most ships, the *Yosemite's* meeting was held in the wardroom.

In this PBFT, my first real one, I was appalled when the meeting extended into the time for the midday mess in the wardroom. Several PBFT members were late and pre-meeting discussions kept the meeting from beginning until 20 minutes after the start time. Everybody had something to say, even if it was unimportant. No one was prepared for the meeting. Topics were brought up off the cuff, and numerous side discussions ensued throughout the meeting. At the conclusion, this new XO asked the group if this was typical. The engineer acknowledged it was and affirmed it often delayed the noon mess in the wardroom like this one had done.

The next day at officers' call, I put out the word about future PBFT's. I said no ship's meeting should last longer than 45 minutes. To accomplish this, I would put out an agenda with responsibility for the topic assigned to a member of the PBFT. That person would be responsible for bringing all pertinent information on the topic. I announced there would be no side discussions and no subjects other than those on the agenda would be discussed. If a need arose to discuss a non-agenda item, we would document it to be discussed at another time. Then I delivered the crushing blow. I declared if any members were more than five minutes late or all of the agenda topics had not been covered, the meeting would be rescheduled after liberty call. Until the end of my tour, all meetings in which I was part never went beyond forty-five minutes. A number of the PBFT members thanked me. The supply officer was profuse in his thanks because the previous overruns had played havoc with the wardroom cooks and mess cooks' schedule.

• • •

I had begun using a spiral notebook for my memos and to-do list on board the *Okinawa*, my previous ship. During *Okinawa's* overhaul when I managed subcontractors and eventually became the ship's overhaul coordinator, my small 4x6 inch "wheel book" in my back pocket for keeping my schedule, notes, business items, personal reminders, my to-do list, and my calendar proved totally inadequate in size. The little green wheel book had been my brains for every command since I was commissioned. But the overhaul coordinator of a helicopter carrier could not put all of his needed information in a wheel book. And for this XO of a ship deploying in less than a month, with women on board, and a ship's company of 900, a wheel book wouldn't hack it there either. I continued using the spiral notebook as I had used on the *Okinawa*, the sportswriter's arm extension. Instead of one page or slightly more for each day, I was filling up three, even four pages daily. In other words, I was busy.

As I settled into my XO role, I tried to put things in order as well as take care of my own needs. My office was on the starboard side of "Times Square." There was a small private head immediately forward which led forward into my stateroom, about twelve by eight feet and including a single rack and closet space.

• • •

One personal goal was to not let the deployment interfere with my running. I had started running daily as early as 1975 and normally ran about five to ten miles at least five days a week. I was never a fast runner but running had become an outlet and my major means of staying in shape. This had not been a problem on my previous ships. The big amphibious ships had places to run. Even the *USS Anchorage* had a flight deck and if vehicles were not loaded, one could run the flight deck down the ramps to the well deck and back up. The *USS Tripoli, USS Okinawa,* and *USS Belleau Wood,* all helicopter carriers, allowed running on the flight deck

XO and Chaplain Poe running on board *Yosemite*

when flight operations were not being conducted. When Marines and their aircraft and vehicles were not loaded aboard the *USS Belleau Wood (LHA 3)*, one could run the flight deck, down the ramp to the helicopter deck, down the ramp to the vehicle deck, down the ramp to the well deck, and back up and run a mile without lapping oneself.

The *Yosemite* had no large decks for such activities as running. After all, she was commissioned in 1944 when the Navy was focused on winning a war, not physical fitness. The "DASH" flight deck aft on the 02 level had been added for testing the Drone Anti-Submarine Helicopters (DASH) in the mid-1960's. The DASH program, after earning the derisive nicknames of "CRASH" and "SPLASH," was discontinued in 1969 after only six years in the fleet. The DASH deck on *Yosemite* was way too small for running but would prove invaluable later on this deployment for other reasons.

After looking over the topside spaces, I decided the ceremonial deck, which wrapped around the 02 level (the second level above the main deck) and immediately below the bridge, would work. If one ran 10 laps from the motor whaleboat docks on the 02 level through the ceremonial deck and back, it would be a mile. I had found my running place. I would run 55 laps every day possible, which worked out to about four or so days a week except when I ran in Diego Garcia or occasionally in liberty ports throughout the deployment. The second day underway from Mayport, the daily Plan of the Day (POD) included this item:

ATTENTION JOGGERS/RUNNERS. The 02 level forward of the motor whale boats, around the ceremonial deck, will be open from 1115-1245, and 1630 to 15 minutes after sunset for running. Future early morning running hours will be announced as we get into areas where sunrise is at an earlier time. Ten trips around from port to starboard and back constitutes approximately 1 mile. You are encouraged to use caution if you intend to run. Take 15 to 20 minutes to warm up. Stretching is critical. Loosen up by holding a slight constant pressure on the muscles you are stretching. NEVER bounce the muscles loose, as some people do when bending to touch their toes. Bouncing may cause a severe pulled muscle.

We didn't get a large number of runners, but we did get some.

• • •

Another problem I discovered was managing traffic into and out of my office. The executive officer is constantly being sought by crewmembers and officers for all sorts of reasons. In addition, I would be in and out of the office during the workday and didn't want people waiting for me behind a closed office door when I wasn't there. I decided to let people know where I was while I was away. I taped two paper clips bent to hold paper pad cardboard backs on my office door.

I took those cardboard backs and made my own crude signs: "On Messing and Berthing Inspection," "Out and About," "With the Captain," and with a running stickman "Out Running." I also tried to convey the situation with folks who wished to see me in my office: "Knock and Enter," "Conference in Session; Do not enter," "XO Mast in Progress," "Quiet Time, Please Do Not Knock or Enter."

After just under two weeks on the job, I realized there were a large number of officers and crew coming to me to solve their problems rather than working on solving those problems themselves. I had read *The Peter Principle* by Lawrence J. Peter about people being promoted to their level of incompetence. I had also read William Onken's *Managing Management*

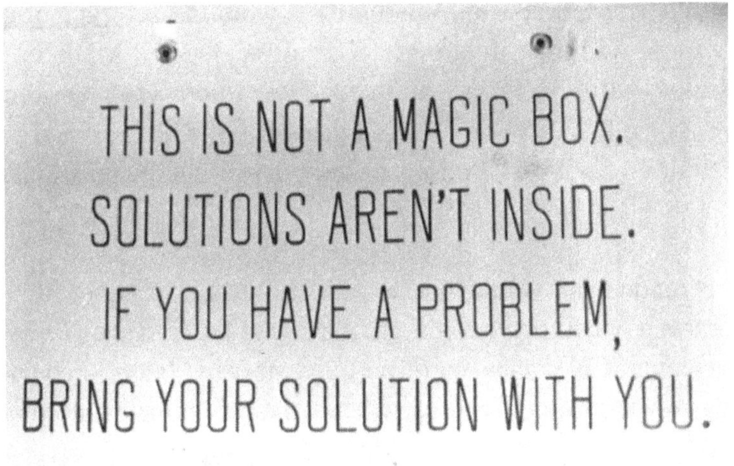

Sign outside XO's office

Time: Who's Got the Monkey? with the anecdote about subordinates passing their monkeys to the manager's shoulder. I had the Repair Department make a Bakelite sign to hang next to the door where my crude cardboard signs hung. It read: "This is not a magic box. Solutions aren't inside. If you have a problem, bring your solution with you." From the feedback I received then and recently, the sign had some positive impact.

• • •

On Tuesday, 30 August, the *Yosemite* got underway, not to deploy, but for "Sea Trials." Shortly prior to deployment, Navy ships go to sea for a short period, one or two days, to check all equipment to ensure all is running correctly, and just as importantly, get the crew used to going to sea. *Yosemite's* sea trial was one overnight trip into the Atlantic. This new XO was ready. I would be just as glad if the ship didn't come back to port and just kept heading east. For as long as I could remember, I found one of the best things about deploying was having no phones. Deployment meant the ship was operating as a sole unit, even with other ships in a group, separated by lack of phone lines (before satellite communication and GPS came into existence). It was where a ship was meant to be: at sea. But this time, I was anxious for the one-night cruise to end.

Maureen and I were married on 30 July followed by ten wonderful days of honeymoon in San Diego. Then I flew East to pick up my car and head to Mayport. Maureen and I thought we wouldn't see each other until the deployment was over in late March, but we decided Maureen should fly into Jacksonville on Friday and spend the Labor Day weekend with me before flying back to San Diego and work. She already had rented a seaside cabin. To say I was anxious to see her was a huge understatement.

• • •

But that rendezvous would have to wait. Sea detail was set at 0800. I took my position as navigator next to the chart table on the bridge as *Yosemite* got underway. Navigating a ship out of port and standing out of a channel was one of my favorite evolutions. For sea detail, the only thing better for me was being the Officer of the Deck and having the conn in an open sea.

Mayport had one of, if not the shortest and most direct, sea details of all Naval bases, just over a mile from the Mayport basin to the sea buoy. My navigation duties ended quickly. The pilot had left the ship. I joined CAPT Boyle and LT Sitton, the OOD and conning officer on the open bridge (the "conning" officer on a Navy ship in those days was the one who was directing the speed and direction of the ship, giving steering instructions to the helmsman and giving speed orders to the lee helmsman who passed those orders to engineering's Main Control, which in turn responded to those orders). The captain became a bit agitated as a number of sailboats appeared from the south crossing the end of the channel. Sailboats were not a usual problem in Norfolk where CAPT Boyle had spent most of his shipboard time while hundreds of sailboats in Long Beach and San Diego fouling up the channel were business as usual. The captain knew well the rules of the road, which included the rules for power ships and boats. He knew the rules for sailboats as well, but he had not had a great amount of experience with them and was not comfortable with those tacking sailboats bobbing on the water dependent on the winds. He knew I had not only had to deal with innumerable sailboats but also had crewed several while sailing out of and into Long Beach and San Diego.

There was some question as to whether *Yosemite* in this case should maneuver to avoid any collision. With the sailing vessels a mile or more away, CAPT Boyle asked me my opinion as to what to do.

"Don't worry, Captain," I replied, "They will maneuver and avoid us. They normally don't want to mess with ships this big. It is the law of gross tonnage."

In less than a minute, the sailboats began to tack and disperse, giving *Yosemite* a clear shot east.

I was relieved and felt good about giving my captain correct information.

• • •

Underway had always been good for me and this was no exception. I was fascinated by the beauty of the sea ever since my third-class midshipman training in 1963. To me, she was beautiful in every mood, and every changing color.

I saw her in the doldrums of the South China Sea when she was a glass sheet of green reflecting the yellow of the sunset when I saw my first "green flash." I saw her off Cape Hatteras dressed in her gray, black, and white of fury where the wind howled for days whipping the sea into waves that crashed up to the bridge 75 feet above the waterline and angry foam making it nearly all white. I have seen her in the blue green of the shallows off of Florida and California with ripples in the tidewaters. I have seen her as clear as drinking water in the harbor of Key West, clear enough to watch the hammerhead sharks prowl along the bottom 30 feet below. I have seen her in her blue-green currents of the Great Barrier Reef of Australia where those currents required a skilled helmsman to hold the ship on course to avoid grounding. I have seen her in the azure waters of Bermuda where pilots conn steel behemoths at 30 knots through treacherous shoal waters. And I have seen her in her deepest blue in the middle of the Atlantic, the Pacific, the Mediterranean, and the Indian Oceans, where there is seemingly no end to her depth, when at night with standard running lights, the moon and stars make it difficult to discern the constellations, hidden in the millions and millions of stars and moons, and comets under the canopy of the black sky.

To me, the sea is beautiful in all of her moods, in all of her colors. In my own way, I love her.

• • •

My first day at sea on the "Busy Lady" went better than I expected. All systems were in working order. After the evening mess in the wardroom, something occurred to set the tone for the entire deployment and for all of my tour as XO.

With the collateral duty of navigator, I walked up to the bridge with the intent of checking out the equipment and the quartermasters for shooting stars. "Shooting stars" is the process of taking angles on certain stars, then using *The Nautical Almanac* to find figures for that particular day, plotting the revised angles to determine a ship's location on the ocean. Shooting stars is normally done at twilight and after first light in the morning. LTJG Noreen Leahy was the assistant navigator. Shortly after we began the deployment, she took all of the navigational fixes. But on this first night at sea for me, I wanted to shoot the stars. The sun had set. It was twilight, the perfect time. As I came on the bridge, I walked past the chart table and quartermaster's station and over to the starboard bridge wing. I looked down and was surprised to see the standing lights were on.

One of the primary Rules of the Road is from sunset to sunrise a ship must not have any lights visible except for standard "running lights." Standard running lights consist of a green light on the starboard side, a red light on the port side, a white light as a stern light, and two forward "range" lights above and in line. This is to allow other ships to ascertain a ship's aspect in order to get an idea of the relative direction she was heading. This aspect determines which ship is the privileged vessel (required to remain on course), and the burdened vessel (required to maneuver to avoid a collision). Other extraneous lights would make it difficult, if not impossible to discern the ship's aspect. In my time at sea, any ship showing more than navigational running lights after dark would be denigrated and called a "cruise ship."

I called to the OOD, "Why aren't the standing lights off?" Recognizing the OOD had much less experience than I had and it had been quite a while since any watch standers had been to sea, I added, "Don't you know the Rules of the Road prohibit standing lights to be on after sunset."

"Yes sir," the OOD responded, "But it's in the Captain's Night Orders to leave them on all night."

"What?" I almost shouted in disbelief.

"Yes sir, would you like to see it?"

"No, I believe you," I responded as I walked over to the sound powered phone and rang the captain's cabin.

"Captain," the commanding officer answered.

"Sir, this is the exec. Have you finished your evening mess?"

"Yes, why?" CAPT Boyle responded.

"Well sir, I was wondering if you could come up to the bridge?"

"Certainly, be up in a minute."

When the captain arrived on the bridge, he asked, "What's up, XO?"

"I'd like to show you something," I said and directed him to the starboard bridge wing.

As he peered over the bulwark and saw the lights, CAPT Boyle shouted, "What the hell? Officer of the Deck, get those damn standing lights off right now. What kind of watch are you running?"

Before I could explain, the OOD repeated, "But sir, your night orders direct us to leave them on."

"They aren't my night orders," the captain responded angrily, "Now turn those damn things off!"

"Aye, aye, sir," the OOD obeyed and ordered the standing lights off.

"Dammit, Jim, I forgot to rewrite the night orders," CAPT Boyle explained. "Those are CAPT Roberts' night orders. I'll write mine tonight and you can edit them so we have them ready for deployment."

"Aye, sir," I agreed, relieved the violation of the Rules of the Road was a product of the previous regime, not CAPT Boyle's.

He and I stayed on the bridge. The captain took his seat on the starboard side, and I stood next to him discussing how the day otherwise had gone and my getting any input for Eight O'clock Reports.

In about five minutes, Master Chief Weaver ran onto the bridge demanding, "Who turned off those standing lights?"

With both the CO and I amazed at the Master Chief's reaction, the captain beckoned him over.

"What in the world are you talking about, Master Chief?" the captain asked, "Why do you think the standing lights should be on?"

"Well, sir," Master Chief Weaver responded, "With CAPT Roberts and CDR Sheffield, we kept them on, and we created a roving security patrol. We wanted to make sure no one was sneaking out onto the weather decks at night for a little hanky-panky."

There was a moment of silence. I was shaking my head in disbelief when CAPT Boyle, with obviously controlled anger said:

"Master Chief, I want you to be sure that every person on this ship knows by tomorrow morning we don't have men on board this ship; we don't have women on board this ship. We have sailors aboard this ship. And we are going to act like that.

"We will observe all of the Rules of the Road as long as I am the commanding officer. And we will all act like sailors.

"Understood?"

"Aye, aye, sir," the master chief responded, then quickly left the bridge.

I smiled and told the captain I had to get below to get ready for Eight O'clock Reports and left the bridge.

There is no doubt CAPT Boyle's philosophy, so well stated that evening, became the watchword for how the ship did business for the rest of the time I was the executive officer. I used the captain's direction that evening as my first guidepost in any situation requiring judgement about male and female personnel, officer or enlisted, that arose during my time aboard the *Yosemite*.

• • •

Upon completion of our sea trial, preparations for the deployment reached a fevered pace. In addition to loading supplies, *Yosemite* needed more materials than a combatant because the Repair Department required a large amount of material, like steel in large sheets and various other supplies for repair and maintenance during customer ship maintenance availabilities.

Cruiser-Destroyer Group 12 was having a change of command, which not only meant the captain would be gone that entire day, but there would be another admiral's brief on board. The discrepancies from the sea trial and a zone inspection needed to either be fixed before getting underway or put in a long-range plan for correction. *Yosemite* also took part in the change of command. She was charged with firing a 13-gun salute in honor of a rear admiral. At the ceremony, CAPT Boyle was sweating during the salute while I was sweating aboard ship with each round from our saluting battery. After an initial glitch from our battery, the gun salute went fine. No one, except us, noticed the glitch.

It was time for a respite. It had been over three weeks since I had seen my new bride. Maureen had decided she should fly into Jacksonville on Friday, 2 September, and spend the Labor Day weekend with me. While I found and reserved a room in the Sheraton Hotel, Maureen had already located and rented a small cabin, a Bed and Breakfast, on the beach. I cancelled the hotel reservation.

We had a wonderful weekend even with ship's business frequently distracting me. We did have one moment that cut into the romance (pun intended). Saturday twilight, we settled into the cottage for an evening together alone and sat down on the couch looking out at the Atlantic past the sand and the small picket fence. I uncorked a bottle of Sauternes while Maureen prepared a wonderful cheese and apple plate. After sitting down, Maureen went to slice the apple, but missed and cut a deep gash into her left palm. What had been planned as a romantic evening was devoted mostly to first aid and laughter.

Even though that Monday was a holiday, I had to do some work. But the newlyweds had some wonderful moments together before I put Maureen on a plane back to San Diego that Tuesday morning.

The clock toward deployment was ticking.

• • •

With days winding down, two more major difficulties arose, one impacted by Navy policy and the other was older than the hills. Both involved sailors trying to avoid deployments.

The first problem arose when the doctor advised me one of the female sailors was pregnant. In these early days of the Women At Sea (WAS) program, the Navy's policy stipulated any enlisted female would be immediately transferred to a shore command. One of the immediate repercussions of this policy was a number of women who didn't want to deploy on a tender would get pregnant in order to avoid the deployment. I knew this policy was a product of politically correct, but misguided thoughts. The *Yosemite* had a capable doctor on board trained in family practice. If there was a problem or health issue, the crew person should be transferred, but the blanket policy produced a lot of unwanted results. It didn't matter. That was the policy, and the seaman was transferred to shore duty. As I recall, only one or two women were transferred due to pregnancy before we got underway for good.

This policy would come into play during the deployment in a much different manner.

The next big problem would plague the *Yosemite* and particularly me for nearly all of the deployment and beyond.

A week before the underway date, a senior chief went to a fast-food restaurant to take home some fare to his family. He spotted a cook in the back, a *Yosemite* sailor who was Absent Without Official Leave (AWOL) at best, a deserter at worst. When Fireman, Machinist Mate, Nuclear Power (MMFN(N)) Edmunds realized he had been recognized, he bolted for the back door. The senior chief tackled him in the parking lot and with the help of shore patrol brought Edmunds back to the ship. The quarterdeck watch allowed them to come aboard and put the fireman on restriction.

When I received the report the next morning, my antennae quickly rose and started vibrating. I remembered LCDR Louis Guimond, a Louisiana Cajun, who was the XO on the *Hawkins*, my first ship. Louis was one of the best if not the best XOs I had throughout my Navy career. One afternoon, the shore patrol brought back a sailor who had gone on Unauthorized Absence (UA) several months earlier. The ship had declared him a deserter. When Louis heard they had the guy on the quarterdeck, he ran out to the quarterdeck and screamed at the shore patrol to take the guy off the ship immediately and to the base brig. The XO knew if the ship accepted the sailor, he would be part of ship's company and the ship's problem. The *Hawkins* would be responsible for the ensuing court martial, and the sailor also would be part of the crew, preventing the ship from getting a replacement.

But Edmunds was on board. I couldn't change that. He had become my problem. I shuddered when I discovered he was a Machinist Mate Fireman (Nuclear). This meant he had been in the nuclear program, most likely on a submarine, and had been kicked out. The nuclear submarine commands, because of nuclear safety and security, had an instruction allowing them to simply get rid of a troublemaker by declaring him unfit for the nuclear program. All such problems were reassigned to…yes, that's correct: they were assigned to a Navy ship. They became the surface navy's problem.

The reason I shuddered was recalling the only nuclear dropout I previously had as a subordinate. I was Chief Engineer on the *USS Hollister (DD 788)* from 1973-75. An MM3(N) reported aboard and was assigned to M division, the division that operates the propulsion part of the engineering system. This new sailor was assigned to main control. Soon he got into some trouble and went to captain's mast. The captain found him guilty, demoted him to MMFN, reduced his pay in half for three months, restricted him to the ship for three months, and assigned him 45 days of extra duty. This was the maximum punishment a ship's CO could allot at captain's mast except for three days in the ship's brig on bread and water, which is an extremely rare occurrence.

As one would expect, the demoted MMFN was not happy. *Hollister* engineers, including me, just didn't realize how unhappy he was. When his duty section had the duty on a Wednesday, he was assigned to roving security patrol. When a ship was cold iron, i.e., not steaming, a roving security patrol was set. This patrol would be on four-hour watches, roaming through the engine rooms, fire rooms, and other engineering spaces to ensure the plant was secure and safe. In the early part of his mid-watch, this MMFN opened up all of the sea valves to allow sea water to come into the space. When it was discovered by the next watch, nearly all equipment on the lower level of main control, which included vital pumps, many with electrical components, were underwater, salt water. The *Hollister* was scheduled to get underway the following week.

The MMFN was assigned a summary court martial. In the process, as chief engineer, I had to provide all the evidence against him, but as his department head, I had to counsel him. It was the most difficult two-headed job I ever experienced.

My machinist mates worked around the clock. We took several of the pumps to a "bicycle shop" in Long Beach, got the ones required to "light off" running and installed in time to get underway. It was an incredibly demanding week, one of the worst I endured in my Navy career.

I think it was natural for me to be alarmed. Fireman Edmunds proved my concern was justified.

Edmunds's young wife was not happy either. She made all sorts of nonsensical claims and demands for Edmunds to be released off the ship and not deploy. She began making protests. She demanded her husband be allowed to stay ashore. As much as I wished we had not allowed him back on board, he was *Yosemite's* problem, and we needed to follow regulations and Judge Advocate General's Corps (JAG) procedures. The ship would have to prosecute him through the proper regulations.

Edmunds went to Captain's Mast. Rather than mete out the maximum punishment a captain was allowed under the Uniform Code of Military Justice (UCMJ), CAPT Boyle assigned Edmunds to a summary court martial. This would take place after the ship got underway for deployment. Edmunds was not happy. He did not want to deploy in the worst way. His wife was perhaps more upset.

This was not my first time to respond to a Congressional Inquiry. But it was the first time for me to respond to a First Lady, Nancy Reagan, which was more critical. Edmunds's wife wrote a letter of protest to the First Lady. Nancy or her staff, in turn, wrote a letter to *Yosemite*. At that time, a ship was required to respond to a congressional or First Lady inquiry within 24 hours, including the vetting process through the chain of command. Guess who had to write the response? The XO. Me.

I guess it was a good response. Nancy didn't call me or otherwise respond. We kept Edmunds on board until we got underway. I'm sure neither he nor his wife were pleased. I thought it was a stunning victory for good order and discipline, and that's a significant part of an XO's job. Little did I realize Edmunds would be a major thorn in my side, not for just the deployment but most of my tour on *Yosemite*.

• • •

Because there were only a small number of officers and sailors who had deployed on a ship before, we began running all sorts of warnings, and instructions in the POD as well as passing the word down the chain of command about what to do and what not do. I kept discussing with the captain, the First Lieutenant, and the engineer about what word to get out to the rookie sailors. It was a new experience for me. All of my previous ships had been manned by officers, chiefs, and sailors who had been on numerous deployments. The department heads, the division officers, the chiefs, and the experienced petty officers made sure new folks knew how the rules at sea were different and also made sure the newcomers obeyed the rules of going to sea on a ship. But for *Yosemite*, there were large numbers of leaders who had not really gone to sea. We passed the word at quarters daily, and we posted notes in the POD.

For weeks, there was a constant reminder to conserve fresh water:

7. CONSERVE FRESH WATER: All hands are reminded to conserve fresh water to keep us from having to go on water hours. Report any fresh water leaks immediately to Damage Control Central. Take Navy showers. For those of you who wonder what a "Navy shower" is, you do the following:
- *Turn on the water to wet down*
- *Turn off the water to soap up*
- *Turn water on to rinse off*

Don't be shy to let someone know about it if they're not following these procedures. Water hours are an inconvenience that we don't want to have to experience.

We warned about safety at sea. We preached about securing all loose items before getting underway to keep them from becoming flying objects when the ship began to roll in rough seas. And a POD note warned:

SAFETY NOTE: Safety! All hands are reminded to think "Safety." This means staying away from lifelines, no "skylarking." Report all safety discrepancies to departmental safety PO's/Safety officer. The main objective is to "Think Safety." If we keep this in mind, we'll all have a safe deployment.

All Navy ships tried to provide entertainment for the crew. In my earlier shipboard days, entertainment was the evening movies for the crew, chiefs, and wardroom. The movies were high-lined from ship to ship until they were replaced by the service force ship, usually an oiler, which had returned to port for a resupply of fuel oil, other supplies, and a new batch of movies. I use the word "new" cautiously because the available movies were older reruns, many black and whites. Occasionally, once or twice a deployment, we would have "steel beach" parties on the fantail and grill hamburgers. That was about it for our entertainment.

But the *Yosemite* needed more. Many of the personnel would not be standing watches. Off hours were dead time. We wanted our sailors not to have time to think up things, which might not be good for themselves or the ship. We found a space for weight-lifting. Several officers and enlisted volunteered to lead group exercises. And we created areas and times for sunbathing:

SUNBATHING: All hands are reminded that sunbathing hours are from 1130-1300. The male sunbathing area is the flight deck (i.e. the DASH Deck). The female sunbathing area is the 03 level aft of the OPS complex. Proper sunbathing attire must be worn. Females must wear one piece suits (no bikinis). Males must wear boxer style suits (no briefs)

To add to such concern, I added a hand-written note at the bottom of the POD:

Remember sunbathers, you are responsible for ensuring against sunburn. Sunburns are not legitimate reasons for not performing work.

As I copy these notes, I keep thinking of the television series and movie "M*A*S*H" and feel in retrospect a bit like Corporal O'Reilly, always announcing something to the crew only my vehicle was the POD and O'Reilly's was the camp loud speaker.

After all, it was a different time and a uniquely different challenge for the *Yosemite* to deploy, unlike all of my other preparations to go overseas.

Our underway preparations were going well until Wednesday, September 7, when the Chief Engineer Ken Clausen, reported the evaporator had gone down. Our scheduled underway on Thursday was delayed. It was not feasible to leave port with no guarantee we could produce fresh water for cooking, drinking, and washing or, most importantly, feed water for the boilers. I was very concerned as I remembered another tender preparing to deploy. The *USS Prairie (AD 15)* in 1974 was about to get underway out of its home port of Long Beach while I was the chief engineer on the *USS Hollister (DD 788)*, also homeported in Long Beach. The *Prairie* suffered a casualty to her Ship's Service Turbine Generator (SSTG). Since the *Prairie* was launched in 1939, many plans and blueprints were not available. The Navy finally flew in an eighty-year-old man from Philadelphia who had helped design the generator. It took about two months to make the repairs. I was envisioning this happening to the *Yosemite* and her evaporators (distilling plants).

But the engineers and Repair Department personnel worked continuously and on the originally scheduled underway day, Thursday, they successfully got the distilling plant running.

Finally, the *USS Yosemite,* the "Busy Lady," was going to get underway for her deployment to the Indian Ocean. It was just under a month after I reported aboard. I had no real idea of how this was going to turn out.

I did however record in my notes my thoughts about what we were about to face:

Now we are gonna take this 39-year-old ship that's got guts so old nobody even makes replacement parts anymore, and we're gonna sail her better than halfway round the world and back. We're gonna take about 750 men and 100 women from a doctor, dentists, and even a Wellesley graduate to those educated in street crime and many more so far away from what they've known they will think they have left the world (i know as i have had that sensation before). We're gonna leave a pier where the ship stayed so long she became locally referred to as "Building 19" and not come back to that pier for more than 6 months, more than half a year.

I expressed my feelings about my own absence for half a year in a letter to Maureen, September 9, 1983:

...Another short note before we go. It looks like we'll make it this time. It's 11:30 a.m., 1130 my time. All our equipment is operating, and we're scheduled to get underway at 1:30 p.m., 1330 my time. It will be a relief in many ways.

Only the thought of delaying our life together causes sad thoughts. I am proving to be a good executive officer, and this time at sea should put it all in order. There is absolutely no one yet to whom I relate as a friend like there was on Okinawa. That is because of my position, the way it should be. Everyone seems so different. That's not derogatory. It's as though they have a lack of experience (not counting the captain). Of course, I am now a senior officer, XO, so that too is as it should be. I have to be a teacher. There's so much to do, and the majority, a large majority of the crew has never deployed before.

My philosophy of life, if you can call it that, is becoming more cynical. People are incredibly naïve about life at sea. I hope this job proves to me they can learn and they have no evil purpose.

Except for you and me. How did I find you? God must exist to allow us to meet, to be together to love as we do.

Take care and write and tape cassettes and laugh on the tapes and walk the beach and think of me. I feel that empty gut feeling coming on. It's loneliness setting in and will exist on its own, independent of all the other things going on and the thoughts I must put to the forefront to do this job right.

*   i love you.*

It was going to be a lonely seven months.

Chapter 4: Crossing the Pond

September 1983: Florida to Rota, Spain, to the Mediterranean

As mentioned earlier, far and away one of the best things about deploying in my time in the Navy was leaving all attachments to land behind. That point in time was announced, even saluted by one prolonged blast on the ship's whistle and the boatswain's mate piping "Attention" followed by his announcement on the 1MC speakers, "Underway. Shift Colors." Such announcements were preceded by two even better announcements: "Let go all lines," and blessedly "All lines clear."

All of this meant the ship was on her own. The "All lines clear" not only referred to the mooring lines, steam lines, and electrical shore power cables, but also the phone lines. Such cutting of umbilical ties meant no phone calls. It also meant no salesman trying to get their foot in the door, no superiors or their staffs coming on board to give direction on how we should operate or address their particular area of expertise, no inspectors coming to check any and all equipment, programs, procedures, etc. and disrupt the ship from getting done what needed to be done, and no dependents coming on board asking for us to do something to help them or their sailor.

"Underway" meant *Yosemite* was on her own to do what she, in 1944, was commissioned to do. As a career surface officer, it was a heady feeling to get underway for a deployment scheduled to last almost seven months.

At 1400, Friday, September 9, 1983, *Yosemite* got underway and would remain on her own power except for hooking up to "shore power" during five brief port visits until 1200, Wednesday, March 21, 1984.

While writing this book, I came upon a shoe box full of letters I had written to Maureen. Many are too personal to include here. But there are some that capture my thoughts better than I could more than thirty years later. The one below, as all those letters appearing here, has been edited for grammar, sometimes to omit an item not really accurate in retrospect, or to delete a negative reference to a shipmate. This one was begun two days after *Yosemite* departed Mayport and was completed the night before we arrived at the US Naval base in Rota, Spain.

Lady,

Underway. Sun so bright; sea so calm: we sail. I cannot hear the engine growl or the boilers rumble from up here on the open bridge – an archaic wonder, this open bridge I have come to love with the wind in my face. Dolphins, flying fish, and a giant sea turtle bigger than a small car, busily nosing about and poking their heads up and sometimes clearing the water in their entirety to peer at this strange sight passing by, this steel mammoth filled with 900 souls, these 900 souls ironically lonelier than if they were by themselves on a deserted isle.

The above was written several days ago – I have already lost track of time – when all was peaceful. A hurricane (Chantal), born in an unlikely area and following an unusual path has reared up to pester us (our pesterers actually are the ones who control our puppet strings from dry land reacting to lines on a satellite picture, not the hurricane herself) and wakens me at all hours of the night to receive reports, analyze the graphs, and then look at the beautiful sea and attempt to read her dark and brooding mind to guess at Chantal's course and speed to minimize our peril, avoid standing into danger. Then in those irregular moments throughout the day, i make recommendations to the captain, a knowledgeable, capable seaman in his own right, a course and speed to keep us on a safe journey east.

But we cannot take the risk of the course and speed we both think is prudent taking us eastward, defying the desk-sitting analysts back in Norfolk, for if we were wrong, there would be hell, ours, to pay with swift retribution from the desk sitters on dry land.

So we avoid a danger that never really existed for us, a hurricane that died in a confused sea, a fate precipitated by her birth in an unusual place for such phenomena while several hundred miles west we fretted away the hours.

i spent my time being concerned about our being subjected to the lack of seaman sense governing us when i realized the captain was relying on my sense of the sea, my knowledge and experience, which was close to equal to his, and certainly greater than anyone else on board. CAPT

Boyle was listening to and taking my recommendations, often seeking them. He commented that I communicated with the sea.

i communicate with the sea.

i had never had it put that way before. And it came from a man who knows. i do not possess the technical knowledge of oceanography and meteorology. i have the basics of sailing the sea and not much more. i, however, can look at the sea's skies and her endless depth of blue, and hear her speak her mood. i used to feel her presence and interpreted the feelings i experienced at sea as an indication that god might really exist. Now, i know it was not a god but the sea trying to talk to me. Mystic nonsense? Maybe.

But maybe it is you who has given me this gift. Maybe experiencing you and our love has allowed me to understand this power of my communication with this frighteningly beautiful force such as she.

i rejoice in the revelation but acknowledge the responsibility i bear along with the talent(?). i am even more responsible for this lovely old ship and the souls on board. i must temper my abandon and romantic restlessness. i live comfortably within my communication with this power and love you even more for allowing me to live with both of you. These people rely on me. They all rely on me, whether they realize it or not, to give their lives a substance, a direction, a purpose.

The Captain is an idol, an object of reverence, a god at sea. i am the force, the dynamic driving force that worms into the spirit of each soul and claims my territory. Unlike many others, but not all, i have attempted to add humor, understanding, selflessness, credibility into this force. i hope i have not engendered fear. i believe I am promoting respect; respect for the Captain, for me, and the ship, but most importantly for themselves.

There have already been mistakes. There will be many more. Hopefully, they will not have any adverse impact. i only hope i don't burn out, don't become so involved i cannot see the humor, pathos, and futility in this game of driving, leading these people down a path that has no real direction except for the immediate and eternal goal of the ship's mission. i already have come to love this job, but i still occasionally wonder if this awesome responsibility of power won't destroy itself, destroy me. i sometimes feel i am Luke, old "Cool Hand Luke" lying on that table, those fifty eggs bloating his stomach, his body resembling a man on a crucifix after he told his prison mates not to lean on him.

i am an image i believe: an image our sailors would like to emulate. They know i am happy. They know i enjoy fine things. They know i am honest and upright, and they know i am married to a beautiful woman. They also know i came from the same roots as they. i can feel they identify with those common roots and see they, or perhaps their son or daughter, can reach this plateau.

The job is consuming. i started this letter the second day out. i started this last part at 0200 the morning before we arrive in Rota. Every morning, i arise around 0530; sometime around midday, go for a run or take a nap (sometimes both); have one relaxing meal (breakfast is a working meal where i read radio messages and prepare for officer's call), skipping the other meal. i normally hit the rack between 2300 and 0100 but already have had a couple of nights with only one or two hours sleep. There will be more. i really am not complaining because i am really into it and feel like i'm having a positive impact.

i've taken very little time for personal things. Sleep is my enemy. i want to stay awake forever and cram all of these things into my life, including being XO. i can't, so i'm trying to be selective and truly prioritize. This deployment provides me the time and requires me, quite willingly, to focus on this ship, crew, and wardroom. My goal is to reach peak organization by the time we reach Diego Garcia. Once i've achieved that, i should have the time to focus on writing, and of course, you.

i am excited. i am excited about performing this job well and absolutely bonkers about us in the future. After these 183 days of deployment, i never want to leave you. i think about actually getting screened and assigned as commanding officer of a ship. It would be reaching my ultimate Navy goal, but it also would most likely mean at least one deployment, and the thought of being away from you that long again does not sit well with me. My wanderlust is fading, but i would accept a CO assignment in a heartbeat. But there would be some regret at the thought of leaving you.

"Whatever else you are, be a seaman, know the ways of the sea and the men who go down to the sea in ships." Unknown

"Our will is to keep the torch of freedom burning for all. To this solemn purpose, we call upon the young, the brave, the strong, and the free. Heed my call. Come to the sea. Come sail with me." John Paul Jones

• • •

I reflected more about my communicating with the sea after I'd finished my letter to Maureen. I vividly recalled when I had first felt that sense of communicating with the sea.

When I first went to sea, I was not a particularly good ship driver. I was decent, like most ensigns and lieutenant junior grade officers, and knew how to stay out of trouble, but my ship handling skills were modest. When I was the sports editor of *The Watertown* (NY) *Daily Times* after my first active duty service, I spent two weeks aboard the *USS Waldron (DD 699)* during my Active Duty for Training (ACDUTRA) in the late summer of 1971. Ironically, she was home ported in Mayport.

The *Waldron* and the other ships in the reserve squadron had not had much experience sailing with other Navy ships. In those two weeks, she was in a major exercise in the Atlantic, including continuous ASW operations. On my first evening watch (2000-2400), I was the Junior Officer of the Deck (JOOD) for a LTJG OOD who had never worked with ASW helicopters. I stood next to him and guided him through a formation of ships and ASW helos hovering while dipping their sonars in the sea.

My experience and guidance to the OOD impressed the captain. He assigned me as OOD soon afterwards. As I departed after my two weeks, the captain gave me a letter qualifying me as a Fleet Officer of the Deck.

That was when I became a better than average ship handler.

When I returned to active duty later that summer, I reported to the *USS Stephen B. Luce (DLG 7),* which was under command of CDR Richard Butts, who later after becoming an admiral, convinced me I should accept my assignment as XO of the *Yosemite.* The *Luce* XO was Ted Fenno, the head of detailing who had played a big role in my getting me assigned the XO tour.

The *Luce* operated in a huge NATO exercise with ships from Britain, Spain, Italy, and Turkey. Almost every time I stood the OOD watch, we would encounter a merchant ship that was not obeying the International Rules of the Road creating situations requiring evasive action on my part. CDR Butts eventually made me the Sea Detail and General Quarters OOD. I felt as if I had become an excellent ship handler with an understanding of the sea.

After *Luce* and department head school at Newport's "Destroyer School," I had my chief engineer tour aboard *USS Hollister (DD 788)* and reported to the *USS Anchorage (LSD 36),* an amphibious dock landing ship. It was on our six- month deployment to the Western Pacific when I gained this sense of what CAPT Boyle had described as my communicating with the sea. There were a number of instances while I was the officer of the deck when I felt the sea was somehow giving me information about her mood and how her currents and the weather were impacting the ship. Perhaps it was just a feeling I got from my experience and knowledge of ships at sea, but it did feel like I understood what the sea was telling me.

• • •

All of my previous transits in the Atlantic had been a Speed of Advance (SOA) of 17 knots. This was primarily because my previous ships in the Atlantic had been destroyers. At one time, the old *Yosemite* with her four 400-pound steam boilers had been capable of a maximum speed of 19.6 knots. But with the age of the machinery and additional weight for new repair equipment, CAPT Boyle and our engineer, Ken Clausen believed her maximum was about 16 knots. The transit from Mayport to Rota, Spain was planned at a cruising speed of 14 knots. I was pessimistic and suspected she would be lucky to grind it out at 12 knots.

CAPT Boyle and LT Clausen discussed how the thirty-nine-year-old ship could handle speed. CAPT Boyle had plenty of experience and knowledge concerning steam ships. He served in three engineering tours, was an engineering instructor at Navy Destroyer School and the Senior Examiner on the Atlantic Fleet Propulsion Examining Board. Ken had already established himself in my opinion as one of the best chief engineers with whom I had served. The two agreed if they used oversized sprayer plates (disks that sprayed the fuel oil into the boilers) those old metal huffing and hissing wonders could put out the needed steam for the necessary speed.

Prior to departure, we had three non-crewmembers board for the transit across the Atlantic. Navy Campus for Achievement provided Mr. Mabry for conducting GED and CLEP tests and other educational services for the crew. The Fleet Weather Center, Norfolk sent a first class and a second-class aerographer's mates (AG's) temporary duty to give us the most current and complete weather information. It was the season for tropical storms and hurricanes.

After our first night underway, AG1 Scollan came to me with a message from his command in Norfolk. A tropical depression off of Bermuda was developing and was being watched closely. In two days,

Darryl Gunter, Boiler Technician, third class petty officer, lighting fires in the boiler.

the depression strengthened into a tropical storm and on 11 September, it became Hurricane Chantal, the one I described in my letter to Maureen.

Looking at the charts, CAPT Boyle and I assessed our options. Both of us had significant experience with hurricanes, typhoons, tropical cyclones, and tropical storms. We believed it would be safest for the ship to cross well ahead of the northern path of Chantal. To remain on the western side of the storm could put the ship in a precarious position without maneuvering room if Chantal moved northeast. The fleet weather center disagreed and directed us to stay east until the hurricane passed.

Frustrated, CAPT Boyle, with my agreement and equal frustration, decided to obey the direction of the weather center. There was a slight chance our crossing north of the hurricane track could put us in a dangerous position. Although we were sure this wouldn't happen, if it did, we would have no leg to stand on in defense of our actions.

By Monday evening, 12 September, Chantal had dissipated and was no longer classified a hurricane, reverting to a tropical storm. We resumed our course to Rota. I was not sure the old "Busy Lady" could make up the delay to arrive on time. She proved me wrong.

Those oversized sprayer plates in the boilers did what the captain and Ken Clausen planned. The old, grey lady made it across the big pond at an estimated SOA of twelve knots. At times, she even topped out at sixteen knots. Beautiful old lady. She arrived in Rota as scheduled, Tuesday, 20 September.

• • •

In all of the other Navy ships on which I deployed, going to sea was an extremely busy time for all hands. Everyone had watches, usually in three or four sections. If it was four sections, the watch sections would rotate through the four-hour watches. If it was three sections, the 16-20 watch was halved or "dogged" into the 16-18 and 18-20 watches. Both methods gave the sections a different watch each day. *Yosemite* was in four-section watches on the bridge, CIC, lookouts, and engineering. But the vast majority of the ship's complement was the Repair, Supply, Medical, and Dental departments, and only a very few of those crew members stood watches. This, to me, was a big problem. What could we do to keep the non-watch standers busy during off hours?

There were a few things we could do to keep them from being idle. CAPT Boyle had determined early on the material condition of the 39 year-old ship was poor. There was a large amount of rust throughout the ship, especially on the weather decks. The First Lieutenant, Chief Engineer, and the Repair Officer came up with a plan to address the problems and bring the ship back to respectable material condition by the time we returned to Mayport. CAPT Boyle approved.

The plan went into effect as soon as we left Mayport. Nearly the entire ship kept busy throughout the transit, and a massive effort by the Repair department was made cutting out rotten metal and welding new throughout the ship.

• • •

I was getting the feel of interfacing with the crew. The Plan of the Day became my daily connection with all of them. The POD was read, or at least was supposed to be read, to all hands at morning quarters. I tried to convey good order and discipline was a primary concern for everyone, but we could take care of business and also have fun. I was learning on the fly.

I also was learning how Navy officers, chiefs, and sailors heeded my cardboard signs I hung on my office door. If the sign indicated I was out of the office and where I was, whoever had come to see me would leave, go back to work, and return later. However, if the sign indicated I was in, I qualified that information with additions. My normal sign was "Knock and Enter." Then there was "Quiet Time: Please Do Not Enter," "Conference in Session: Please Do Not Enter," "XO's Mast: Please Do Not Enter," etc. All of these admonitions to stay out were routinely ignored.

As president of the wardroom mess, I would sit at the head of the wardroom table. On one of the first days at sea at the end of the noon mess, I arose and announced, "I hear the rack monster calling. It is time for a "NORP" ("rack" was the sailor term for beds, which had been canvas bottoms tied to a metal frame). The old salts knew about the "rack monster" even though the new officers didn't understand, and no one knew what a "NORP" was. When they inquired, I explained "NORP" was the acronym for "Naval Officer's Rest Period."

CHENG and the First Lieutenant got together with the assistant Repair Officer. They had the Repair Department make a Bakelite sign. This one was blue framed with a gold edge. Instead of letters, Navy signal flags were painted on the blue background for November, Oscar, Romeo, and Papa. One had to know the signal flags to read it, but soon everyone on board knew it spelled "NORP."

NORP sign

As noted, most of the officers and crews did not pay attention to any of the other signs and would barge into my office regardless of what the sign said. However, when I hung the "NORP" sign on my door, no one dared to enter. It worked and continued to work until the day I left the ship.

• • •

One particular incident occurring on the transit to Rota was related to later events. The Repair Department had an informal leader who was a positive influence on the crew's morale. Second Class Petty Officer, Electronics Technician (ET2) Padelsky was constantly involved in supporting the ship's policy. He was a leader in group physical fitness workouts and other social activities.

One late morning after I had conducted my messing and berthing inspection, Padelsky knocked on my door and sat down. In the POD that morning, I had inserted my hand-written assessment of the previous day's messing and berthing inspection. In it, I had named a culprit of having a gross rack in the engineering berthing. Padelsky decided the new XO needed a lesson in leadership. He told me it was not right to identify poor performers in public, adding the old saw that I should praise in public and condemn in private.

I listened politely and then told Padelsky his idea might work somewhere else, but we were in the Navy and should be held accountable. I could put the poor sailor with the gross rack on report, which would lead to a rather lengthy non-judicial punishment (NJP) process, which was silly, or I could point out in public the rack-maker was creating a bad and unhealthy atmosphere for the others in his berthing compartment, which should put pressure on him to clean up his act.

I thanked Padelsky for his input and told him I would consider his advice in future POD notes.

• • •

On the fourth day after leaving port, a chief came to the bridge to report two sailors, male and female, had been found in a locked compartment. Apparently, nothing of significance had happened yet, but the situation was grossly inappropriate considering one of our biggest concerns. The two went to captain's mast and were dismissed with stern warnings.

This occurred as the captain and I were discussing how we should deal with male and female relationships when they went on liberty throughout the cruise. I went through the regulations concerning women at sea. We considered an incident during the previous regime when two crewmembers, a male and female kissed each other while crossing the brow to the ship. The sea trials incident of standing lights on after sunset, and the recent incident influenced our discussions.

As far as I can recall, we never wrote any of these rules down officially, but it was known throughout the ship these rules were in effect throughout the deployment and continued once we returned stateside:

1. There are no female or male sailors and officers aboard. There are only sailors and officers aboard, and we were all going to act like sailors and officers.
2. No two sailors or more shall ever be inside a compartment locked from within.
3. No affection will be demonstrated between crew members on board or in any area controlled by the ship including the pier or landing areas for liberty boats.

For many of the 900 sailors on board, rules were made to be broken. Sailors are sailors, and especially male sailors are sailors. Sailors can figure out how to get around any rule. We never caught any sailors involved in fraternization, romantic relationships, or sex. We suspected all might be occurring to some extent. We came close to discovering some liaisons but never did. Frank Kerrigan later told me he was handing out birth control pills like candy. But on the surface, it appeared the sailors were abiding by the rules. I am glad, as XO, I never found out what was actually going on. I do not know the extent of relationships between the men and women on board. But our rules worked.

• • •

It was a different time, different cultural mores and different fashion. An example was in my POD note:

6. Shaved heads. General regulations on grooming standards state that the standards are based on "neatness, cleanliness, safety, military image and appearance." While shaved heads might be clean, they do not project the military image and appearance. This is especially important when Yosemite enters foreign ports and represents the US in our sailors' appearance and conduct ashore. Consequently, no personnel with shaved heads will be allowed ashore after ROTA.

• • •

On September 16, captain's mast was held for several sailors put on report. MMFN(N) Edmunds, the deserter whose wife required me to write a letter of explanation to the First Lady, was one of them. The Captain assigned Edmunds to a Special Court Martial.

At 1000, Thursday, September 20, *Yosemite* entered Rota Bay and tied up port side to the pier at Naval Station, Rota.

By the captain's and my assessment, the transit had been successful. There remained a long way to our destination of Diego Garcia. The first of the four legs had gone pretty well. We had made our projected arrival date at Rota on time in spite of the threat of Hurricane Chantal. The crew had gotten their sea legs, and nearly all fared fairly well. From our experience with this new idea of women on ships, we had been able to formulate some rules. Perhaps the crew had bought into the idea they were sailors, regardless of gender.

It was time for a short port visit and to prepare to cross the Mediterranean.

Chapter 5: Rota, Gibraltar, the *New Jersey,* and Palma

September 1983: The Mediterranean, Palma de Mallorca, and the Suez
11 days deployed, 183 days to home

Rota, Spain is a coastal town with just shy of 30,000 inhabitants. In some ways it is like San Diego with a dry climate and the Canary current coming down Europe's western coastline providing a cooling effect, although not as strong as the Japanese current's impact on San Diego. I thought it was a sleepy town in 1968. Many of the citizens worked at the joint U.S. Navy and Spanish Naval base. It has become a tourist mecca for Europeans. I did not go ashore during this port visit, but when I spent two weeks there waiting for transportation to my first ship, I enjoyed the officer's club and the golf course, and frequented both often.

• • •

As I set the times for expiration of liberty, I couldn't help but mull over my first experience with liberty. In 1963 as a third class NROTC midshipman from Vanderbilt, I went on a summer training cruise out of Newport, Rhode Island on the *USS Lloyd Thomas (DD 764)*. Our first liberty port was in Sydney, Nova Scotia. I was astonished when they announced the different liberty expiration times based on rank.

Liberty for sailors (E1-E6) ended at 2200. Chiefs and midshipmen, both first and third class middies, were to be back at midnight, and officers' liberty expired at 0700 the next morning. I did not understand why I and my fellow midshipmen weren't allowed to stay out all night. After all, I had just finished my freshman year in college.

Even then and certainly after I became an officer on ships, I recognized enlisted personnel were a little crazier and a bit more cavalier than most chiefs and officers. After all, they were younger. The idea of having them returning early was a good idea and minimized the number of missed movements (not getting back to the ship before she got underway), reduced the number of fights in another country, and cutting down on international incidents due to overdrinking.

With the captain's blessing and inputs from others, including Master Chief Weaver, I was the one setting the limits according to rank. The first decision was easy. There would be no separate categories of liberty expiration based on gender. This wasn't even a discussion. Our first liberty for our one day stop in Rota, Spain was lenient. Liberty for all hands expired at 0715, the morning we got underway for Palma. There were no changes due to having a male and female crew. Like all of the overseas liberties I can remember such as my midshipman cruise, the junior enlisted liberty expired earlier, the first class petty officers were sometimes given a bit more time before liberty expired, the chiefs had additional time ashore, and officers nearly always had significantly more liberty time, often until the next morning.

Strangely, for a reason I cannot explain, the times for expiration of liberty arc not included in the POD's, the ship's logs, or my notes other than my handwritten note in the POD while we were in Rota. As I recall, liberty expiration times were generally the same for all the ports we visited during the deployment: 2200 for E1-E5 (all sailors below first class petty officer); 2300 for E6 (first class petty officers), 2400 for chiefs, and 0730 the next morning for officers.

• • •

Liberty in Rota was quiet. Being our first liberty out of home port, I was a bit nervous. Perhaps it was because the mixed gender crew would be going on liberty in an international port for the first time.

Perhaps it was because of my initial visit in 1968 to this southwestern port city of Española. I took a Morale, Welfare, and Recreation (MWR) tour to Seville and watched a bull fight. Except for that excursion, I played golf (poorly) almost every day on the base's very dry course, and every evening, I would wander from the BOQ over to the officer's club. On my second Saturday, I hooked up with a couple of aviators and several of the nurses at the O-Club bar after dinner. We went to one of the nurse's apartments in downtown Rota, the only time I was off base during those two weeks except for the tour. We played a drinking game called "Indian." I shall not go into details, but the other officers drove me back to the base in the wee hours of the morning and poured me out of the car. I stumbled into my quarters and proceeded through the worst hangover in my life. On the following Monday, I received instructions to catch a morning flight to Malaga, Spain where I would board the *USS Hawkins (DD 873),* my very first ship.

Needless to say, I did not have fond memories of Rota and had concerns some of *Yosemite's* personnel might follow in my experience fifteen years earlier.

The town was no longer off limits. The crew and officers went into town and enjoyed the sights, returning to the ship in good shape (as far as I knew). Several of the officers, including Doc Kerrigan and Linda Schlesinger, our Disbursing Officer, drove about 45 minutes to Cádiz. Cádiz is a larger city directly south of Rota across the Bay of Cádiz. The provincial capital of Andalusia had a fairly large casino. Linda had stood watch during sea detail, then pulled shore patrol duty before joining Frank at the casino. She later told me she fell asleep at one of the gaming tables. When she woke up, all her chips were gone.

• • •

We pulled out of Rota in the morning. By the time we reached the straits, the world of the sea had turned gray. Crossing the Straits of Gibraltar into the Mediterranean or back out to the Atlantic Ocean was one of the most majestic sights I saw in my 15 years of sailing the seas aboard Navy ships. By now, I had transited the straits four times. This time, it appeared the transit was going to be just gray mist and black seas with no sighting of Gibraltar's promontory likely this time. There were some dim lights through the mist at the foot of Gibraltar and to the south, lights on the Morocco shore. If you knew where to look as I did, you could barely make out the shadow of the awe inspiring peak.

Then came something better than seeing a rock. We gained communication with a radar contact on a parallel course eastward. It was the *USS New Jersey (BB 62). New Jersey* was one of the Iowa class battleships known for their powerful and accurate 16-inch guns. She participated in World War II, the Korean War, Vietnam, and in the Persian Gulf. The *New Jersey*, with a speed advantage, soon became visible, a specter of a magnificent past silhouetted in the gray mist. We crossed into Mediterranean waters side by side. It was more awesome than it would have been had it been a beautiful sunny day. We didn't need that Spanish rock. We were in the company of a legend, and she was breathtaking for this mariner.

I was even more impressed with CAPT Boyle when he sent a flashing light message to the *New Jersey's* commanding officer, CAPT Rich Milligan. Milligan had been promoted to Rear Admiral and was CAPT Boyle's immediate superior in a follow-on command. Milligan became the Commander, Cruiser Destroyer Group Two out of Charleston. CAPT Boyle was Commanding Officer, Readiness Support Group, Charleston, a direct report to RADM Milligan. They became friends and golfing buddies.

Their flashing light messages made me smile. They discussed the durability of the older Navy ships like destroyers, *Yosemite,* and *New Jersey*, compared to the new ships, an appropriate observation even more applicable today. And they were doing it by flashing light messages as these two ships of World War II vintage crossed from the Atlantic into the Mediterranean.

• • •

After parting ways with the *New Jersey* and before we arrived in Palma de Mallorca, we had an event that was upsetting to say the least. After we had secured from sea detail, we conducted a "unit sweep," a drug test for all hands.

As we got underway from Rota, we announced the unit sweep. The Navy belatedly had begun a "zero tolerance" program for drug abuse. In 1973-76 during my time aboard *USS Hollister (DD 788)* as chief engineer and later on *USS Anchorage (LSD 36)* as first lieutenant, drug usage had been epidemic. There were many crazy incidents involving marijuana and harder drugs on both ships, but it had been particularly rampant on the *Hollister*. During my years aboard those two ships, the Navy's policy was unclear, at least in my mind. On the *Hollister*, I took the position that if a sailor used drugs off the ship and his drug usage did not impact his performance on the ship, I would not take offense. But if they used drugs on the ship or the use ashore impacted their ability to perform, which in engineering is a definite ship safety concern, then I would do all in my power to take them to mast or a court martial and use every means available to get them off my ship.

My approach didn't work. I was at peace with the way I handled it, but drug usage did not abate on *Hollister*. On the *Anchorage* when I was First Lieutenant, drug usage remained a significant problem, but the wanton disregard for policy had abated somewhat. For an operator, sailors using drugs continued to be a scary proposition for many reasons.

After nearly four years as the Senior Naval Officer at the Texas A&M NROTC Unit and two years in my amphibious squadron staff tour, the military's zero tolerance for drug usage was a concern of mine when I became weapons officer on the *USS Okinawa (LPH 3)* in Perth, Australia in September 1981. Usage seemed to have decreased.

The military established a zero tolerance for drug usage in late December 1981. The policy used random testing and "unit sweeps" to find drug users and initiated punitive actions including courts martial or administrative separation for drug use. Drug checks included testing for marijuana, cocaine, heroin (opiates), amphetamines, barbiturates, methaqualone and PCP. The Navy's version of the edict was issued with the catchphrase, "Not on my watch, not on my ship, not in my Navy."

From my perspective as a ship's department head and later as executive officer on *Yosemite,* the zero tolerance greatly improved my ships' performance and greatly reduced the dangers associated with drug use on ships.

As part of the regulations including military justice, the procedure included the command's ability to process out of the Navy on an "Administrative Discharge" any Navy personnel who had tested positive twice. It was a step in the right direction. Using or taking anything with the probability of debilitating one's effectiveness at performing their job at sea on a warship was and remains an unacceptable risk. I believed that then and I believe that now. Even though I drank alcohol when ashore on liberty, I never had a drink aboard any of the Navy ships on which I was stationed. To me, there was and is a distinction between alcohol and drug use, but not on a warship.

I was all for the Navy's new zero tolerance stance. Another advantage of the policy for a ship's executive officer was it gave me a clear and unconfused procedure to follow.

There was only one sailor who "popped positive" on the test: ET2

Padelsky, the second class who had admonished me for calling out another sailor for a gross rack during a messing and berthing inspection. It was Padelsky's first drug offense.

When Padelsky appeared before me at Executive Officer's Inquiry (XOI), I asked him why he would violate the Navy's zero tolerance program. He told me he was raised in a family where they did not consider marijuana harmful, and they all used it as a matter of course. He continued by explaining he did not agree with the Navy's policy. I thought his explanation was a lame excuse and did not bear any weight. He knew the consequences, and he had violated the rules. I was sad a productive sailor who had been a positive force for the command had chosen to violate the drug enforcement policy. In addition to being a key, effective member of R-4 Division in providing electronic equipment repair and maintenance, he was the division's leading petty officer. As stated earlier, he had contributed positively to the ship's "*esprit de corps.*"

That made Padelsky's act even more severe from my perspective.

CAPT Boyle, if possible, was even stronger in his belief than I was about drugs having no place on Navy ships. Following his own guidelines, even though Padelsky's division officer and department head recommended leniency, CAPT Boyle held firm to his belief and administered the penultimate maximum punishment at captain's mast: reduction in rate to Electronic Technician, 3rd Class (ET3), half-pay for two months, forty-five days extra duty, and restriction to the ship for sixty days. The harshest punishment supposedly was three days in the brig on bread and water, but most commanding officers, including CAPT Boyle believed the long restriction and reduction in rate would have a more significant impact on the offender. I thought the captain's action was right on target.

If a *Yosemite* sailor had a second offense for drug usage, CAPT Boyle's policy was to refer the offender to a summary court martial. He believed, and I agreed, someone who used drugs and endangered the ship should leave the Navy with a "bad conduct" or "dishonorable" discharge. An administrative discharge would get the sailor out of the Navy but with a "general discharge under less than honorable" conditions. That was not sufficient punishment or enough of a deterrent in our minds.

I thought the incident was over: case closed. I was wrong.

• • •

There was another incident leading to disciplinary action also with a long term effect.

I worked until past midnight almost every night underway, sometimes as late as 0200. As a break, I would call the radio shack and ask for the latest messages to be delivered. Reading them would give me a jump on the next morning.

Petty Officer Moore, a radioman 3rd class petty officer (RM3) arrived shortly afterwards with the requested messages. She was a pleasant, smiling delivery person. I thought she should progress up the ranks quickly. Little did I suspect she would become one of my greatest headaches for almost my entire tour, at least equal to the problematic Fireman Edmunds's headache quotient.

Petty Officer Moore was a single mom. She had left her child, a daughter if I remember correctly, in the care of her mother when she deployed. What I didn't know was when we hit Rota and began the transit to Palma for our liberty ports, she had "fallen in love."

Apparently, she became infatuated with the second class radioman who was married. She made a run on him while the ship was in Rota. He wasn't interested and spurned her advances. This upset Petty Officer Moore. She decided to get revenge.

After almost 40 years, I cannot fathom how Moore came to her decision about how to exact her revenge.

It was before the morning mess after we had passed Gibraltar and before we reached Palma, when LTJG Leahy called me. She informed me she had already reported to the captain that the daily "crypto cards" were missing. ("Crypto cards" were the encoding and decoding pieces changed daily, usually after midnight Greenwich time to match with the crypto systems on other military forces' platforms.) They were highly classified and intelligence sensitive. About the only thing guarded more closely was the system for safeguarding nuclear weapons.

LTJG Leahy has sent me redacted copies of her letters to her new husband, Jim Leahy, who was the Main Propulsion Assistant of a frigate in Mayport. Below is an extract of one of those letters describing the incident (CMS is the abbreviation for Classified Material System):

Made it to Palma and approach went smoothly. My nav team is pretty sharp!...

Speaking of CMS – bad news. The other day one of the radiomen ...got angry at her watch supervisor and maliciously destroyed day 24 of the weather broadcast key card. I didn't find out at first. They first learned of the missing card during the watch to watch inventory at noon. They didn't tell me until I navigated the straits (good move I thought). Anyway they told me the next morning. I had a heart attack. Well anyway, I gathered all of the radiomen together and asked (begged) for info concerning the lost card. I told them that I suspected foul play and the entire shack would stay on board and undergo lie detectors. Well, 10 minutes later, this daffy chick admits she did it 'accidentally'. She was boohooing, etc. I was relieved that I knew what happened. Of course I had to send a message immediately. The CO/XO were pretty understanding considering. There was nothing anyone could do. I pulled her TS (Top Secret) clearance and pulled her from radio.

As Noreen wrote, she and Kathy Rondeau, the Operations Officer, reported the missing cards to higher authority. The failure to find what happened to the cards could have jeopardized the entire crypto system. An even worse result would be for them to have been stolen by a foreign agent, not likely on a ship at sea.

The details began to emerge. The captain and I were flabbergasted. LTJG Leahy and LT Rondeau were distraught but handled everything properly in reporting the incident and dealing with the aftermath.

After her Top Secret clearance was pulled, Petty Officer Moore was taken out of radio and assigned a Special Court Martial, and with the help of our admin officer and legal officer, Mike Jackson, we began the process of an administrative discharge.

The administrative discharge was an executive officer's best friend. If someone failed to meet standards, such as two drug usage offenses, this allowed the command to administratively discharge an enlisted person with a "general" discharge. The administrative discharge could also be used to discharge someone who had been to Captain's Mast, non-judicial punishment several times, or a court martial if the command made a good case the individual had become a disciplinary or administrative burden.

The admin discharge was a quick and effective way of getting rid of a problem. During my tour on *Yosemite*, the process also gave me a clear picture between the roles of a commanding officer and executive officer. CAPT Boyle and I would discuss the use of this tool in a number of situations throughout my tour.

But like the MMFN's Unauthorized Absence, the crypto card incident would have a long and troubling existence, lasting long after the deployment had ended.

14 days deployed, 180 days to home

On September 21, we set the sea detail to enter Palma de Mallorca, a beautiful European jewel of a city on the Spanish resort island less than 200 miles directly south of Barcelona. The uniform for entering port was "Service Dress Blue."

I took my post at the navigator's chart table in the after part of the pilot house on the starboard side. Soon, the pilot came on board, walked up to the bridge, and proceeded to the open bridge to join the captain. The navigator's job became pretty much a backup safety measure after that, but I continued to work diligently with the quartermasters and LT Leahy to ensure we were not standing into dangerous shoal waters.

As mentioned, the sea detail uniform was service dress blue. The doctor, LT Frank Kerrigan, new to the Navy, had received instructions on what "service dress blue" entailed from at least two of our prankish prone women officers. Frank came on the bridge and over to me in the proper uniform except he had on the navy blue long sleeve shirt underneath his service dress blouse, not the required white dress shirt. He looked like he might have hired out to Al Capone. I doubled over in laughter. Frank recognized his faux pas and started to leave the bridge. I stopped him and said he couldn't leave without the captain seeing his outfit. Protesting slightly, Frank

LT Kerrigan, Yosemite' medical officer in unusual uniform entering port of Palma de Mallorca

accompanied me to the open bridge. I tapped CAPT Boyle on the shoulder as he stood by the pilot before we passed the breakers into the harbor.

"Sorry to interrupt, Captain, I said as he turned around, "but you gotta see this." When he saw the doc, he laughed also, but it was more controlled compared to my original outburst. The captain quickly gained his composure and resumed his work with the pilot.

With the doc by my side, I walked to the ladder aft of the pilot house, and muttered something to him about how I understood he was new to Navy uniforms. Embarrassed, Frank went below.

With the navigation detail essentially having completed their duty, I turned to my executive officer duties, seeing the bridge watch was shipshape, and then doing a quick tour of the topside spaces to ensure everyone on the weather decks was in the appropriate uniform and no "looky-loos" were sticking their heads out of hatches, wearing dungarees or work coveralls rather than the proper uniform.

We moored pier side. I was back in Palma, one of my favorite liberty ports of all time.

The other time I had visited Palma de Mallorca, the island's large city, was in 1973 after I had become the ASW Officer aboard the *USS Stephen B. Luce (DLG 7)* in early autumn, 1972. Mallorca was the epitome of my vision of a Mediterranean island.

The city of Palma is as old European as you can get except for the weather, which was always Mediterranean and perfect in my time there. The perimeter of the island was composed of separate beach communities of different nationalities filled with tourists on vacation. On that previous port visit, a shipmate and I traveled the perimeter, stopping every five miles or so when we could detect a community of a different nationality: Spanish, German, Dutch, French, Italian, and so forth. Better yet, all of the beaches did not require tops. And nearly every commune had a disco.

It was fun, but I was married with a brand new daughter back in Paris, Texas. I had a drink and watched. There was great shopping back when a sailor could get a bargain in Europe. Best of all was sitting around at the tapas bars on the streets and drinking Sangria.

This time, it was different. I was the XO, in charge, and leading by example. We greeted the welcoming party, which included US expatriates in the Navy League. The Navy League has good and bad points. I had been exposed to both on previous tours. I was a bit wary, but the expatriate Navy

League members in Palma were anxious to reach out to help the sailors have a good time. Even though I was somewhat concerned with Palma being the first real liberty port for this ship with women in the crew and thought I should remain on board and monitor the situation, I could not evade a dinner at the home of an elderly Navy League couple when they invited CAPT Boyle and me to their home for dinner two evenings later.

It turned out well for me. The dinner was delightful, and the Navy League couple set me up with another Navy Leaguer for a round of golf at the private Mallorca Golf Course. It was a wonderful break. The gentleman picked me up at the ship. We drove to the middle of the island. I played the beautiful course poorly. My host put up with my play and bought me a gin and tonic with hors d'oeuvres before driving me back to the ship. Even though my golf game was its usual awful, I was in high cotton.

The first night of liberty gave me my first inclination of how having women as part of the crew could be beneficial. The wardroom officers on liberty had taken off to various attractions in the city and the island. I went into the "gut" with George Sitton, Ken Clausen, and Steve Strzemienski to check out how our sailors, men of course, were behaving.

The "gut" is Navy slang, somewhat of a generic term for an area in a big city, mostly in Europe, where sailors liked to hang out. It usually was an area filled with cheap bars and floozy women. It might even be labeled as a "red light" district. In many places, like Naples, Italy, it has been declared off limits to sailors by Senior Officer Present Afloat (SOPA) or the shore commander because of the unsavory and even dangerous reputation, certainly deserved in most "guts" I knew. Of course, sailors of the old guard loved to go to those kinds of places.

But not *Yosemite* sailors on this voyage. The "gut" was essentially empty of our sailors. We finally found an old, spacious bar in a back alley named "Texas Jack's" with our sailors, about a half-dozen of them. But they were chiefs, not junior enlisted. Master Chief Weaver, our command master chief; Master Chief Brewer, the leader of the huge R-2 Division, and the heart of the Repair Department, *Yosemite's* main producer of repair and maintenance work; Chief Johns, the boatswain 's mate chief who was always annoyed that most of the other chiefs had not been on a deploying ship before; Senior Chief Personnelman (PNCS) Delcogliano, the enlisted leader of the administrative department, and several other chiefs sitting around a large table, drinking beer.

They asked us to join them, and we did for a couple of beers. It was an enjoyable hour or so. Master Chief Weaver, after an inquiry from me, acknowledged he never drank any alcohol except beer. He told me he quit the hard stuff because it made him crazy and angry and only got him into trouble. The chiefs were the only *Yosemite* crew we saw that night.

But they were the only sailors we ran across in "The Gut." Apparently, most of the men had followed the women. Not having a pack of sailors in such places removes a lot of anxiety for any XO.

Palma was a very successful port visit. I was amazed. There were no liberty incidents. I had never been on a ship that did not have some kind of an international incident during liberty in an overseas port, and my liberty ports in foreign countries were extensive. I was also astounded when I received the Welfare and Recreation report of tours. Over three-quarters of enlisted personnel had gone on ship scheduled tours. No ship I had ever been on had more than twenty percent, if that, to go on tours.

I simply hoped all of our port visits would have the same happy ending.

• • •

From that day back in Mayport when I took over as the XO and throughout our voyage to Diego Garcia, XOI and Captain's Mast were frequent occurrences, often twice a week.

When someone was charged with a violation under the Uniform Code of Military Justice, the accused would be screened by the XO. The XO could either dismiss the charges or send the accused up the chain to Captain's Mast. While the executive officer was not supposed to mete out any punishment, this prohibition was often circumvented with threats like "…if you don't want to go see the captain, then I'll put you in hack (stay on board the ship) for three days."

When I first came into the Navy, liberty cards were dispensed at quarters or after the working day to all personnel who did not have the duty that day. They had to display those cards before they were allowed to go ashore. Those precious cards were often "missing" when a sailor had done something to displease the lead petty officer (LPO), CPO, division officer, etc. and the sailor had no option but to remain on board. During my early Navy days, the old system of *Rocks and Shoals* had not completely disappeared at the lower levels. It was not uncommon for an offending sailor to be taken to the boatswain's locker and return black and blue from an unofficial disciplinary beating. Many sailors considered that a better option than being sent to captain's mast.

I never employed corporal punishment, but I was involved with others delivering such punishment several times when I was a junior officer on the old destroyers. I certainly didn't offer punishments or threats during my XOI's on *Yosemite*. However, I became pretty good at chewing sailors out and then dismissing the charges before captain's mast. After all, I previously had many opportunities to watch executive officers and commanding officers do some pretty amazing acts to scare or intimidate sailors at mast before dismissing the charges. To put it another way, I had learned from the masters.

Even though the rules and regulations for shipboard discipline had been spelled out and there were few options for the XO to mete out discipline, he could be an effective disciplinary force in other ways.

The word about my ability for chewing out sailors at XOI quickly became known in the wardroom, especially by the seasoned warrant officers. By the time we reached the Indian Ocean, over two months, my ability became so well known, a warrant officer would sometimes call me aside to tell me he had put a sailor on report and was sending him to XOI but the case shouldn't go to the captain.

On one occasion, the warrant officer explained, "XO, this kid I'm sending to you is a pretty good kid who did a stupid thing. He doesn't need to see the captain; he just needs a good ass chewing; and you are the best at that." After I gave the sailor a superb chewing out and as the party was leaving my office, the warrant officer turned to me with a smile and gave me a "thumbs up."

There was one occasion after the deployment where the sailor who appeared before me had been four hours late in reporting aboard from liberty. He limply explained he was sitting in his apartment waiting for his ride from another sailor. When I asked him why he had not called the ship to tell his superiors he would be late, or why he had not called his ride to find out if the ride was coming, he told me he thought it was best for him to just wait.

"Are you telling me you just sat in a chair in your apartment doing nothing for four hours and thought that was the best way to handle the situation?" I asked.

When he meekly nodded yes, I arose from my chair behind my desk and walked into my small head leading forward to my cabin. The mirror above the sink faced aft and could be seen from the position before my desk where the sailor stood at attention during XOI. I looked in the mirror making sure the sailor was watching my reflection. I studied my face, twisting it, looking at it from different angles in the mirror before returning to my desk.

"Do I look that stupid?" I yelled, "I don't think I look that stupid. Do you think I look stupid enough to believe your story?"

I then chewed him up and down for his stupidity for about five minutes, going on a rage, pounding my desk, before finally turning to him and his chain of command to announce, "This time I'm going to dismiss this case. But if it ever happens again, I will see you go to a court martial. Got that?" I yelled.

When the sailor nodded numbly, I announced, "Case dismissed. Get him outta here."

But there were some difficulties with my tough guy XO image.

There were a couple of people who always attended XOI. The legal yeoman, YNC Lucy Gwinner recorded the proceedings. Also attending XOI was the admin/legal officer, ENS Mike Jackson to provide Navy legal advice; the command master chief, representative for the crew; the chief or the leading petty officer (LPO) and division officer of the accused; and the Substance Abuse Coordinator (SAC). The *Yosemite's* SAC was Electrician's Mate Chief Petty Officer (EMC) Paul. She was the only female chief electrician in the Navy at the time. She had had a rough time with alcohol but had gone through a recovery program and wanted to help others. Chief Paul had a perfect mindset for the job of counseling sailors concerning drug abuse, the recovery programs available, and the options sailors had. She attended XOI in case I needed her expert opinion on what we should do when drug or alcohol abuse might be involved. She also was also there to provide counseling for the sailor, possibly ending with the sailor entering a recovery program. EMC Paul was also tough as nails. She was old Navy. I admired and respected her.

She also knew my act.

When I went into my tirade act, she knew I was on stage performing at the top of my game. Occasionally, I would do something, like the "mirror-looking-stupid" stunt that she found humorous. It was difficult to continue with my rage charade when EMC Paul was stifling her laughter in the after section of my office behind the accused.

There were a few times when a female sailor came before me when I had to strike the fear of US Navy justice in her heart. Male sailors could break down. I not only could handle their breaking down, it fueled my performance because I knew they were absorbing the lesson. But when the female sailor began to break down and cry, it was a hard act for me to continue in my tough guy role. EMC Paul laughed at that as well.

Once when she started laughing quietly behind the accused's back, I lost it. Another sailor had done something really stupid and ended up reporting to duty late. After hearing another long winded and worthless explanation, I started beating the desk with my fists, but stopped and asked Chief Paul if she knew what diseases the doctor could handle.

Chief Paul looked puzzled.

Then, I explained, "I need to know if he can cure terminal dumbness because this guy has it so bad, I'm afraid he's going to die right here."

Chief Paul began to shake while muffling her laugh. Seeing her, I could feel myself losing it. I spun my chair around and began laughing into my handkerchief, hoping the sailor would think I had a coughing spell. Finally, I turned around and dismissed him with my usual fit of an angry warning.

Then, Chief Paul and I both shared another good laugh.

Chapter 6: The Big Watercourse

September-October: Sicily, the Mediterranean, the Suez Canal

Wrapping W — When we moored in Palma, I had been the XO for 40 days. The *Yosemite* had been on deployment for two weeks. I continued to learn how to be an effective executive officer. After Palma, we steamed overnight to Augusta Bay, Sicily. Our stop was brief. We anchored in the bay, refueled, and got underway. It would be our last refueling until we reached Diego Garcia. I was amazed at the old girl's legs. This is not a sexist comment as ships are referred to in the feminine gender; *Yosemite* was old; and "legs" in this usage refers to how far she could travel without refueling, the distance she could cover on a full tank of fuel. On all of my previous ships, we refueled frequently. Of course, we normally had oilers steaming with us, and we were required to maintain our fuel above 66 percent of our capacity. CAPT Boyle, the engineering expert, noted that he never worried about *Yosemite* running short of fuel.

• • •

It was difficult being Number Two, essentially subjugating my natural inclinations to the captain, and in many ways, adapting my behavior to most effectively lead and manage all of my subordinates while simultaneously demonstrating the behaviors he expected and deserved from me as his Number Two. I expressed my frustration in a long letter to Maureen:

Lady,

I almost lost it somewhere in mid-Palma until tonight {October 14}. I could feel the edge creeping in, the desire to not be where i was, the frustration, the lack of confidence all waxing toward the surface. There was no place to breathe, no one to talk to. The box (cassette tape) *i spoke into was only a box. It did not respond. The letters i placed on the paper were cold and flat, dull nothings that said less. i perceived all around me shrinking into their protective envelopes, not working together for the whole, lobbying for their interests, and i could feel all of those good feelings ebbing, not gone, but i could feel myself sliding into the mire.*

(Another day). But i caught it, stopped it, put the world in perspective, thought of you, loved you, thought of how long it would be before i saw you.

Then came another malady. Plague immunization came for me as we readied for entering the Navy port of Augusta, Sicily. The shot slowly went from having the expected sore arm into a touch of the plague (Anytime I was on a ship that visited a port with questions about the quality of health there, especially in a country noted for having diseases not found in the U.S., everyone on board was required to take a "plague" vaccination) *driving me down into a slight fever; my work hours caught up with me and the combination demanded sleep as retribution. i yielded amidst the silly mast cases of drunks, malcontents, malingerers, and young, good sailors losing their heads over their first piece of bona fide foreign tail and explained to me at XOI: "I met this girl and my friend and hers went back to her apartment and accidentally fell asleep. She didn't have no clock, and I didn't have no watch."*

So, i see this twenty-year old sailor, and i try to imagine the inept, drunken groping and all else that went on, and i wish i could tell him some things, but i know he would never understand even if he listened and most likely will never learn.

• • •

One of my goals after taking over as XO was to update the ship's instructions and eliminate duplication of instructions issued by higher authority. The first night after CDR Sheffield had departed, I hung my photograph of Maureen, arranged the office to my liking, and began to examine my surroundings. There was a built-in bookcase behind my desk, about six feet tall and about five feet wide. It held two-inch and three-inch loose leaf notebooks. The notebooks were filled with *Yosemite* generated instructions, some dating back probably to when she was commissioned in 1944. I wanted to leave after my tour with a set of ship instructions that were current, logical, and built upon existing instructions from our superiors, not parroting or duplicating them.

I didn't think I could complete them in what I anticipated to be a two-year tour, no more than three. But I was going to try.

The only time to work on this was each evening underway after I had briefed the captain following 8 O'clock Reports. This meant I would usually start around 2200 because after my meeting in the Captain's cabin, there was always a department head or someone else who wanted to talk to me. I enjoyed these conversations at the end of the day and didn't discourage them. Chaplin Poe was a great confidant. We would share stories and discuss potential problems and complain to each other. George Sitton was another frequent visitor in the evening. George and I respected each other's knowledge of the sea and deck seamanship, and he was an old style sailor like me with a caustic humor.

There were others, but I most welcomed Frank Kerrigan, the doctor. As mentioned earlier, Frank was brand new to the Navy. The powers that were back then had not sent him to "knife and fork school," which we laughingly referred to for an indoctrination period for officers who had no prior Navy experience like doctors, attorneys (JAG), and chaplains. Frank graduated from Michigan State on a basketball scholarship. Although he never made the varsity squad, he scrimmaged against Magic Johnson. That made him a superior athlete in my opinion. We both loved sports. Frank was the one person on the ship with whom I could talk about things without my position of number two having any impact on my duties as executive officer. For Frank, I was able to explain many things about the Navy no new officer without any indoctrination would know. To further solidify our bond, we were both recently married. It was a great relief to spend a couple of hours with no pressure.

But Doc and the others had lots of things to do, and all were gone most of the time before taps. That's when I would pull down a notebook from the bookshelf and begin shredding it, checking it for being current and for duplication. Arduous work but somebody had to do it. Actually no one *had* to do it, but I thought it should be done.

• • •

I was experiencing growing pains as the executive officer. I was an old seadog compared to 95 percent of the crew and wardroom. My Navy of the past had been on combatants where officers and sailors alike worked hard on board, and played hard ashore, but getting the job done. Working toward meeting the ship's mission was always paramount. Even on my ships during the escalating drug problems and student protests of the mid to late 70's, getting the job done overrode all other considerations for my shipmates and me. But now, I was faced with not only women as part of the crew and wardroom, but with a crew that were mostly those who had put in their workday and gone home every night, more civilian in nature than like my seadog days.

The doc was concerned with taking care of people, and the dentists were there for the same reason. The chaplain was even more focused on helping the troops. Repair and maintenance were the reasons we were on this deployment, not to go out and fight. Even supply was taking care of other ships and ensuring the repair department could do its job rather than focusing on meeting our own needs to allow them to be an effective fighting force. Our mission was a noble one and all of these people were excellent in performing their part of that mission but vastly different from my past experience. I was learning to adjust and play on a different playing field.

As much as I liked the captain and agreed with most of his policies, I was finding it difficult to be a complete supporter. I disagreed with several of his ideas and thought he was too harsh with our personnel in some matters and too lenient in others. I recognized this likely was true to some extent in every CO and XO relationship.

I tried not to show my frustration to CAPT Boyle and was even more careful in revealing my feelings with anyone on the ship. I knew I had to support him and his policies regardless of how I personally felt about them. After all, that was the true job of an executive officer on a Navy ship.

I was also a newlywed. I had been on this ship longer than I had been with Maureen since we married. It was eating at me.

I understood all of that and gritted my teeth when realizing there were about seven more months I would have to endure.

I expressed my concerns to Maureen in a letter before we arrived in Augusta Bay. She was my outlet for whining:

Maureen,

I'm extremely frustrated right now. My officers have not been staffing their administrative work plus they have been extremely parochial in their jobs. As a consequence, i've had to tighten down, forcing myself to be more dictatorial. All of this has been accented by the Captain's being rather particular and unyielding in the last several days. The results have produced some very tense and very long work hours for me.

This has to be the only correspondence for Augusta. I apologize not so much to you but to me because there are so many things i wanted to write to you. Please contact all, especially Blythe (my daughter from my first marriage, who lived in Austin, TX at the time with her mother) *and my parents, and explain why i've been so bad about corresponding.*

Our next mail will go out in Diego Garcia on October 14. Add several days for mailing before expecting any other letters from me.

Jeezus, i feel lonely. i love you and want to be with you. i want us to make love and forget the world for a few moments. Right now, all i can think of is what a screwed up deal it is to be away from you.

Maybe the long transit to our destination will settle me down, get my mind straight...

• • •

23 days deployed, 171 days to home

Other than the crypto destruction, the drug case, and my adjustment, the two-day journey to the southeastern part of the Mediterranean Ocean was mostly uneventful. The ship arrived at Port Said, the entrance to the Suez Canal, just before midnight. Immediately, it was confusing. The anchorage held an uncountable number of ships with their standing lights shining like a sky with thousands of stars. I don't recall seeing any other area of the seas with more ships than the entrance to the Malacca Straits near Singapore. For some reason, this mass of every kind of ship and vessel imaginable struck me as more ominous.

The next morning, ships began entering the canal at 0100. *Yosemite's* turn in line came early, getting underway at 0400. We steamed to the entrance and took the pilot on board. The Navy had warned us about taking on board other parties, even if recommended by the pilot. The other parties usually claimed extra lighting was required and then charged exorbitant fees for essentially useless floodlights. Even though we had briefed the key sea detail personnel on this warning, a team of five Egyptians were allowed to board with the pilot. When the captain and I were informed, we instructed our personnel posted at the entry to the ship on the port quarter to quarantine the Egyptians in a small room for the duration of the transit.

CAPT Boyle quite rightly was conservative in his view of foreign nationals being aboard the ship. He was graciously accommodating to guests but also protective of his ship and his crew. His recollection of the Egyptian pilot:

My most vivid recollection is the pilot. Somehow, I became aware that he had been disrespectful of our female officer, (Linda, I think) as she escorted him to the bridge. I was furious and had as little contact with him as possible. He was less than worthless foisted on us by the Egyptians. As I recall I directed him to your chair on the bridge and for him to remain there and that he had no further interaction with our women crewmembers.

Having spent lengthy times in Subic Bay, I was very aware of the deceptiveness and the thievery of foreign natives boarding Navy ships. I was quite angry that our personnel had allowed the Egyptian floodlight team aboard. The Egyptian pilot blustered his indignation at our not allowing his team to have free access aboard the ship, but we remained adamant. I was not pleased with the pilot sitting in my bridge chair, but I seldom sat there. It was not a big deal, just rubbing the salt in the sore.

• • •

CAPT Boyle remained on the open bridge almost through the entire transit of the canal. Although he relied heavily on the experience and expertise of LT Sitton to serve as OOD and conning officer, he allowed others to conn the ship under his or George's oversight. I suspect when our female officers, LT Kathy Rondeau, LT Sharon Carrasco, LTJG Noreen Leahy, and LTJG Emily Baker took the conn, they were some of the few, if not the first females to drive a capital ship in the Suez Canal.

Yosemite crew members taking in view of the Suez Canal and other ships in transit

Botton: A view of life along the Suez Canal

If I can get past the hubris of the pilot and the unethical, if not illegal boarding of the floodlight team, the passage through the Suez was remarkable and thought-provoking.

Even though I had witnessed the conglomeration of ships waiting for entry into the canal, the never-ending line of large ships of every type was just incredible. I considered all of the languages used in the necessary communication with the canal transit operators astounding. Once in the transit, I was not only staggered by the numbers but concerned about safety. The distance between ships was 500 to 1,000 yards. I worried of another ship's going Dead in the Water (DIW) due to engine malfunction or, because of a language barrier, a miscommunication between a ship's master, the pilot (especially if they were as all incompetent as ours), canal operations, and another ship creating a potential collision. These were not comforting thoughts. I was positive my concerns were echoed by CAPT Boyle although he kept his concerns to himself.

When I could divert my concerns about the shipping, the canal itself was stunning. The engineering effort required digging a watercourse 120-miles long and a width that easily can accommodate the U.S. Navy's newest aircraft carriers, was, to say the least, impressive. My everlasting impression of the journey was sand, sand everywhere like a colossal and unending beach. There were other emotional reactions. Shortly after clearing the passage through Port Said, evidence of the 1967 Six Day War and Israel's sudden victory was evident, even 26 years later. Destroyed tanks and armored vehicles partially jutted from the sand. It was sobering to consider how swift and deadly the Israelis took the Gaza Strip. Not too much later, we passed small villages. The citizens, mostly youths, sat on the canal wall with their feet hanging over the edge laughing and yelling as *Yosemite* passed by. It was a different world than ours, almost as if they were from an earlier century, and at that moment, only yards away.

At 0900, eight hours after beginning our transit, the column of ships anchored in the Great Bitter Lake. It is a saltwater lake, and it was barren then. Ship columns would anchor there to allow the columns transiting in the other direction to pass and reenter the one-way canal on the other side. Four hours, we stood at anchor, then getting underway heading south at 1343.

The rest of the transit was uneventful. But when we dropped off the pilot and the band of thieves and cleared the canal, we all breathed a sigh of relief, especially the captain and I.

Chapter 7: The Red Sea, The Indian Ocean, and Crossing the Line

En route Diego Garcia:
33 days deployed, 161 days to home

Transiting the length of the Red Sea was rather uneventful although I knew this relatively unarmed U.S. Navy ship was sailing in a less than friendly area. The Gulf of Aden transit was no less daunting although it felt more like being at sea than anything in the Canal or the Red Sea.

Looming ahead was a significant concern of mine. I decided not to discuss it with anyone, not even the captain. It was going to be what it was going to be, and my discussing it would not change it. On Wednesday, 12 October, *Yosemite* would cross the equator. The ship would experience "Crossing the Line." "Crossing the Line" was a time-honored and rough initiation in the old Navy. It had the potential to get out of hand, and that could become a huge problem for a ship with 106 enlisted women, two female chiefs, and six female officers.

In general, the Navy had been cracking down on hazing, which for centuries was a major part of the initiation of "pollywogs" (those who had not crossed the equator) by "shellbacks" (those who had crossed the line and gone through the initiation). I knew. I was a shellback.

In 1979, I flew to Hobart, Tasmania to join the staff of Commander, Amphibious Squadron Five as Current Operations Officer aboard *USS Tripoli (LPH 10),* a helicopter carrier. Our staff numbered about 30, the ship's complement was just short of 700, and the number of embarked United States Marine Corps (USMC) personnel on the landing force commander's staff and the marine air unit numbered around 600. The ship had crossed the equator en route to Tasmania. The number of pollywogs was significantly more than the number of shellbacks. It was a raucous two days.

The number of personnel, i.e., pollywogs, reporting in Tasmania included about 100 enlisted marines and one lieutenant commander, a.k.a. me.

Tripoli departed Hobart and went to Sydney, Australia for a week. Following Sydney, we made a port visit to Port Moresby, Papua New Guinea. After New Guinea, we headed for Subic Bay, Luzon, Philippines, and the equator. The transit produced another Crossing the Line.

The officer I was relieving, LCDR Conrad Bormann, knew Crossing the Line could be very rough for me. Out of 100 pollywogs, I was the only Navy type and the only officer. The 900 or so brand new shellbacks were excited about being on the giving part of the initiation, especially to initiate the one Navy lieutenant commander. Conrad gave me the lowdown on what was going to happen, how I should pick out my shabbiest working khaki to wear backwards for the ceremony, and how to act. He went an extra mile by promising to escort me through the initiation line to prevent some overzealous new shellback from hurting me.

After getting up an early hour, I dug out my oldest and most stained khakis (having been a chief engineer, I had managed to soil a number of working khakis), turned them inside out, and pulled them on backwards. I reported to the mess decks and was met by Conrad. I pretty much faked eating the "green" eggs and other supposedly gross breakfast fare. I figured I didn't need anything on my stomach for what was going to happen next.

Conrad escorted me to the gauntlet of eager new shellbacks excited about getting to lay on to a lieutenant commander with their shillelagh's (lengths of fire hose cut to be flexible paddles).

The shillelagh-wielding gang did not disappoint. I was amply whacked as I crawled along the flight deck, confident and assured Conrad was watching to make sure it would not get worse.

On my knees, I was ushered to the boatswain, one of the…how shall I say this, ahh… most stomach-ample sailors on the ship. It was time to kiss the "Boatswain's Belly." He grabbed my ears and forced my head into the folds of his belly. This could have been really bad, but Conrad had it stopped before I completely lost my breath.

It was bearable, and I was confident as I approached the last two steps. It would soon be over. Conrad's escort was a blessing. Then, as I approached the chute filled with garbage we had to crawl through, Conrad, after a messenger had run down to him from the flag bridge, nudged me and said, "We just received a top secret op-immediate radio message. I have to go read it, then brief the commodore and chief staff officer, but I'll get back as soon as I can."

As I faced the jury rigged tube stuffed with the previous night and morning messes garbage, my confidence dimmed a bit. But it was only about fifty feet, and one more event. I made it through and was spitting and trying to clear gunk out of my eyes and ears. I saw the final event was being hoisted in a cargo net along with three or four other pollywogs and being blasted by a firehose stream. Considering all of the slime I had all over me and filling most of my pores, that didn't sound too bad.

But as I headed to the cargo net's final indignity, they stopped me. I was informed that as an officer, especially a lieutenant commander, the only officer on the ship who was a pollywog, I would have to kiss the boatswain's belly and traverse the chute to finish.

Being a good sport, I went through the ordeal once more. This time with that unholy garbage mess filling the pores of my pores, I once again

Crossing the Line initiation station

Crossing the Line: final station, washdown

headed for the cargo net. Once again, I was stopped. Once again, I went through the line. I was beginning to wonder, but Conrad finally came back, saw what was going on, and guided me to the cargo net and my hose down cleansing.

Back in my stateroom, I stripped out of my inside out khakis, violated the Navy shower rule with a non-stop fifteen minute drenching, trying to wash as much as I could off me. Finished and dressed, I gingerly held my initiation uniform away from me, walked out to the weather decks and tossed them into the sea.

Therefore, I was very aware of what could happen at the Crossing the Line initiation.

32 days deployed, 162 days to home

We used every way of communicating to keep things under control, including a POD note:

1. Crossing the equator: (the initiation)

General safety guidelines: "crossing the equator" is a time honored tradition in which an initiation ceremony is performed to introduce the slimy, greasy pollywogs to trusty shellbackism. It can and should be fun for all hands. It can also be unnecessarily injurious and humiliating if common sense is not applied to tone down the physical and mental acts which are involved. Shellbacks must guard against being overzealous when applying those well-deserved wallops to the hind sides of the slimy pollywogs. The safety regulations shall be strictly enforced and any personnel violating those regulations will be required to forfeit any participation in the ceremony. The 'wogs watch committee has the overall responsibility for the safety of both pollywogs and the shellbacks on the forecastle. All senior personnel on committees have overall responsibility for the safety of both the pollywogs and shellbacks in their assigned areas. The following general safety guidelines shall apply:

1. *fire hoses shall not be used inside the skin of the ship.*
2. *fire hoses shall not be sprayed directly toward pollywogs.*
3. *no foreign matter of any kind will be rubbed into eyes, ears, or nose.*
4. *wallops, to the hind sides, shall be made with care to an area below the waist and above the crotch and shall only be administered in the designated "shillelagh line."*
5. *care must be taken to avoid directing water toward electrical boxes and outlets.*
6. *activities incident to "crossing the line" will be conducted on weather decks only. All areas inside the skin of the ship are off limits to initiation events.*
7. *pollywogs will walk up and down ladders.*
8. *shower shoes or rubber pads will be taped to the knees.*

I considered adding some comments to the above note concerning sexual abuse of any kind being cause for NJP. The greased bosun belly step particularly concerned me. I remembered our watchwords of not having men and women but sailors aboard and decided against such a warning.

CAPT Boyle, Master Chief Weaver, who would be King Neptune in the ceremonies, and I had numerous meetings on security and how to handle any misconduct. The word got out. It was not a patty-cake initiation. It was pretty much the way I remembered them. The major difference of Crossing the Line on *Yosemite* was that some women pollywogs became shellbacks that day.

The ceremony, I thought, was really good for morale. Everyone had gone through the ordeal or meted out the initiation rites together. Everyone was proud of getting through the two days, and everyone on board was a certified shellback.

• • •

It was time to get ready for Diego Garcia.

As we approached Diego Garcia, the captain and I wanted to be sure our sailors understood our rules. After discussing liberty on Diego Garcia, I published the following note in the 4 October POD, and it ran daily until we reached the lagoon:

> *Fraternization: The following USS Yosemite regulation is provided for the information of all hands: Fraternization between crewmembers of the opposite sex is prohibited on board or on the pier controlled by Yosemite. There will be no displays of affection, physical contact, or other type of conduct except that which is normally expected in a military environment. Off ship, public display of affection between Navy members in uniform is prohibited.*

Not counting the Suez Canal transit and the refueling stop in Augusta, Sicily, we had been out of port since leaving Palma de Mallorca, 27 September, the longest continuous time at sea, 16 days, for the vast majority of *Yosemite's* crew.

We began our preparations for entering port in earnest. A fresh water wash-down of the entire weather decks was conducted that morning. A navigation brief for entering port was held in the wardroom in the afternoon. We took a break when the Captain cut the cake on the mess decks to celebrate the Navy's 208th birthday and then we held a brief on boat operations, especially liberty boat runs, presented on the ship's closed circuit television in the evening.

Entrance to Officer's Club on Diego Garcia. LT Steve Strzemienski, Weapons Department Head, and LT Jack Campbell, dental officer.

35 days deployed, 159 days to home

1425, Friday, 14 October 1983: *USS Yosemite (AD 19)* anchored in the middle of the lagoon of Diego Garcia. Known to sailors as the "Footprint of Freedom," Diego Garcia had a significant US Navy presence in the British Territory, the largest island in the Chagos Atoll Island chain.

There is not much there. However, I had said during my previous stop there in 1981 on *USS Belleau Wood (LHA 3),* it was my vision of the island I would like to be on if marooned.

It was just as enchanting this time around.

Chapter 8: The Footprint of Freedom

October 1983: Diego Garcia

While entering into the lagoon through the toes of the "Footprint of Freedom," I recalled my other visit with pleasure.

I was there as the Current Operations Officer of the Amphibious Squadron 5 staff aboard the *USS Belleau Wood, (LHA 3)* in 1981. Sitting seven degrees south of the equator, the atoll measures just over eleven square miles. From the air, the land mass around the lagoon looks much like a footprint, which is where its nickname originated among sailors.

The weather is best described as muggy. Although there is considerable wind, I never considered either the humidity or the wind as problems. The oppressiveness of mid-70 lows and mid-80 highs throughout the year is mollified somewhat by those ocean breezes. Although the annual rainfall was slightly over eleven inches, the humidity and the dew points produce categories of "muggy," "oppressive," and "miserable" all year long. In spite of the small amount of rain, the humidity produces jungle thick vegetation if not held in check. I found it livable, even bearable in the shade, and I thought if I ever were marooned on an island, I would want it to be like Diego Garcia.

But it wasn't deserted. The base had a gym, complete with racquetball and basketball courts, weight rooms with spas and saunas in the dressing rooms. There were enlisted, chief, and officer clubs, as well as a "seaman's club" for the merchant marine. The Navy exchange was small but adequate.

Diego Garcia is the largest and only inhabited island in the Chagos Archipelago, which consists of approximately sixty islands. It has been a British Indian Ocean Territory (BIOT) since 1965 when it was detached from being a part of the British colony of Mauritius. The local population, consisting largely of former slaves on the coconut plantation on the eastern side of the island, were forcefully deported to the Seychelles and Mauritius in order for the British to make the island a forward military operating station in the Indian Ocean for the United States.

The island population of U.S. military, merchant marine, and contractors has grown to 4,000.

It is a beautiful atoll. The various clubs would provide a release for all of our personnel. The beaches were beautiful, although swimming in the lagoon or the outer beaches was discouraged. Hector, a 35-foot plus hammerhead shark had made the lagoon his home and was considered a pet, a part of the mystique of the place. Even still, it was not a good idea to swim with Hector.

Sharks were also plentiful in the waters surrounding the atoll. In addition, as LT Sharon Carrasco described:

...it was extremely dangerous to swim off shores surrounding the island. The land plunged suddenly down just off the shoreline creating a shelf where a swimmer could get trapped under if currents were bad. Sharks were numerous.

The British military maintained a presence with a unit of about 30 male personnel as the United States Navy became the dominant presence on the island. A significant number of deployed United States Naval Ship (USNS) cargo ships were anchored there to provide immediate equipment and supplies to US forces in any surprise conflict in the Mideast or other Indian Ocean areas, particularly in the Persian Gulf. The Navy also commissioned a "Naval Air Facility," (NAF) at the time used primarily by the Air Force for long range bombing capability throughout the Indian Ocean as well as supply aircraft for Naval forces in the Indian Ocean.

Once *Yosemite* anchored in the middle of Diego Garcia's lagoon, base personnel brought out a large barge to serve as our departure point from the accommodation ladder to the waiting liberty boats to take our crew and officers to and from the island.

Diego Garcia had some new buildings at the base. The transition to new barracks was completed, but the old wooden buildings where base personnel originally had been housed remained standing. They reminded me of many of the WWII buildings used for training at OCS in Newport, Rhode Island, or perhaps more so like the barracks in Asia during WWII depicted in movies, with wood siding on the outside and interior open bays, all on stilts. They were located near the toes of the "footprint". The Officer's Club was just beyond them on a point that was like the big toe of the footprint. The club was small yet provided a brief escape for officers, as did the Chiefs Club, the Acey-Deucy Club, and the Enlisted Club for all of the ranks. The O-club bar and dining area looked out toward the northeast where the "toes" of the "Footprint of Freedom" were visible. The "toes" were West Island, Anniversary Island, Middle Island, and East Island. The "O" Club had a great view, was comfortable, had passable food, and occasionally gave one the opportunity to have some contact with someone outside of the command.

• • •

I was a bit anxious. Liberty on Diego Garcia would be different from Rota or Majorca. To begin with, there were some Navy female personnel presently assigned to the Naval Station there. Our male and female sailors would be going on liberty together in addition to mixing with both sexes who were ashore. And there were no orphanages for painting, no tours to occupy liberty time. An island perfect for romance. I tried to conjure up how I would have behaved in that situation as a single officer fifteen years earlier. Yeah, I was worried.

I had also noticed there were a few men and women who were spending more time with each other. There was nothing against regulations or against our few rules about male and female relationships, nothing that could, on the surface be categorized as "fraternization." But the consistent pairing off was evident, and I wondered what else was going on when there was no one watching. I knew sailors were good at finding places where no one was watching. They would have a whole island to find places where no one would be watching.

We were expecting to be there for almost three weeks, transit to Perth, Australia for liberty, then back to the atoll before a transit and short period anchored off Masirah, Oman in early December.

• • •

Maureen was never off of my mind. At Parron-Hall Office Interiors where she was an account executive, one of the principals was Bob Long, who was also an excellent photographer. For a wedding/going away present, Maureen gave me some beautiful photos Bob had taken of her. We framed one large one, the one I hung on the after bulkhead of my office so I could look at it anytime I glanced up from my desk.

I looked at that photo a lot. After all of my work had been put to bed, I would write Maureen a letter, perhaps adding to it every night until it we had a mail call, when I would send it to her. Sometimes I would write just for me. Here is a poem I wrote and sent to her between *Yosemite* clearing the Suez and arriving in Diego Garcia:

To Maureen, the Beginning of an Epic Poem
Indian Ocean phosphorescence,
glowing wave in the night
awes me not,
i have seen this glow in other oceans,
while young sailors shout in delight
at their sighting the sparkling waves;
i, unamused, return to my stateroom
with better things to do
like dream visions that were real:
there should have been a diaphanous mist,
ethereal, mystical,
flowing about her
when she walked toward me
the first time
(mind, do not play tricks on me:
i desire to remember the moment
exactly as it was,
clear, finite).
her dress a gossamer gown,
softly caressing the elegance of her body;
her hair curled and falling to her shoulders gracefully,
framing her delicate, fine yet soft features;
eyes, oh eyes that drew me in, took my breath,
suggested more than my mind could comprehend,
grasped my soul
and
told Scherazade's thousand tales,

drawing me into a bottomless pit of emotion
before I knew emotion could have no end,
allowing me to float suspended in her beauty.
i was afraid to speak,
afraid I might fall from suspension,
might break the image before me;
then we got down to business;
what in god's name did I think, I think;
perhaps suspicious of her beauty,
certainly awed;
i made a joke.
did she notice i was nervous?

oh, little boy,
walk away
if you are merely making a furniture deal;
walk away happy with the thought
you will see her at least one more time.

i am deep into the Indian Ocean night;
i have learned to gauge the depth of the night
by the strength of the coffee;
now, the coffee is knock-your-socks-off strong,
burnt grounds black;
the work seems endless;
the sea is infinite;
yet i smile
when i dream of her.

• • •

Before we had arrived in Diego Garcia, I decided to let Maureen know our schedule.

I hedged on rules about confidential material in a quick note to Maureen. I felt a bit guilty. I would have been screaming mad, (or at least faked being screaming mad) if a junior officer or sailor had divulged such information to a spouse, but I also knew from experience, ship's schedules, although it was confidential information would become quickly available to just about everybody. I overcame my guilt when I thought our schedule was set. I sent it to Maureen with trepidation:

Boggs,
Here's the schedule as we know it:
14-24 Oct: Diego Garcia
25 Oct– 2 Nov: Transit to Perth
3-7 Nov – Perth, Australia
8-16 Nov – Transit to Diego Garcia
17 Nov – 7 Dec: Diego Garcia
7-12 Dec – Transit to Masirah, Oman
13-25 Dec – Masirah, Oman (anchorage, no liberty)
26-31 Dec – Transit to Diego Garcia
1-10 Jan – Transit to Mombasa, Kenya
11-17 Jan – Mombasa, Kenya
18-23 Jan – En route to North Arabian Sea
29 Jan-9 Feb – Ops North Arabian Sea (i'm guessing we'll be at
*   anchorage in Karachi,*
Pakistan with some liberty)
10 Feb-21 Mar – En route Mayport (Best bet is one stop in the
*   Western Mediterranean:*
we plan to ask for Malaga, Spain. If we could stop in the eastern
*   Med, it would most likely*
be Athens or Korfu, Greece.

• • •

The first morning after arriving in Diego Garcia, we had our "turnover" with the *USS Cape Cod* (AD 43). When a ship relieves another on deployment, they have a "turnover" when the ship leaving will provide information about duties required, the operational situation, and any other information that would be useful for the ship relieving the one now leaving. It also might include the passing of materials or paperwork pertinent to performing on station. Our "turnover" was brief. The tender we were relieving had not had one period of maintenance for a Navy ship. The Captain, department heads, and I were appalled. The thought of sitting at anchor in the lagoon with nothing to do was not a comforting thought. My concern about all of the free time our men and women could enjoy in various ways increased my concerns.

CAPT Boyle thought of a way to make us more effective and was determined to make it happen. He forwarded his proposal to Admiral Butcher, our immediate operating superior and the Commander, Task Force 73, and Admiral Hogg, Commander, 7th Fleet, the senior Navy officer for operations in the Western Pacific and the Indian Ocean

CAPT Boyle recommended *Yosemite*, rather than remaining in Diego Garcia except for one December week off Oman and the liberty trip to Perth, Australia as scheduled, sail immediately to anchorage off Oman's island of Masirah and provide maintenance and repair services to ships of Battle Group Echo, the *USS Ranger (CV 61)* carrier group for the bulk of our time in the Indian Ocean.

The chain of command realized CAPT Boyle's idea had merit and ordered *Yosemite* to get underway and head to an anchorage off the island of Masirah, Oman much earlier than scheduled.

As is usual for the Navy, our main enemy was distance. Nearly all, if not all of the US combatants in the Indian Ocean were operating in the North Arabian Sea or in the Persian Gulf, over 2,000 miles from Diego Garcia. For a ship to receive maintenance and repair services, she had to transit more than 4,000 miles from her area of operations to reach Diego Garcia and return. That's over ten days. Adding the repair availability, normally two weeks back in the states, would make a ship unavailable to meet operational requirements for over three weeks.

Going to anchorage off the island and staying there until Christmas made good sense. Compared to Diego Garcia, Masirah is much closer to the primary operation areas of US forces. A ship could reach *Yosemite* within a day of being on station, sometimes less. Since *Yosemite* would be at anchor, essentially at sea, with no liberty, time for services to be completed could be compressed into much shorter periods. Such a move would allow *Yosemite* to be effective in accomplishing her mission, i.e., providing support services to combatants in a forward-deployed area.

The change made perfect sense. I suspected wanting to be at sea rather than in a port might have played a small part in the captain's idea. We would be performing our mission of providing services to our fleet.

I was elated. We would be at sea again. The CO and XO would have much more control over ship's company, and the change would, in fact, allow us to do our job better and more frequently.

 JIM JEWELL

Yosemite's liberty boat with passengers

Bottom: Liberty party going ashore in Diego Garcia

On the other hand, this would also affect our schedule, most significantly our liberty port visit to Perth, Australia.

Perth was one of my all-time favorite ports of call. I had spent over two weeks there when I joined the wardroom of *USS Okinawa (LPH 3)* and earlier as the Current Ops Officer on the Commander, Amphibious Squadron Five staff aboard the *USS Belleau Wood (LHA 3)*. I was single, and Perth was a wonderful place to visit for a single US Navy officer.

As with all things related to Navy ship's schedules, that schedule did change. The departure from Diego Garcia to a longer stay off Masirah made a voyage east to Perth impractical.

With the loss of Perth as a liberty port, the captain and I lobbied through radio messages to the chain of command for the *Yosemite* to return to Mayport at the end of the deployment by going east, around the world. Of course, we both wanted to circumnavigate the globe. We also mistakenly believed it would be a public relations coup for the Navy: the first Navy ship to go around the world with women as part of ship's complement. The chain of command, not too excited about getting positive public relations for the Women at Sea program, denied our request.

• • •

We would be headed north shortly. We might have been the first tender to operate in a forward operational area for an extended time since the Korean War. After that conflict, tenders and other support ships usually remained far from the area where operations were being carried out. But *Yosemite* would be closer to the action at Masirah. That made missing Perth and not going around the world a little easier on me.

As the plans were changing, we continued to operate as other tenders had in the "Footprint of Freedom." Liberty launches began their round trip circuits at liberty call until the expiration of liberty. Our few rules about fraternization apparently worked. Senior personnel, including myself, observed our crew. Our sailors would go to the Navy clubs and have a good time. As they left the clubs and headed back to the liberty boat landing, a number of couples could be seen walking with their arms around each other or holding hands. As they walked toward the liberty launch pier, they would gradually move away from affectionate postures and by the time they arrived at the liberty launch, they would be mixing with everyone else as if they were not a couple. More than anything, the possibility of an unplanned pregnancy loomed as a problem that might torpedo the entire program due to bad press.

Having liberty meant having problems, even on an atoll in the middle of the Indian Ocean. One medical report in the ship's logs for 16 October is proof:

Received injury report on Moore, Joe. S., MM3 procured head injury from falling out of his rack. Urinalysis to follow.

Even with alcohol available in the clubs and apparently marijuana and possibly other drugs available through sailors not abiding by Navy regulations, we had a minimum of liberty problems. I attribute some of that to male sailors behaving better when they were on liberty with female sailors.

• • •

Yosemite had business to address before leaving the atoll.

The captain made official calls to the commander of the British detachment, CDR Tony Hodgson, Royal Navy (RN). CAPT Boyle also rode his gig out to the *USNS Jupiter (T-AKR 11)* to give his official regards to the senior master in charge of the civilian manned forward deployed flotilla.

There was a requirement to refuel. It had been a long way since Augusta Bay when we last took on fuel. Combatants, for all of my time aboard them, refueled at sea.

In my early Navy years, refueling was done from a Navy oiler. Back then, the surface Navy had the destroyer, amphibious, and service forces. The service force consisted of ammunition ships, cargo ships, and oilers. Refueling at sea was a tricky evolution, bringing a ship alongside an oiler, passing hoses from about 120 feet apart, maintaining course and speed (usually 12 knots) with the combatant maneuvering to maintain station on the oiler. The refueling usually took an hour or so depending how much fuel the combatant needed to top off. The refueling was usually accompanied by a high line between the ships with the oiler delivering supplies and mail and swapping movies, and occasionally personnel would ride on a "bosun's chair" transferring between the two ships.

It was a demanding operation for all hands from the engineers to the personnel on station. The crew would have to latch up the refueling rigs

Yosemite in Diego Garcia with *USS William Bates* (SSN) alongside

and tend the lines. For the conning officer on the bridge, keeping station was a mark of good seamanship.

By the time *Yosemite* deployed, most of the service forces had transitioned out of the Navy and had become Military Sealift Command ships manned by the merchant marines, not sailors. The amount of refueling at sea had greatly decreased with most refueling being accomplished in liberty ports. It really didn't matter as *Yosemite's* capability to refuel at sea had been removed a number of years before we deployed. In a way, I was relieved. Even though we had the best LDO Bosun I had ever met, a CO who was an expert in such maneuvers, and I was a conning officer with tons of experience, we had enough on our plate without having to go through refueling at sea.

On Monday, 17 October, we weighed anchor, moved to the Petroleum, Oil and Lubricants (POL) pier and commenced an all-day refueling, returning to anchorage in the late afternoon.

Maintenance for USS William S. Bates (SSN 680), 18-19 October

Yosemite's mission was to provide repair and maintenance services to forward deployed ships. The first Navy ship was not a destroyer type, but a nuclear submarine. The *USS William S. Bates (SSN 680)* came alongside and tied up the next morning. The one-day alongside allowed us to perform some minimal maintenance and repair work. The *Bates'* primary need we provided was reprovisioning her food supplies. Linda Schlesinger, our ship's store officer at the time, remembers the sub's provisions were down to hot dogs and brussels sprouts.

It was our first time providing maintenance since we had deployed. I thought it somewhat ironic that our destroyer tender was providing repair and maintenance services as well as supplies to a nuclear submarine. I was also well aware of the high jinks submariners could initiate. Their wild liberty escapades were well-known sea stories among surface sailors. Those submariners had spent long, long days and nights submerged without any contact with females. Some of their antics on liberty, and even antics of their own commanding officers, were legendary. Yet no incidents from the submariners reacting to the women crewmembers occurred, at least as far as I knew.

• • •

As noted earlier, it was easy to forget Diego Garcia was not a paradise. It was a beautiful tropical atoll, if humid and far away from where we came. I personally experienced such an awakening on my first stop there for those four days in 1981. I had escaped from other officers and had stopped my vehicle on the side of the road past the Naval Air Facility. At that point, the atoll was less than a half mile across. I walked over a dune to the beach on the ocean side.

I stumbled upon the carcass of a long dead fish about six feet long. I surmised it was a tuna of some sort but it had disintegrated into being unidentifiable even though there was some skin attached to the bone. The thought of wading in the ocean quickly vanished with my discovery.

I decided to just walk the beach. I was at peace, almost meditating as I walked slowly along what I thought was a pebbly sand surface. Then I sensed I was having a stroke or something. The long stretch of beach appeared to be pulsating, undulating, moving. I became dizzy. I wondered if it was a slow earthquake or if the volcano from which the atoll was formed was awakening. I wasn't afraid yet, but I was paying attention to this feeling.

I kept observing. I looked down at my feet and realized the source of the strange movement. The entire beach was covered by tiny hermit crabs. They were all moving, producing the undulating movements for as far as I could see. I watched fascinated, trying to get my bearings before I finally left. I never went to the ocean side beaches again.

Maintenance for USNS Catawba (T-ATF 168), 18-19 October

Later that morning, the *USNS Catawba (T-ATF 168),* a MSC fleet tug came alongside to port. She refueled and got underway the next morning.

After *Catawba* departed from refueling, I went ashore. I went on a run of about ten miles with the doc. We showered and changed at the gym and then went to the Officer's Club for dinner. I sat down at the bar for an after dinner drink. Sitting next to me was the master of the *Catawba.*

I have no record of his name nor remember it. We talked over a couple of drinks. I remember most of the conversation well because I was thinking about my future.

The master related he had been a second class quartermaster on a destroyer with six years in the Navy. He got out, used his navigation experience in obtaining his third mate's license, and quickly moved up to master of a fleet tug in his early thirties. The salary for a master of any sea-going merchant marine ship was almost three times what I was making as a commander and executive officer with 15 years of service. In addition, the *Catawba* master's contract was to work at sea for six months with the next six months off at home each year.

Being on a ship at sea had become a passion for me. If my quest for command at sea did not materialize, a real possibility, I was looking for another option for continuing a life at sea. My first executive officer tour (my last of three years of obligatory service after my first tour aboard the *USS Hawkins (DD 873)*) was with the MSC. I experienced life in the Merchant Marines. My MSC Unit One rode the *USNS Geiger* and later, the *USNS Upshur* carrying Republic of Korea troops to Vietnam and back to Pusan, Korea. The Navy transport unit officers consisted of a commander CO, the XO, two doctors, and a chaplain. The medical team consisted of a chief and six corpsmen. Two "storekeepers" were assigned to the unit. One second class yeoman, a boatswain's mate chief and two seamen rounded out the unit.

On that tour, I considered finishing my obligated Navy service of three years, attaining a third mate's license with the merchant marine and spending my life at sea. My career goal was to be a sportswriter, and an offer from my good friend from Vanderbilt, John Johnson, to become the sports editor in Watertown, New York, was too good to turn down. When my active duty obligation ended in January 1971, I separated from the Navy and became a sportswriter and then sports editor of *The Watertown Daily Times*. At that time, I no longer considered obtaining my third mate's license.

Kathie, my first wife became pregnant while we lived in Watertown. The possibility of earning enough money to support my wife and a child on the way was not going to happen unless I moved to a larger paper, which I wasn't ready to do. That's when I requested a return to active duty.

Talking to the master of the *Catawba,* that possibility of remaining at sea crossed my mind as it had a dozen years before. I had always wanted to be on an ocean-going minesweeper and a fleet tug was similar in size and more of a working ship. It should be, fun. But I dismissed the thoughts quickly. I was married and wanted to spend as much time with Maureen as possible.

Maintenance for USS Lynde McCormick (DDG 8), 18-19 October

The next day, the *USS Lynde McCormick (DDG 8)* came alongside for repair and maintenance services. The planning conference went well. CAPT Boyle invited the *McCormick's* CO for dinner later that evening. The conference and the dinner led to another first during our transit north in the coming days.

As we concluded *McCormick's* maintenance period, radio messages from Commander in Chief, US Pacific Fleet (CINCPACFLT) confirmed our schedule change. The *Yosemite* would head north in three days, arriving off the island of Masirah, Oman on 1 November.

As mentioned earlier, the bad news was the scheduled liberty port visit to Perth, Australia was cancelled. The crew was not happy about not going to Perth but instead going to sea and working. Neither was I.

I had flown to Perth from Subic Bay, Luzon, Philippines on a C-130 in September 1981 to report aboard *USS Okinawa (LPH 3)* to relieve Ken Manni and become the weapons officer.

The flight was one of the most miserable in my Navy career. Being the only officer on board other than the flight crew and dressed in my service dress blues, I sat on a cargo jump seat in the back of the aircraft and concerned about my appearance when reporting to *Okinawa*, I remained there during the flight while a number of the enlisted passengers climbed atop the large amount of cargo and slept sprawled out for most of the initial ten-hour flight. The pilot announced we would land at an Australian air base in Queensland to refuel and have breakfast prepared for us at the air base's enlisted mess. This was welcomed news as our only in-flight meal was a box lunch we had been handed while boarding. It consisted of a ham and cheese sandwich on white bread with a bag of chips, an apple, and a stale cookie. The flight crew handed out cokes and cups of water sporadically throughout the ten hours.

Unfortunately, no one had told the Australian galley of the plans. The breakfast did not occur and we re-boarded for the remaining twelve hours.

But the miserable flight led to one of my two liberties in Perth. The second time was even better, one of the best I had during my time at sea. After the *Belleau Wood* had moored in Fremantle, the port of Perth, a group of officers hired two cabs to go to Eagle Wools, a sheepskin plant outside of Perth. I was not interested in purchasing any sheepskins but decided it would be good to mingle with my shipmates and tagged along.

Eagle Wools consisted of a warehouse where a number of ladies were sewing sheepskins into various items, mostly hats and slippers. Much later, the company became the manufacturer of Ugg boots. The warehouse boasts a modern showroom with Ugg products on display.

We were greeted by Phil White, the plant's manager. He pointed the other officers to product sales material and turned them over to the ladies. When he asked me what I was interested in buying, I responded I wasn't interested, just along for the ride. Phil then took me over to a 1950's era refrigerator filled to the brim with cans of Emu Beer. We had both had about three while the officers finished their shopping. Phil offered to give me a tour of Fremantle and Perth. A great friendship was formed.

Phil White gave me the "cook's tour" of Perth and surrounding areas, while his wife dined with the two of us for the rest of our liberty stay. I went to pubs that might as well have been in Britain. Phil took me out to an Australian Rest and Relaxation (R&R) inn in a park where Australians and Americans had escaped from the rigors of battle in World

War II and Vietnam. There after a hearty lunch, I had face-to-face time with kangaroos, koalas, and wombats. The couple also introduced me to several enchanting Aussie women. It ended the night before *Okinawa* sailed with Phil and me back at Eagle Wool with the two of us swapping tall tales. After not intending to buy any wool products at the outset, I left my last evening with Phil with four two-hide sheepskin rugs and a couple of wool hats for gifts. To top it off, Phil gave me a great price on a nine-piece sheepskin, which I purchased for myself. I used that piece as a rug in front of my bachelor apartment fireplace, a bed cover, and something to make me warm when needed. (My younger daughter, Sarah, has it now).

I was looking forward to escapades with Phil one more time, but it was not to be.

• • •

I developed a good relationship with CDR Tony Hodgson, the head of the British detachment in control of the island. One night after an afternoon run and a racquetball contest with Doc Kerrigan, I met Tony at the officer's club for dinner. Our conversation led to beers and darts at the small, all-hands club in the British compound. We discussed the island's history and the deserted coconut plantation, which had been worked by slaves, at East Point on the other side of the atoll. We also discussed *Yosemite's* rather incredible capabilities.

Seeing an opportunity to recapture the deserted plantation from the jungle vegetation, Hodgson followed up with a request to the ship. He asked if we would be willing to participate in a restoration of the plantation's main house. We agreed to go to the site and check out the possibilities.

The remarkably capable CWO2 Ken Dawson, the assistant Repair Officer LCDR Frank Fortson, and I met Tony at the liberty boat landing. He drove us out to the east side of the island, parked, and we walked toward the plantation grounds through what had been a bumper crop of coconut palms. As on my last visit to Diego Garcia, I was beginning to feel dizzy, like the earth was moving, but this time it was not the millions of tiny hermit crabs moving across the beach and making it appear to undulate. This time, there were hundreds of coconut tree crabs in an area between the trees. And these crabs were all the size of a large dinner plate, all quivering in a large pile.

House of manager on Diego Garcia's coconut plantation worked by slaves.

I immediately thought of my father telling me about his time in the Philippines as a Seabee in World War II. He also ran into those coconut tree crabs, actually having one crawl upon his chest in the middle of the night while he was sleeping in his sleeping bag.

Our group moved on to the plantation proper. First, Tony took us to the slave quarters, which was used for the "apprentices" after slavery was supposedly abolished. It was depressing. The living quarters were open to the weather and bare, of course. The slaves obviously spent a great deal of their time in a large and open communal area when not working. Tony pointed out an area slightly apart from the rest of the slave living area that had been their "hospital." In the center was a concrete table. The top was slanted down at about a ten-degree angle with a hole in the bottom. Tony explained they performed their surgeries there and the slant and the hole was to allow the blood from the cuts made in the procedure to run out and down so as not to pool and interfere with the surgery. He then added the table was also used for embalming those who died.

In a way, it was macabre. I was in some "time machine" movie where the different times and folks from different cultures collided.

The British eliminated slavery on this island in the mid-1800's. However, the conditions for the "apprentices" who worked for their former slave owners on the atoll's plantation remained pretty much the same until they were forcibly evacuated off the island. The British had agreed to provide the US military a forward base in the Indian Ocean for quick response to any threats to US interests. The agreement provided "unpopulated territories" for US use, stipulating "each island so used would be without a resident civilian population." Even though it was the British who effected the forced evacuation of Diego Garcia, the US State and Defense departments were fully aware of the action. The evacuation and the US moving onto the atoll took place by 1973. More than 2,000 islanders from the Chagos chain (they are called Chagossians) were relocated to Mauritius.

According to Wikipedia, for those islanders up until the evacuation, "… it was common for local plantation managers to allow pensioners and the disabled to remain in the islands and continue to receive rations in exchange for light work. Children after the age of 12 were required to work."

I was standing where essentially slavery by a different name had been practiced only a dozen years earlier. The residents were removed in 1971. Pets were taken from them and gassed en mass. Brutality to humans and animals, which should have disappeared from the earth a hundred-plus years ago was extant. I was a mariner who wanted nothing more than to be on Navy combatants for the completion of my active duty. Now I was a leader in the cutting edge of a new movement toward equality: women on US Navy ships. The juxtaposition of the mistreatment of the Chagossians, my continuing pursuit of command at sea, and my job in this women at sea program struck me as ironic.

I shook off my thoughts as we moved to the main plantation house. It was in bad shape with misuse, rot, and the wear of the tropical weather and invasive local plants, insects, and animals. The wooden floors were unsafe for walking, the tin roof was badly damaged and leaked like a sieve. Frank Fortson and Ken Dawson assessed the work required. Essentially, to bring the house back to a suitable condition would require a complete rebuild.

Regrettably, we told the British representative any significant improvements could not be done with the time we would be at the atoll.

• • •

With the news of our schedule change, our stay in Diego Garcia took on a different tone, shifting to preparations for getting underway for an extended at-sea period.

The ship's in-port business continued as usual. Liberty ran as usual. We ran "I-Division" indoctrination for new crewmembers reporting aboard. The ship's basketball team played games against different base organizations' squads including the "All Island" team at the base gym. The ship's softball team played several games including one against the "Near Term Pre-deployment Force." Small arms qualifications were being conducted. Preparations and study for advancement exams were underway. And civilian instructors for the Navy's Program for Afloat College Education (PACE) were conducting a number of courses for crew and officers.

The ship also conducted the Physical Fitness Tests (PFT) over a period of three days. The Navy's PFT program was created in 1976 over concern many of our sailors were not physically able to perform in combat or other dangerous situations on ships. This PFT effort was a follow-on to the "JFK" physical tests introduced in the 1960's by the sitting president, John Kennedy. Ships made a gesture of complying, but there was no concrete corrective action required in the program, and it was mostly ignored, gradually disappearing.

I was all for the new standards of physical fitness. I remembered a few enlisted shipmates from previous ships who were too obese to get through the smaller hatches. The new requirements not only required passing the minimum standards of pull-ups or push-ups, sit-ups, and a 1½ mile run, they established a "body fat" minimum." At the time, failure to meet the body fat standards or to pass the PFT could be cause for the service member to be administratively discharged. Later, there were more teeth put into the program with on-board remedial programs for failures, and if that was not productive, the service member could be sent to a Navy program for failure at body fat reduction much like the earlier established drug and alcohol rehab programs. The program was quickly labeled the "fat farm" by sailors (In my final Navy tour, I had a most rewarding experience when I required a senior chief to go to the "fat farm" when, after returning to the command, he thanked me for saving his life). If all of these failed to produce results, the service member could be administratively discharged.

ENS Emily Baker, our Damage Control Assistant (DCA) recalled the *Yosemite* included push-ups in our PFT, not pull-ups. Linda Schlesinger, one of our stars in the supply department, remembers the command master chief, BMCM Weaver crossing the finish line of the run with a lit cigarette hanging out of his mouth.

• • •

Chaplain Poe held Roman Catholic Mass every Saturday and two masses on Sunday. He also led Protestant Services on Sunday, Protestant Bible Study on Wednesday, and "Free Worship" on Sunday evenings, two Church of Christ lay services on Sunday, and Latter Day Saints lay services on Sunday. He was a busy man.

Military Justice also had to be served. This was not a crew of angels. Sailors were sailors and always will be. The results of Captain's Mast on Friday, 21 October, were listed in the next day's POD and make this point for me:

9. *Captain's Mast: The following are the results of Captain's Mast held on 21 OCT 83:*

Rate   Viol. UCMJ   NJP Awarded
FN ART. 92 Derelict in duty   30 Days Restriction to
USS Yosemite,
30 days extra duty, RIR to E-1
SN ART. 86: UA from unit (2 specifications)
ART. 87: Missing ship's movement
ART. 134: Breaking Restriction   Awarded Court Martial
SA ART. 89: Disrespect to a commissioned officer
ART. 128: Assault (3 specifications)
ART. 134: Communicating a threat (3 specifications) Awarded Court Martial
SA ART. 86: UA from unit
ART. 87: Missing ship's movement   45 days restriction to the USS Yosemite *45 days extra duty, Forfeiture. of ½ month's pay ($286) per month for 2 months, RIR to E1*
SA ART. 92: Failure to obey a lawful general regulation, 30 days restriction, to USS Yosemite, *RIR to E1*
SR ART. 86: UA from ship
ART. 87: Missing ship's movement   Awarded Summary Court Martial

• • •

Diego Garcia provided its own challenges. The following POD note demonstrates beach liberty could be dangerous:

Safety Note – Cone Shells
Venomous Cone shells can be found in the Diego Garcia area.
They have a highly potent venom apparatus and their stings have caused paralysis, coma, and death. <u>Avoid these shells.</u>

It was easy to forget Diego Garcia was not a paradise. It was a beautiful tropical atoll, if humid, far away from where we came with its own dangers.

• • •

It was late October. We had been away from our families for a month and a half. For many of the crew who had not deployed before, it felt like we had been gone for an eternity. Christmas was two months away. But we were reminded we were not going to be like Elvis and be home for Christmas. We had set up a studio for videotaping Christmas messages back home. Those crew and officers who wished to send a message back home could be taped and the videos would arrive back home for the holidays. The tapings brought the realization of not being home for Christmas into clarity.

Although I did not make a video tape for Maureen in San Diego or my daughter Blythe in Austin, Texas, I also was lonely. I had made three deployments from 1979 through 1981, but I had been a bachelor then and viewed them as long, hard work interspersed with lots of fun. However, I was married. My new wife and I had been together for a whopping two weeks. I expressed my feelings in a 20th October letter to Maureen:

Lady,
i have decided, quite on my own, there is no way possible, no way, you can be the woman I think you are.
i mean, I mean, really mean I look at your pictures. By the hundreds, I look at your pictures and know, no matter how gawdawful (Southern term) good looking I think you are, how much more I think you are good looking in the first person.

There ain't no possible way a woman could be as wonderful as I know you are. So what must i do?

Spend as much time for the rest of my life trying to be with you, at least enough to figure out how you can be this wonderful and how (god bless office panels (we met when I bought office panels from her for my ship's quarterdeck)*) I could have found you.*

Love, scooby dooby doesn't hold a candle to our love, scooby dooby.

• • •

The possibility of sexual liaisons among crew members continued to concern the command, i.e., the captain, department heads, the command master chief, and me. Although we knew men and women forming romantic relationships would never be stopped, we decided we needed to keep them at a minimum on our ship. I knew such goings-on could lead to some difficult problems and possibly create friction in the crew. One of the main functions of my job as XO was to promote good morale. I also was the figurehead for good order and discipline. Both could be threatened if amorous relationships went south. We had already learned that lesson with Petty Officer Moore and the radio "crypto card" problem. Another important aspect was our charge, specifically the Captain's and mine as well, was to make the Women at Sea program successful. Pregnancies while deployed, any negative impact on the ship created by relationships between men and women crewmembers (as well as in the wardroom), fraternization between male and female sailors of different ranks, especially between officers and enlisted, would have disastrous effect and possibly destroy the program. I should add that such problems would leave an incredibly bad mark on the Captain's and my Navy careers.

We didn't want to throw threats at the crew or continually remind them of keeping their distance. After all, that would be going against the mantra of not having women or men on the ship because they were all sailors first. Reminders of acting like sailors would help. The ship held "Military Rights and Responsibility," "Culture Expression," and "Women at Sea" workshops on a regular basis. I also would frequently add POD notes reminding all hands the weather decks were off limits after taps even during in-port periods.

• • •

We didn't forget our families back home. We mailed out our first "Familygram," a six-sheet newsletter, complete with photos to crewmembers' families. The newsletter described our journey east, our liberty ports, and praised many of our sailors for their hard work.

• • •

Yosemite was engaged knee deep in preparing to go to sea. We had no real idea of how long it would be. We had to prepare accordingly. Departments were ensuring they would have the needed supplies for the voyage north and our stay off Masirah (with no definite end date set yet). It was a busy time, but considering all, it was pretty much that way the entire deployment.

On Monday, 24th October, the *Lynde McCormick* moored alongside to refuel in the morning. That afternoon, *Yosemite* returned to the POL piers to refuel herself and then returned to her anchorage.

0800, Tuesday, 25 October 1983, *USS Yosemite* got underway for the North Arabian Sea and the island of Masirah, Oman. A new chapter of Navy history had begun.

46 days deployed, 148 days to home

Chapter 9: Passage to a Different World

October: En Route Masirah, Oman
Underway.

There is nothing, nothing in the world like being underway at sea, especially on a Navy ship. Aboard the *Anchorage,* the *Okinawa,* and the *Yosemite* "underway" was particularly enjoyable to me. Those ships and their officers and crew were doing the job they had been built to do. *Anchorage's* job was to load and unload equipment and troops by landing craft, boats, or helicopters. *Okinawa's* job was to fly helicopters. *Yosemite's* job was to provide repair and maintenance services.

The umbilical cords had been severed. Underway, the ship had become its own entity. True, orders from above dictated where the ship was to go and what it was to do when, but it was the ship and her commanding officer that determined how she would accomplish her mission and how well she would fare.

I loved my time aboard five destroyers *USS Lloyd Thomas (DD 764), USS Hawkins (DD 873), USS Waldron (DD 699), USS Stephen B. Luce (DLG 7),* and *USS Hollister (DD 788).* They were true "greyhounds of the sea," and could do so many things uniquely. They were either practicing in exercises or providing a forward presence for the most part. One could feel the sea when on a "tin can." The landing ship dock, the helicopter carrier, and the tender were working ships. On cans, I felt like I was cavorting as none of those ships were involved with gunfire support in Vietnam. On *Anchorage, Okinawa,* and *Yosemite,* I felt more like I was working in my service for my country.

Yosemite was underway. She felt good underway. Although I did not know how long we would be near Masirah, from experience I knew our being at work when we reached our destination would make the time go

LTJG Emily Baker at the conn of *USS Lynde McCormick*

faster. Being at sea was a good time for this XO. I would partially escape from my desk and piles of paperwork. My inspections would be reduced to be part of operations. The line of officers and enlisted outside my office would be less for they too would be working. And I would be spending more time on the bridge watching junior officers at the task I had enjoyed throughout my career: maneuvering a ship.

• • •

Shortly *Yosemite* would be part of another first in US Navy history. As discussed between the two commanding officers when *McCormick* was alongside in Diego Garcia, we transferred two of our women officers, LT Sharon Carrasco and LTJG Emily Baker, by small boat. The seas were calm, and the boat transfer went off smoothly.

They were undoubtedly the first women officers on a deployed combatant in the US Navy. The plan, as I remember (but cannot find a source to verify) was for the two officers to remain on the *McCormick* until the day before we reached Masirah, a period of five days. However, we sent a radio message noting the transfer to our chain of command. We received a responding message with the order to transfer them back immediately because there were to be no Navy females, neither officers nor enlisted, on combatants. It should be noted the commanding officer does not recall any such adverse orders and remembers Sharon and Emily's time on *McCormick* was the scheduled three days and two nights, which was their actual time aboard the guided missile destroyer. My recall, which can be spotty, may have been impacted by my sense most senior officers in the Navy did not want the program to succeed.

Regardless, the *Yosemite's* time with *Lynde McCormick* was good for our officers and crew. We had the opportunity to let our junior officers get a feel of Navy ships maneuvering. The *McCormick* began to make approaches alongside, giving their conning officers and ours training in what was a staple of ship handling in my time: underway replenishment.

Yosemite, serving as the replenishment ship, maintained course and speed, normally twelve knots into the seas while the *McCormick* made approaches to approximately 120 feet off of our starboard beam. *McCormick's* conning officer would attempt to maintain station while our conning officers, under the watchful eye of LT Sitton and CAPT Boyle, would ensure we maintained steady course and speed.

There is no doubt in my mind our crew was excited and impressed and the junior officers learned a great deal about ship handling.

The two *Yosemite* officers aboard *McCormick* learned even more. After departing our company that day, they went off to do exercises at speeds the *Yosemite* could not approach. On the morning of the next day, *McCormick* conducted "man overboard" drills.

A man overboard drill was one of the first exercises I experienced as an ensign aboard the *USS Hawkins* on her way back from a Mediterranean deployment in 1968. Admittedly, it took me a while to figure it out. The drill consists of throwing "Oscar," which were kapok life jackets assembled together to look like a person, over the side. Someone then yells, "Man Overboard, Starboard (or Port) side!" The word is passed to the bridge where the conning officer immediately begins to maneuver to clear the propellers from "Oscar" as the dummy passes down the side, then reversing course to find "Oscar" and maneuvering to bring him alongside. "Oscar", the life jacket dummy was often snared out of the water with a grappling hook rather than life buoys (on bigger ships, small boats are used for the actual retrieval of "Oscar"). When *Yosemite* performed the drills, which was nearly always right after getting underway, CAPT Boyle wanted the junior officers to learn difficult maneuvers and required them to get the ship close enough to retrieve the dummy with grappling hooks, not deploying a small boat for the recovery.

Once "Oscar" is near, the conning officer maneuvers the ship as close as possible. If done correctly, the ship stops with "Oscar" right next to it. This is no easy feat. Knowledge of the ship's turning radius, the engines' action to take effect at different speed orders, the rudders' responsiveness to turning, and the sea and wind conditions all must be factored in determining how to get close to "Oscar."

LT Sharon Carrasco at the conn of *USS Lynde McCormick*

LTJG Emily Baker, now married and is Emily Black provided the following narrative of her experience during the drills on the *McCormick:*

...the Lynde McCormick*'s CO decided to hold man overboard drills. All the junior officers were assembled on the bridge wing and the fun began. It was a windy afternoon, which played havoc with the maneuvering. All the attempts resulted in some combination of being downwind of the dummy, surging past it, being dead in the water too soon, etc. Much backing & filling was required to retrieve Oscar each time for the next JO. The CO put me near the end of the line-up, which gave me ample time to study the wind and get a feel for how much the ship continued to swing after a turn and its momentum after stopping the engines. Finally, it was my turn and I took the con. As we got back up to speed, I noticed that topside became quite crowded with sailors, compared to earlier in the exercise. Apparently, word had flown around the ship that one of the female officers was about to try her hand, and everyone wanted in on the show. I felt really confident*

and loved conning such a responsive ship. (Sorry, Yosemite, no disrespect intended!) After Oscar was tossed into the drink, I brought the ship around perfectly. We were at right angles to the wind, motionless with Oscar on the leeward side exactly below the bosun mate on the fo'csle. All he had to do was drop his grappling hook straight down to snag the dummy. The CO watched all this with a completely neutral face, then when Oscar was safely back on board he turned to his JO's, raised an eyebrow, and said "Well, boys, you've just been shown up!"

I felt on top of the world, and obviously I'm still feeling the glow decades later!

This story continues to live on in family lore. I had my children at the tail end of my Navy career, and as a result they have no memories of my being on active duty. However, as they were growing up, my husband and I told them many stories of our military service. (My husband, John, was also a Navy SWO, although he didn't stay in for an entire career.) When my younger daughter started high school, her English teacher assigned the class to write a profile of someone they considered a hero. My daughter decided to write about me. She called her essay "My Navy Mother" and focused on how unusual it was in the early 80's for women to serve on ships. She also included this story of the man overboard drill.

I recall Emily recounting this story when she returned with Sharon on the small boat transfer. I thought to myself then that being a conning officer on a ship does not require a man. I remember not only feeling like we were proving women on ships would work but more so feeling proud of Emily and Sharon and the *Yosemite*.

While the officers were gone on Thursday, October 27th, we lost our gyro. Long before GPS positioning, ships relied on the gyro compasses for navigating the ship. Celestial navigation was the definitive backup for the gyro system and used daily to compare and verify the ship's position. Dead reckoning, using the ship's courses and speeds as well as any available knowledge of current's impact, was a much rougher estimate of the ship's position on the ocean, but that type of navigation also relied on the ship's course, i.e., the gyrocompass readouts. In other words, the gyro compass was critical for us to get where we wanted to go. But the loss was only momentary, lasting less than half an hour. But for me, as the official navigator, this was a frightening few minutes.

The next day before we received the two female officers back aboard from the *McCormick,* at 0509, the port shaft overheated. As I had learned earlier with the evaporator problem just before we left Mayport, it is a good thing to have your own repair department on board. The gyro and shaft problems might have been corrected by a combatant, but *Yosemite* could address such problems quickly and did in both of these situations.

It was a good transit. At "1708 OCT 30, 1983," the *USS Yosemite* anchored just over three miles off Masirah, Oman as had been agreed with the Omani government and our superiors in the chain of command.

The next chapter in her deployment was about to begin.

53 days deployed, 161 days to home

Chapter 10: Entering Uncharted Waters

November-December: Off to Work We Go

The night before the ship anchored off Masirah, I made a challenge that worried me for two months. Each autumn, Navy commands conducted the "Combined Federal Campaign" (CFC) fund drive. The *Yosemite's* had been running for about a month.

The ship's goal was to get 100 percent participation in giving to the fund and to give more than other commands. I thought I might influence both goals being met. At Eight O'clock Reports on the evening of Thursday, 28 October, I put my foot in my mouth. I mildly chewed out the department heads, command master chief, etc. for not getting more crew members to donate. Then, I announced the greatest contributor to the campaign would be my guest for dinner at our first liberty port. I followed that up by posting it as a note in the POD the morning before we reached our anchorage.

Almost immediately, I began to have doubts. I wondered what I would do if the crew member gave the most so he or she could bend my ear about how bad I or another superior was treating them. I was concerned a malcontent might do the same just to make one liberty night miserable for me. I thought of how I might handle this tactfully and project the appropriate image if a female crew member won a dinner with me. And I wasn't looking forward to spending one of the few evenings I would have to relax ashore with a crew member I might not enjoy. But most of all, I worried I might have encouraged a sailor to spend a lot more than they could afford just to have dinner with me.

The possibilities continued to bother me even after the winner, a male fireman in the Repair Department, was announced at the conclusion of the CFC drive.

As we went to our anchorage, my problem of who I might take to dinner disappeared from view by my becoming even busier than I expected.

Once anchored, the world of *Yosemite* changed quickly. We were at a place where we would remain for an undetermined amount of time. The operation of the Omani air base primarily was managed by British Air Force personnel. Through government channels, we learned what was expected of the ship while anchored in Oman territorial waters and when any of our personnel went ashore. Our Supply Officer, CDR Tim Allega had worked on the coordination for us. Most of the coordination on the Omani side was done by the British.

We were just off the coast of what was for all of us a strange land. We would find out more as the ship's personnel went ashore. We attempted to give the crew some ideas of what we could and couldn't do while offshore from this strange land.

What we could and couldn't do was pretty straightforward, especially for one item: trash. The word we received from shore was emphatic: there could be no trash floating up on the shore of Masirah. In case you haven't been on a ship, especially ships of that era, they did not get regular service from garbage and recycle trucks. It was before Navy ships had Collection Holding Tanks (CHT's) for holding waste and treating it in order to become environmentally safe. Ships had to deal with it. For my entire time at sea, the way we dealt with it would give today's environmentalists a heart attack. We dumped our trash over the fantail and watched it float away on our wake or sink. The waste from our toilets, urinals, and sinks were flushed with salt water through scuppers on the side of the ship into the ocean.

But *Yosemite* was not underway. There were no garbage scows or other vessels to collect our garbage. We had a problem. The CAPT, department heads, and I put our heads together and came up with a plan. It was explained in the 01 November POD:

9. Trash/Garbage Procedures for Masirah Anchorage: While at the Masirah Anchorage, it is imperative that we take necessary steps to ensure all trash is bagged, sinkable, and dumped at optimum tide conditions. Accordingly, the following procedures will be applied.

The fantail is the only authorized trash dumping station. No coke cans or other items of trash are to be discarded over the side except as specified below.

All trash and garbage will be held on station until the authorized disposal time.

All trash will be compacted to the maximum extent possible and bagged in such a fashion as to prevent the load from coming apart before it sinks. (e.g. coke cans or aerosol cans floating loose).

Take extraordinary steps to ensure no radio copy (classified or unclassified) or any classified material is mixed in with the trash.

Times for dumping trash will be published in the Plan of the Day. During the trash dumping period an EDF [Enlisted Dining Facility, i.e. the mess decks] petty officer will supervise at the fantail dumping station. He will make the determination as to whether or not a package is in compliance with the above procedures. In making this determination, he is exercising a watch responsibility and will not be overruled by a more senior petty officer. Any dispute over what is approved for dumping and what is not will be resolved by the quarterdeck OOD.

If it becomes necessary to send a boat to retrieve a package which did not sink, the offending division will provide the personnel to ride the boat and fish out the mess.
Trash Dumping Hours for Today are:
0600-0700
1830-1930

We announced daily the times for dumping trash coinciding with the outgoing tides. We thought we had solved the problem.

This was just the beginning of the extra work we had due to our unique situation.

• • •

Everyone aboard the "Busy Lady" was learning on the fly, especially this XO. It was going to get busier.

It was a new world. We were attempting to set up a routine, or routines that would work with constant changes in an unknown environment. Those routines began to fall into place. It was busy, very busy. Yet, it felt good. The "Busy Lady" was doing what she was supposed to do. We didn't yet know exactly how many ships we would benefit from our maintenance and repair work, but they would certainly be more than if we had remained at Diego Garcia, the "Footprint of Freedom." Being busy would make the time go faster. I felt this was the best place to be.

Even though I was satisfied with how the crew was faring in this new world and even though all the activities created 16-18 hour workdays for me, I continued to consider my situation of being an executive officer of a repair ship managing 900 sailors and Naval officers, including women, while anchored in the North Arabian Sea.

Here I was an old sea dog, one who would have been in hog heaven if I had been assigned to another combatant with no female situation to consider except when on liberty. I think I could have done that the rest of my life and been happy. I had accepted I was likely to be single the rest of my life. Being a Navy officer on a ship at sea always had been an adventure to me, challenging but fun.

But I had met the love of my life and married. Then, I became the number two officer on a ship of 900 in the beginning of the process of integrating women on ships. It was a strange place to be, and, I admitted, I opted to do this as a last chance to achieve my ultimate goal of becoming the commanding officer of a combatant. Sometimes my frustration showed, but only in letters back to Maureen, not to anyone on the *Yosemite*. I had a role to play, and irony did not suit that role. In my 20 October letter to Maureen, I let her read the irony and my frustration:

...i mean i'm sitting here on a ship. Some silly ass ship that is anchored off al Masirah island near Oman for goodness' sake. I mean i'm sitting here thinking I am pretty good at this and wondering why I think i'm pretty good and why i'm going to spend twenty-one days sitting on a ship at anchor off of this island to fix other ships that will go out to bore holes in the ocean and watch aircraft fly off the carrier unless a war starts when they may sink

Personnel being lowered during Vertical Replenishment (VERTREP)

another ship or get sunk. And I keep thinking what would this basically defenseless ship, with a few small guns, do if the real shit hit the fan. And then, I think about all of the paperwork i've generated and how I can see the light at the end and may, just may be getting this organized. And through all of that thinking, I think about you and ache to be with you and accept the ache is good and warm to miss someone, you, like that. And I think about all of that stuff when I run across a radio message from a crew member before it goes out. Essentially, I am censuring their messages as I have to screen all such messages for security. When reading such personal feelings for someone else, it makes me wonder how I became the father-manager or whatever to damn near a thousand souls who can do heavy crime or "turn to Jesus." I could enjoy it if I didn't stop and think about it and consider they are really good people and need someone to help them. And I think of you throughout all of this thinking, and I love you. Think I will take a walk around the weather decks and look at the stars over Oman (not quite a song title) ...

Reflecting after all of these years, it is amazing to me I had the time to think at all.

• • •

Even before the *USS Fletcher (DD 992)* came alongside for our first TAV (Tender Availability) off of Masirah, we began a routine for Tuesday and Saturday that would last throughout our time in the North Arabian Sea. The transfer of supplies, mail, and personnel (and often fuel) was termed UNREP for Underway Replenishment. One form of an UNREP sans the fuel transfer was VERTREP or Vertical Replenishment.

Early each Tuesday and Saturday morning beginning the first of November, the ship would set Flight Quarters at 0630 or earlier to receive helicopters from a supply ship. The helicopters would hover aboard the deck constructed for DASH (Drone Anti-Submarine Helicopter, a program that lasted about four years in the late 1960's) lowering supplies and transferring incoming and outgoing mail.

This also would be our method of transferring personnel who had completed their tours on *Yosemite,* had medical problems requiring specialists beyond the capability of our doctor and medical staff, or others who had been granted emergency leave. The personnel would be hooked into a lifeline and hoisted from our deck to the hovering helicopter, taken to the Masirah air base, then flown to Diego Garcia on Navy aircraft for further flights out of the "Footprint of Freedom" to various airports before eventually reporting to their intended destinations. It was a grueling and tediously long journey. We also received our new or returning personnel in this manner.

Before the VERTREP began, the captain and I would go to the bridge just before "Flight Quarters" was set. We would observe what we could from the bridge wing and be in constant contact via sound- powered phones with George Sitton, who ran the operations of the DASH deck, offloading the supplies and shuttling them to the working party, which would further transfer the goods, usually to supply or repair personnel. The DASH deck crew also would hook up the transferring personnel into the helicopter and receive new personnel being lowered to our deck. Depending on the amount of supplies received, this was normally a three or four hour evolution. Infrequently, the event could take more than six hours.

Supplies for storing during VERTREP

CH 46 from *USS Camden* (AOE 2) delivering stores to *Yosemite*

Bridge team and onlookers during VERTREP

• • •

The physical effort required to move the supplies off the DASH deck and then to the area of the ship where those supplies would be used or stored varied from light work to some very heavy lifting. As with all of the tasks on the ship with one exception, the women sailors did all they were physically capable of doing. Some could not handle the heavy lift requirements. Some could. Those that could did the required heavy lifting along with their male counterparts.

• • •

The first VERTREP lasted just upward of an hour. The supply ship for the first one was the *USS San Jose (AFS 7)*, a combat stores ship. *San Jose* and her sister ships would be vital in our stay off Masirah, providing not only supplies and material for our work at hand but also bringing us personal necessities and entertainment materials sold in our ship's store. Of course, the greatest morale booster these ships brought us was mail.

In my opinion, of the three surface communities (the destroyer force, the amphibious force, and the service force), the service group had the most arduous sea duty during those days. Today, most of the service ships are not "USS" but "USNS" ships manned by the merchant marine, government civilians.

Service ships (oilers, tankers, combat stores, ammunition ships, etc.) would conduct their transfers to carriers, cruisers, destroyers, and amphibious ships. Then they would steam back to a port to replenish their supplies in a quick turnaround and head back to the combatants at sea. Their in-port time, unlike the other deployed Navy ships, was spent essentially working round the clock rather than liberty. It reminded me of the grueling routine of the merchant marine ships I rode in 1970 as the executive officer of a transport unit in charge of the embarked Korean troops being carried to and from Vietnam.

Those Service Force ships and the USNS ships had my utmost respect.

Chapter 11: A Bunch of Garbage

November - December: The "Busy Lady" Is Busy, Real Busy

It was time for us to resume the work the old lady was commissioned to do in 1944. In Diego Garcia, we had provided maintenance to the *Lynde McCormick,* and some minimal work for the *Catawba* and the submarine *Bates.* We were about to accomplish major work for combatants in a forward operating area, almost non-stop.

The first one would give us a good idea of what it would take to do the job, what problems we might encounter, and what would be different from the availabilities we conducted in the states.

Of my special concern was how the all-male crews and wardrooms would deal with our women. The captain and I discussed our rules concerning relationships between our crewmembers, especially the women, and the all-male crews of the tended ships. We had established the guideline there were only sailors on the ship, not men sailors and women sailors.

The one exception to the way we did it on *Yosemite* was deep hole engineering, the firerooms and engine rooms. The Navy's policy was to not assign women the ratings of boiler technician (BT) or machinist mate (MM), ratings whose work was primarily in those main engineering spaces. This did not make sense to me as women were assigned to the deck department. Deck evolutions often required the same amount of physical effort as those in engineering, if not more. Those women assigned to the deck department did all that they could do. Some performed the more difficult tasks right alongside the men. Having been both a chief engineer and a first lieutenant (in charge of the deck division or department), it appeared to me the only difference in the physical requirements was engineering spaces were hot and humid, very hot and humid.

• • •

Maintenance for the *USS Fletcher (DD 992)*

The helo ops, the *Fletcher* coming alongside, and the arrival conference were just a few of the items on my list. My spiral notebook action list went from one or two pages to four to six. My tasks varied. Concern for the crew's morale included providing them the opportunity to record tapes to send home to family and keeping the heat on department heads for submitting enlisted evaluations on time. In navigation, the assistant navigator, LTJG Leahy and I calculated tides to determine the scheduling of garbage dumps, and we monitored the condition of the auxiliary gyro compass. In regards to tasks pertaining to health and safety, I oversaw the safety requirements when our divers cleaned our own hull, managed urinalysis procedures, and even had to count all of the prescription drug pills in the medical inventory. In public relations with the ships alongside, I had to ensure ship's plaques were available when needed. Other duties included coordinating with the Repair Officer the repair of the commanding officer's cabin air conditioner, reading radio messages, responding to higher authority, and enforcing smoking and coke can debris rules.

· · ·

This *Fletcher* arrival conference led to a reunion in a faraway place. I had quite a few such occurrences in my career.

First was John Sweatt, a guy who became my support in my sophomore year of varsity football. John was a post-graduate and also a "town boy," a cadet at Castle Heights Military Academy who lived at home, not a boarding student. He taught me the ropes and looked after me. In my first week of OCS in Newport, Rhode Island, John visited me. John was a Lieutenant Junior Grade aboard the *USS Basilone (DD 824)*. When he found out I was at OCS, he came to my barracks after his workday. This was at the end of that first week, which was no fun, no fun at all, and appropriately nicknamed "hell week" by the Officer Candidates. The OCs were awed by a Navy officer coming to see me. John's visit put things in perspective and gave me a calm I had not had since reporting. John's last ship tour, like mine, was XO of a tender, the *Samuel Gompers (AD 34)* homeported in San Diego.

Another unlikely of such connections occurred in the stag bar of the "Town Club," the Navy's officer's club in downtown Sasebo, Japan. My ship, the *USS Anchorage (LSD 36)* was in the Navy's Ship Repair Facility undergoing repairs to our stern gate. Several of the officers had gathered at the stag bar for drinks and shuffleboard games. While we yakked at the bar, someone at the far end asked quietly, "Are you Jimmy Jewell from Lebanon?"

The question came from Bob Hamilton. He was a couple of years younger than me. He also attended Castle Heights Military Academy in our hometown of Lebanon, Tennessee. Bob was a division officer on a destroyer in port Sasebo for liberty.

Robert Hamilton had completed his active duty service, earned his law degree, and became the General Sessions Judge in Wilson County. I did not know there were any other Navy officers from my hometown of Lebanon other than the aforementioned John Sweatt; one of my best friends growing up, Earl Major, who played sports with me all through our school years; and Lee Dowdy, another friend from my youth who was the editor of the award winning Castle Heights newspaper while I was his sports and executive editor, and Lee was my executive editor when I edited the annual.

But this connection with the *Fletcher* makes me smile.

When I reported aboard the *Anchorage* in early 1975 to become the First Lieutenant, my concerns about taking over the department head post primarily responsible for all amphibious operations and deck evolutions, I was comforted with the knowledge I would have a Chief Warrant Officer Boatswain to show me the ropes. Bosuns or "Boatswains" have existed since the early days of ships at sea. In my Navy, Boatswains were Warrant Officers or LDO's like *Yosemite's* First Lieutenant George Sitton. The warrant Bosuns were highly respected for their knowledge and expertise, especially in all aspects of boats and deck seamanship. Having spent all my operational tours on destroyers up to that assignment, I essentially knew nothing about amphibious operations, especially well deck operations. But I knew a bosun would be an expert in all those things, and I could lean on him until I got a handle on it.

Unfortunately, the *Anchorage's* Bosun had been transferred a month before I arrived with no replacement. As a First Lieutenant with no amphibious experience, I had no bosun, nor any chief boatswain's mates. I did have two superb first class boatswain's mates, but when a Landing Ship, Tank (LST) lost her deck leading petty officer the chain of command decided to transfer my most experienced first class boatswain's mate to fill that void. We did get another just before we deployed to the Western Pacific. I had one junior officer, a LTJG, who had one deployment under his belt. With the JG, the two other first class boatswain's mates, and immense help from Bosun Joe Messenger and his first class boatswain's mate who rode *Anchorage* as part of the Beach Master's Unit, I made it through an incredibly challenging deployment, including "Frequent Wind," the military's code name for evacuation of Vietnam.

About two months after the ship returned to our home port of San Diego, we finally had a bosun report aboard. This bosun was a brand new chief warrant officer, CWO-1, the lowest rank of the four warrant levels. His prior experience had been in submarines, not with boats and deck department functions on surface ships. I introduced him to deck and amphibious operations. He was extremely capable and a fast learner. I was glad he was there for the oncoming First Lieutenant when I rotated to my next assignment.

When the *Fletcher's* officers began to come aboard, I discovered my *Anchorage* bosun, Richard Stevenson, had continued upward in his career and was *Fletcher's* Chief Engineer. We had some great conversations and revisited some great times on *Anchorage*.

When we finally got back to the States, Maureen showed me a Christmas note Richard had sent to her after the *Fletcher* completed her time alongside the *Yosemite:*

Dear Maureen,

You don't know me but Jim and I are old friends. I used to work for him in 1976. I am on the San Diego based ship the Fletcher. *I ran into Jim in the middle of the Indian Ocean. My ship spent four days alongside the* Yosemite *for some repair. I had dinner with him in the wardroom. He showed me your picture and asked me to give you a call when we returned to San Diego. But that will not be until 29 February '84.*

Hope to meet you someday.

Have a nice holiday,

//Lt. Richard Stevenson//

He had included a postcard with a photo of the *Fletcher.* It was a nice gesture and I appreciated it greatly. It was a good reunion. I appreciated his reaching out to Maureen. Unfortunately, when Maureen and I finally returned to San Diego in 1985, we did not reconnect with Richard and lost contact.

But in the North Arabian Sea, the unlikely reconnection was good for my morale.

• • •

After the VERTREP, the *Fletcher* made her approach alongside. It was a difficult maneuver. *Yosemite* was at anchor, maneuvering enough to stay as stable as possible in tides and currents. When ships came alongside, it was usually with the ship being moored pier side and a tugboat assisting. But not at the Masirah anchorage. The *Fletcher* did a splendid job. Her approach was flawless. She moored alongside with no difficulties. The *Fletcher*" arrival conference" for her maintenance availability began right after the noon mess.

After she was safely alongside and the brow was passed between the two ships, the *Fletcher's* commanding officer met CAPT Boyle in *Yosemite's* captain's cabin, a procedure which would be de rigueur for all of the availabilities during the deployment. I would attend the bulk of those meetings.

The "arrival conference" was a detailed, expanded version of the beginning of "Restricted Availabilities" (RAVs) *Yosemite* and other tenders conducted back in the states. Critical repairs and maintenance were discussed. Work priorities were set, the coordination of the tender's and ship's force personnel was delineated, and a schedule was laid out to complete the work on time. During our time in Masirah, we also added some requirements for the tended ship's personnel with our female sailors.

With the Fletcher through the mooring alongside and the conferences, we were satisfied with the results.

Our work in Masirah had begun well.

• • •

Then, the *Yosemite* took on some more. On Tuesday, November 1, the *Ranger (CV 61)*, the flagship of Battle Group Alfa, suffered a fire in the number four main engine room during a fuel transfer. With her in the area near Masirah with the rest of the battle group, we quickly learned of the fire and its severity. Six crewmen were killed, thirty-five others were injured, and the ship lost the use of one of its four propeller shafts.

It was a tense time. Many of our experts in a number of fields, including damage control were ready to go over to the *Ranger* and assist in repairs. But a carrier has incredible capabilities to address casualties, and the *Ranger* got everything under control except for one major problem. *Yosemite* was ready to answer the call.

Chief Warrant Officer Ken Dawson, a congenial, fun guy who also was one of our most capable repair types, headed up the contingent of a half-dozen of our sailors who had a unique capability. Ken and his team were certified to perform asbestos removal and replace lagging on pumps and other equipment. On Thursday, November 3rd, they were lifted by helo and transported to the *Ranger.* They worked for ten days, removing the dangerous asbestos lagging and replacing it with modern rubber-based heat reducing covers.

Once again, *Yosemite's* sailors were lauded by those for whom we had provided services.

• • •

I was in all-ahead-full running mode. Sometimes late at night after Eight O'clock reports and my evening meeting with the captain, I had three frequent visitors, the Chaplain, the First Lieutenant, and the doc drop by my office. After those visits, I continued my quest to streamline and update the ship's regulations, which was usually interrupted by writing another letter to Maureen. I realized I really enjoyed this stuff. I was a great example of Maslow's highest stage of "self-actualization." In its own way, working on the regulations and instructions was an escape.

A Navy officer at sea is a busy man (or woman). There is little time to dwell on the loneliness of being away from home. Previously for me, the grind was interrupted by standing bridge watches or conducting amphibious or anti-submarine operations, but as XO, it was all management and administration except for the rare moments when I would participate in an evolution like navigation or bringing ships alongside.

The rigor probably kept me sane.

My frequent evening visitors also helped me maintain my mental state. Frank Kerrigan, our Medical Officer, had become a confidant. We were both big sports fans and had a lot of common interests. His newness, and some ways, remoteness from the Navy way of doing things allowed us to help each other. I explained Navy things to him and talked to him about things I was not comfortable discussing with anyone else on the ship.

Chaplain Poe gave me great advice about the crew and always found the right thing to say to boost my spirits. His attitude and commitment to his numerous roles were inspiring.

George Sitton, as noted before, was old school Navy. He was my connection to the wonderful but politically incorrect old deck plate humor and sea stories. Our shared experience in the West Coast amphibious Navy gave us a constant source for reminiscing. I had been First Lieutenant twice before, and my tour on *Anchorage* immersed me in boats, cranes, and deck evolutions. There were guys we both knew in the West Coast amphibious Navy. We laughed a lot.

• • •

I was playing my role and understood the XO was the bad guy, the enforcer. In Thursday's POD, November 3rd, my hand-written note showed me baring my fangs:

If the XO finds coke cans or cigarette butts and ashes as plentiful about the decks as he did today, the smoking lamp will be put out throughout the ship and the sale of cokes and cigarettes will be halted. No joke. No game. Get hot. No smoking in passageways nor topside. Violators will be put on report.

Cleanliness, good order, and discipline were the responsibility of the executive officer. I was getting used to the role.

Refueling from *USNS Passumpsic (AO 107)*

On Friday, 4 November, the *Fletcher* concluded her availability and got underway at 0800. An hour later, the *USNS Passumpsic (T-AO 107)*, an oiler and former Navy ship, maneuvered alongside for refueling *Yosemite*. It had to be the first time these two ships tied up together in an open sea. Neither had the mobility of the cruisers and destroyers. *Yosemite* received *Passumpsic* alongside to port.

The evolution was the one time I forgot the admonishment CAPT

Roger Newman had given me when I departed the *Okinawa* for my change of duty to the *Yosemite.*

In my time at sea, one of the signs of a good ship handler was bringing his ship alongside a pier with no tugboats assisting. In today's Navy, the increased size of the ships and the cost of repairing any damage if there is contact between the ship and pier has pretty much eliminated this maneuver without tugboats. In the case of tenders, their size and lack of maneuverability compared to destroyers and many amphibious ships in the early 1980's, required them to nearly always use tugboats. The *Fletcher* had handled the challenge well. The same challenge applied to the *Passumpsic.* Yet the *Passumpsic,* an oiler, was a big, slow, and difficult to maneuver ship, like *Yosemite.* We were in Masirah, at anchorage, not alongside a pier. There were no tugboats.

For ships to come alongside and tie up for their maintenance periods, the conning officers of the approaching ship had to demonstrate exceptional ship handling capability as had those on the *Fletcher.* As she had done with the *Fletcher* and would do so for all of the ships who joined her at Masirah, *Yosemite* had to maneuver, if necessary, to provide a stable and consistent position as much as possible. This would be even more of a challenge with these two ships.

Passumpsic was approaching our port side at 0900. This would not only test the seamanship of her conning officer but would also put me through one of the worst experiences of my tour.

As *Passumpsic* made her approach, our line handlers were responsible for passing the "messenger" lines ("ropes" to landlubbers) to the *Passumpsic* line handlers on their forecastle, amidships and on the stern. The *Passumpsic* line handlers would tie the messenger lines to their mooring lines and our line handlers would pull the mooring lines back to *Yosemite.* When the *Passumpsic* moved into her mooring position (our rubber fenders were out over the side to buffer the ships from actual contact), the mooring lines would be secured.

Passing the messenger lines was usually done by one of three methods. One method was to simply throw the heavy mooring lines to the other ship if the two ships were close enough. The next method was to use a smaller "heaving line" with a weighted end to the other ship. And finally, a "shot line" was attached to a projectile in a special gun and fired to the other ship. Use of a shot line greatly increased the distance the messenger line could

USS Passumpsic (AO 107) alongside *Yosemite*

travel. The heaving line or shot line was attached to the larger "messenger line," which in turn was attached to the mooring line. The receiving ship would pull over the shot or heaving line and then the "messenger" line, and finally the mooring line.

Our operation was in an open sea and bringing a ship alongside another ship at anchor required lines being passed as quickly as possible. The mooring lines were passed quickly on the forecastle. However, even though the larger heaving lines had been passed between the ships, the seas had separated the two sterns out from each other. The fantail line handlers had not been able to get their lines across by any method. The captain began to become more forceful in his orders through his sound-powered phone talker to the fantail. George Sitton, the First Lieutenant, spoke to me with some urgency. He said the line handlers aft couldn't get the lines across, and we should use the crane to pass the lines. I agreed. We suggested this to the captain. He did not agree and became more forceful in his commands to pass the lines aft. As George and I became more belligerent in our recommendation, the lines were passed as the captain had ordered without having to use the crane.

The lines were tightened and *Passumpsic* was secured alongside. We secured from sea detail but before going below, the captain asked me to come to his cabin. I followed him and sat in the chair in front of his desk.

"XO," he began, "Don't you ever question my orders in front of our crew or officers again! I cannot tolerate that kind of show of disrespect. If you disagree with a decision or order of mine, we can discuss in private, but never do that again."

I not only knew he was correct in admonishing me. I was embarrassed I had forgotten the parting advice from CAPT Roger Newman as I left *Okinawa:* "You know when you become executive officer, your most important job is to support the captain," he explained, "It doesn't matter what you think about his decisions, if you don't like his actions, or even if you don't like him. Your job is to support him, to do anything to make him successful, to be his voice, his mirror reflection. That is your primary job."

I had forgotten. I had made a major blunder in my mind. It may have been done with good intention, but it was something an executive officer should never do.

I immediately responded to the captain, "Aye, aye, sir. I understand and apologize." As I was leaving his cabin, I vowed I would never disagree with him in public.

The refueling went off without a hitch and *Passumpsic* was underway early that afternoon.

Maintenance for the *USS Stoddert (DDG 22)*

The next day, flight quarters were set at 0630. At 0700, the *USS Benjamin Stoddert (DDG 22)* came alongside for our second maintenance availability. As soon as *Stoddert* was tied up to our starboard side, flight ops with the *USS Camden (AOE 2)* for transfer of our personnel to Masirah and then on to Diego Garcia were conducted, followed by helo ops and supplies and personnel transfers with the *USS Ranger (CV 61),* the flagship for Battle Group Alfa. The captain had the CO of the *Stoddert* over for lunch in his cabin and the second "arrival conference" was held at 1300. And to keep things hopping, another round of flight ops was conducted with the *Camden,* beginning at 1500, for another two hours.

The evening after the *Stoddert's* progress conference in the afternoon of 9 November, a mixer was held with the two ships. It included a steel deck picnic, a talent show, and the two ships competing in boxing and wrestling matches.

An incident, which would have made it tough on me had I known, occurred during the boxing and wrestling contests. *Stoddert* completed its 45th consecutive day at sea, which qualified for a beer day, more commonly known among sailors as a "beernic."

Drinking of alcohol except for medicinal purposes in small quantities aboard U.S. Navy ships was banned in 1914 by Secretary of the Navy, Josephus Daniels. Many stories have evolved around the use of booze on board ships since then. Then in 1980, the Secretary of the Navy at that time, Edward Hidalgo, put out the policy, later modified, that if a ship had spent 45 consecutive days at sea and had at least five more days before reaching a port, each crewmember and officer would be allowed two cans of beer that day.

The *Stoddert* had hit that point. The beer was distributed to the crew while *Yosemite* sailors watched from their weather decks. LT Carrasco was in attendance for the evening entertainment when she saw the following incident:

One of my favorite moments was when the Stoddert *was tied alongside, and a boxing arena was set up on their flight deck.*

It was their turn to have their "beernic." We did not. Many of us were standing at the rails watching the boxing below. One of their sailors held up his beer to us and taunted that they had beer and we didn't. One of our crew put his arm around one of the female crew and taunted "That's okay, we have the women."

Upon reflection, I am glad I was in the dark.

• • •

The crew was getting into a busy routine. When ships were alongside, which was nearly all of the time, the Repair Department adopted a "port and starboard" routine. To accomplish all the work in short order, half of the repair personnel worked for six hours, and the other half would work the next six hours. This was around the clock work until the maintenance availability was completed. The Medical, Dental, Supply, and Administration departments, who did not go into the "port and starboard" routine," were also constantly busy.

I believed it was a good thing. We needed to keep them busy. And they certainly were busy in their first week off Masirah.

But they were missing home. We attempted to assuage the loneliness, especially for the majority of the crew, who had never deployed before without means to communicate back home. A POD note let them know of another method to contact home:

11. Want to send a message home?? The Yosemite *has a service onboard that not too many people are familiar with. It is called the Class "E" message service. The Class "E" message is a service provided by radio in which any crewmember stationed onboard the* Yosemite *can send a message to any person ashore they desire (i.e., wife, husband, girlfriend, boyfriend, parents, and anyone you desire, provided they reside in the Continental United States. There is a charge for this service. The reason for the charge is these messages are transmitted thru the Western Union Telegraphy Co. This service can only be provided when the ship is away from its homeport.*

I had spent 11 years at sea and did not know (or did not remember) Class "E" messages were available. For me, that was okay. One of the best things about going to sea was the ship becoming my primary focus. Connecting with folks back in the States was for late night letters and crazy all-night waits in foreign liberty port telephone stations for expensive and short calls back home.

The Class "E" messages also had to be reviewed. Who got that job? Why the executive officer, of course. I was the censor and the security screener for such messages. There was really no censuring involved and there were not a huge number of those messages. I was not supposed to divulge the content to anyone (of course, if there was a security matter contained, I would consult with the captain). Reviewing the content made me aware of how lonesome some of the crew actually were. There was some real drama in numerous ones I read, and admittedly, some made me laugh out loud.

61 days deployed, 133 days to home

Hearing from Maureen was my greatest escape. Early on, she discovered telegrams could be sent in the form of a "mailgram." 9 November, she sent such a missive. I received it four days later:

PMS CDR J R JEWELL
 USS Yosemite (AD 19) Executive Officer care Naval Communications
  Washington DC
  My dear Commander, Received your wonderful thought. A

crispness in the air invites long walks with you along the beach. It also invites a nice warm romp in the sun. So, is it a date? Loving you in the Biblical sense and any other sense.

    Maureen

I responded:

Ms Boggs Jewell
6840 Caminito del Greco
San Diego, CA 92120

    Telegram. Cassettes. Cards piled high. Your feelings are mine. Controlled and uncontrolled. Three plus months is really a thousand years. Oceans and continents are mere strides across the room to be with you. Yet thoughts aren't good enough as long as I am without you.

    Always,
    Jim
    USS Yosemite

Her notes added another meaning to "short but sweet" for me. Getting any type of correspondence from her gave me a lift.

• • •

Although it made great sense and allowed us to perform our mission, when our schedule was changed to Masirah and the port visit to Perth was cancelled, almost every sailor had been greatly disappointed.

CAPT Boyle and I discussed possibilities of mollifying that disappointment.One of us, I don't remember which one, came up with a new idea. We thought it made a great deal of sense, would provide an exciting opportunity, and would be readily accepted by the chain of command, especially the public relations staff because of the historic first it would achieve.

We sent a radio message proposing a different route for going home in March. Instead of returning westward, retracing our track from the voyage to the Indian Ocean, we could set out eastward, stopping in various ports en route for refueling and liberty. It would be about 4,000 miles longer to transit the Panama Canal rather than the Suez and return to Mayport from there. But the positives certainly made the alternate route very appealing. Undoubtedly, *Yosemite* would be the first Navy ship with women as part of the crew to accomplish a round-the-world voyage.

I was excited. It would add something from this mariner's career bucket list to my achievements, but more importantly, it would give the crew and officers something to boast about for the rest of their lives. I thought it would be a slam dunk, an unparalleled opportunity to gain unprecedented press coverage for the Navy.

I hadn't digested the fact that Navy senior officers were resisting having women at sea. Such a voyage would show off the success of the new program, not cast a negative. The flags, old macho men in my estimation, didn't want that.

Our request was quickly denied.

The two of us begin to consider our options for going home westward. But we put it on the back burner. There were many other things on our plate.

• • •

Daily, we tossed our garbage (and there was a lot of garbage with a crew of 900) timed to the outgoing tide. We were making the effort to keep any of our trash from floating ashore. This was not easy, even if we stuck to the ebb tide schedule. We put one or two of our small boats in the water to watch for wandering garbage.

I still have a hand-written POD note praising a busy sailor in particular:

> *Busiest sailor of the day: SN Warren who worked helo ops, handling cargo loads to helicopters, then was part of the boat crew to sink the wandering barrels (of trash).*

The hard work and the loneliness were somewhat assuaged by the evaluation the *Fletcher* sent to *Yosemite* and our chain of command arriving by radio message on Monday, 7 November (and passed along to the crew via the POD):

> *Overall Evaluation of TAV (with* Yosemite) *is outstanding.* Yosemite's *efforts, spirit, and professionalism was impressive as the statistics above demonstrated.* Yosemite *is a can-do ship that*

does...Ref A (TAV report from Fletcher*) details the astounding amount of work completed by* Yosemite *during* Fletcher's *four day TAV. The pride and professionalism exhibited by all concerned was obvious from the start of the availability and proven by the quality and quantity of the jobs completed. We are proud to have had the opportunity with you and wish that you were San Diego based. All of us in America's finest destroyer salute you.*

Similar praises continued from every ship receiving *Yosemite's* services for the rest of the deployment. For me, this kind of evaluation from ships and sailors made my decision to report to *Yosemite* a good decision.

I felt good about what we were doing. I felt good about how I was doing my job. There were numerous frustrations, but overall, we were doing well. The crew was handling women as part of the crew in the right way. I remained wary.

But our wrestling with the garbage was not over.

• • •

As with all things, the one constant applicable to *Yosemite's* stay off of Masirah was change.

These changes were doubly hard on me, I think. I was trying to make all things work, and recalled a comment, illustrated by a cartoon from a former captain.

CDR John Kelly, later CAPT Kelly, was the commanding officer of *USS Cayuga (LST 1186),* which was a ship in Amphibious Squadron Five out of San Diego in the late spring of 1980. I was Current Operations Officer on the squadron staff. At the conclusion of a Wednesday morning "message meeting" of the staff, Commodore Jim McIntyre asked for a volunteer with no explanation. The staff of two dozen officers and enlisted were silent. After several seconds, I raised my hand, thinking "What the hell?"

The Commodore looked surprised and then said, "The *Cayuga* needs an executive officer immediately. Come to my cabin after this meeting, and we can discuss."

When I sat down with the Commodore, he was amazed I had volunteered, especially since I was the only officer on the staff he could have selected for the job. There were only two lieutenant commander surface warfare officers (required to fill the LST XO billet on the staff) and the other was the material officer up to his knees in alligators in the maintenance of squadron ships.

CAPT McIntyre explained, "Jim, CAPT Kelly is desperately in need of an executive officer. His XO was taken off the ship in a strait jacket to Balboa (the San Diego Naval Hospital) this morning. He had a complete mental breakdown. The *Cayuga* has had a lot of problems.

"While they were in the yards at Long Beach, a personnel man (PN) hanged himself in a fan room. The Philippine community was up in arms and began protesting at the yard gates and the entire mess made the newspapers and the LA TV news.

"Then about two weeks ago, a boatswain's mate was killed when the deck department was conducting UNREP training on a barge operated by a mobile training team. A line parted and the boatswain's mate was hit in the head by a block and tackle that broke loose. They apparently did not set up the rig according to blueprints. The First Lieutenant is under investigation by JAG.

"They start Amphib refresher training next week," he explained and paused, then asked,

"You still want the job?"

I replied, as a good Navy officer should, "Aye, sir."

I interviewed with CDR Kelly the next day and was accepted. I reported aboard on Thursday morning.

Judging by the "In" and "Hold" baskets on his desk in the XO's cabin/office, the outgoing XO had not done any paperwork in six months. Personnel advancements had not been forwarded. Critical reports had not been sent. On my first "messing and berthing" inspection, I found total disarray. Racks were not made. Dirt, paperwork, leftover food, coke cans, cigarette butts, and ashes were everywhere. Roaches and grease ruled the galley and the mess decks.

I held an all-officers meeting in the wardroom, took feedback from all of them, and laid out a plan, reporting the plan to the Captain. I stayed on board for two months, going to my apartment once a week to collect mail and check on my belongings. I actually stayed at my place three nights, giving myself a break once. The other two nights at home were to run the Fourth of July Coronado half-marathon, which I had entered the day before I "volunteered." I was also too busy to train after becoming XO, and the half-marathon, my first, was a killer in the rare 95 degree heat of Coronado. But I made it, slept off the effects that evening and limped back to the *Cayuga* the next morning.

As the two months neared the end and *Cayuga* had successfully completed the refresher training, CDR Kelly recommended to the officer detailers in the Bureau of Personnel I remain the XO and complete a two-year tour. The Commodore endorsed the recommendation, but the Bureau explained they already had a Naval Academy graduate in the pipeline who had completed the pre-XO training course.

I transferred back to the flagship as the squadron was en route to Esquimalt, British Columbia, the Canadian Navy port for Victoria on Vancouver Island. I rode a hydrofoil to Seattle and met my daughter Blythe at the airport the day after we anchored. The two of us visited the Space Needle and a couple of other high points in Seattle and then took the hydrofoil back to Victoria. After that, we rode a ferry to Orcas Island to be with my friend Cy Fraser on Orcas Island and returned to Seattle from where the two of us flew to San Diego.

When I departed, CDR Kelly had drawn a cartoon of me. It referenced a conversation we shared near the end of my stay on board. He told me he was amazed at how I performed. It was like I was dribbling a half dozen basketballs at the same time. I replied it was more like a dozen basketballs and most of them were only half inflated.

It had been a rigorous two months for me. I was disappointed the Navy did not let me finish the tour as it would have completed that check for advancement and put me back on track for command at sea, my ultimate goal. In the late nights as *Yosemite's* XO, I often reflected on how my experience on *Cayuga* had given me the right experience, the right perspective, and made my current XO tour a bit easier to digest. Simultaneously, I realized it was unlikely I would have met and married Maureen nor would I have been sitting in this stateroom anchored off a strange island.

I found myself continuing to dribble an increasing amount of half-inflated basketballs as *Yosemite's* XO.

• • •

Maintenance for *USS Fife (DD 991)*

Sitting at anchor at the top of the Indian Ocean was not a pleasant prospect. When we learned our initial ten days off Masirah had been extended until 1st January, I was upset and even lonelier when I wrote Maureen a note:

Lady,

New word. Schedule has changed again. I didn't believe it possible, but it's for the worse. We are now going to stay anchored in this miserable place for a long time. It has been requested we remain here through January 1, 1984. I guess I don't mind. This is all marking time until I get back to you, but the crew will be bug shit by the time we hit a liberty port. Sure wish I had a tape to tell you all of my frustrations.

Mail call yesterday and none from you. Terribly disappointing but i've not been as good as you in writing. I really do go up and down in this job. Hope there's some mail from you Saturday, even a lecture would be welcomed. Did Blythe tell you I called her? I may talk to you on MARS if we get the reception back, but I greatly dislike exchanging thoughts with "over" interrupting.

My god, how I love you.

Got a great letter from Joe (my brother). *I may send you a copy. This is a note getting out of hand.*

i love you.

jim
Al Masirah, Oman
November 9, 1983

My focus was on our unique situation: 100 enlisted women in a crew of 900 and 6 female officers in a wardroom of 44 on a ship anchored off Masirah, Oman for what appeared would be at least two months. Our rules for male/female relationships were clear and in place. I was glad there had been no overt violation of those rules but didn't know how effective the rules actually were. I and my admin staff were also aware the women were young sailors but women, nonetheless. We attempted to keep them informed about uniforms and dress. This was a new world for me. An example was one POD note:

7. <u>Grooming Standards (women)</u> <u>Hair pieces</u> — Hair pieces or wigs, if worn while in uniform or on duty status shall be of good quality and fit, present a natural appearance, not interfere with the proper performance of duty, not present a safety hazard, and shall conform to the grooming standards set forth in these regulations.

<u>Cosmetics</u> — Cosmetics shall be conservative and in good taste.

This POD entry reads strange and out of touch as I copy it 35 years later.

• • •

Occasionally, I could get away from the work and my concerns. In one evening discussion between Kathy Rondeau and me in my office, we moved from ship's business to music. I had a Jimmy Smith cassette playing on my small stereo. Kathy commented she also liked jazz. After Kathy left, I sent a note to Maureen capturing our discussion:

This is a discussion between Kathy Rondeau, our OPS officer, and me this evening. Her parents live down the street from Blythe (in Austin, Texas).

> *i say, "Maureen likes jazz."*
> *Kathy says, "It seems to fit (looking at the picture of you i have hanging in my office); it seems she has a lot of class."*
> *i say, "Yes, she does. She is a thoroughly classy nut."*
> *Kathy giggles, "Like you, XO?"*
> *i smile, "Yeah, like me."*
> *Kathy says, "It seems she really compliments you."*
> *i beam, then say, "i believe it's the other way around."*
> *She says (damn near wisely, i opine to myself), "That's the way it's really supposed to be: both ways."*
> *i say smugly, happily, and proudly of my relationship with the most fantastic woman in the world, "yeh."*

Executive Officers need that kind of conversation every once in a while during long at-sea periods. And this at-sea period was a doozy.

We were in unknown waters in many respects.

Chapter 12: Thanksgiving and More Garbage

November - December 1983

The POD for Thursday, 10 November backed up the previous day's announcement to all hands:

4. NO TRASH DUMPING UNTIL FURTHER NOTICE!

The notice was in reaction to the protests coming from the Omanis as a bag or two of garbage had escaped our control and washed up on the beaches. The Brit's running the Omani Air Force base protested mightily

The next morning at 0746, *Yosemite* weighed anchor and moved to an anchorage outside of the "territorial waters" limit of 12 miles.

Our move was to be outside Omani's control as we were inside their territorial waters. It was also another effort to ensure no garbage washed ashore again on the island and continue to service the battle group ships with maintenance periods and receive limited supplies from the Navy's service force. Not having access to the frequent C-40 flights to and from Diego Garcia would make things very difficult. Those flights provided personnel transfers and frequent and larger resupply than possible with just service force ships. Even though we were not in their waters, we were obliged to play by the Omani's rules or risk losing those critical flights.

In addition to moving the anchorage, we came up with a new way to handle the trash problem. In a discussion among the officers, I believe it was the two LDO's, George Sitton and Ken Clausen, who came up with the idea of burning the trash that was flammable and dumping only the trash that would sink over the fantail after being closely inspected by a responsible monitor.

The "Trash Burn" hanging off *Yosemite's* crane, a nightly occurrence off
Masirah, Oman from early November until the ship departed her island
anchorage in February 1984.

Another view of the nightly "Trash Burn."

The first attempt, as described by CAPT Boyle, did not go so well:

...we tried launching a gasoline soaked large cardboard carton filled with burnable trash. We lit the carton expecting (foolishly as it turned out) everything to burn to the waterline. This resulted in launching all boats in a futile attempt to recover all floating trash.

The problem was discussed, and the next reiteration was launched the following night. I could not remember exactly and could not find any references in my own sources but thought the second solution was a metal burn cage, loaded, lit aflame, and then hung from the ship's crane. I thought this "Burn Box" lasted for a week or more before failing and falling into the sea, once again causing our boats to be launched and as much floating trash as possible being retrieved. LTJG Emily Baker, the Damage Control Assistant and division officer for the Auxiliaries and ship's Repair divisions, has a much clearer recall of what happened:

Burn Basket #1. It sank on its maiden burn, lasting more like 10 minutes than 10 days! The fire got going, then the basket plunged into the ocean with a loud sizzle. There were crowds lining the railings and a big communal groan went up, followed by some good-natured cat calls. I remember an officer next to me (maybe George Sitton?) saying "That was like watching a car sink", referring to the value of all the metal plate that had just disappeared.

The basket itself was fine, but the problem was the way it had been rigged to attach to the crane. The cable was looped around itself, then just one length went up to a single attachment point. The intense heat from the fire weakened the cable, then the weight of the basket caused the cable to cut right through itself. The cable was also very short, so that pressure point was right above the hottest part of the inferno. The riggers from Repair were very embarrassed and stood there with hang-dog expressions, because they felt they should have known better.

Undaunted and recognizing the problem, the Repair Department constructed a heavier gauge sturdier metal basket. The First Lieutenant, with the advice and recommendations of other officers and crewmembers, came up with an improved method of rigging the box to the crane. Emily recalls the effort:

...Burn Basket #2 had a new & improved rigging method. Each corner had its own cable that went up to some sort of multi-point attachment device that evenly distributed the load. The cables were also much longer, allowing the heat to dissipate somewhat.
The nightly burn was definitely a source of entertainment!

We had solved the trash problem, a major sore point between the *Yosemite* and the Omani's. "Burn Basket #2" was used for the rest of our time both before we returned to Diego Garcia for Christmas, and when we returned after Christmas until we left for the voyage home.

•   •   •

The Captain and I were always concerned about keeping the crew occupied. "Idle hands are the devil's workshop," was never far from my mind. I knew Navy men from my earlier sea time enough to not trust them. I wanted them to have as much entertainment as possible. *Yosemite* was a different breed of ship than the combatants on which I previously served. Entertainment is much less frequent on combatants. The crews and officers of combatants nearly all stand four-hour watches and are underway the vast majority of the time. Consequently, the ship does not have a lot of down time. The officers and crew of combatants are extremely busy all the time.

A large segment of our Repair Department was essentially in port and starboard work teams with six hours on and six hours off when conducting the repair availabilities with the combatants, but a large part of the crew had large chunks of leisure time. Entertainment was a good solution for reducing idle time. Yes, I was concerned as much about male and female dalliances in idle time as I was with keeping up morale.

The evening trash burns became an unplanned source of entertainment. Conducted each evening around sunset, the burns went well past dark. After the evening mess, crewmembers would gather along the rails and watch the huge blaze in the darkness, a modified fireworks show.

Watching from the ceremonial deck above, I had several thoughts. I wondered what the Masirah natives were thinking. Even 12 miles away, they could certainly see the blaze or the light from the fire below their horizon. There must have been a great deal of wonder and curiosity, perhaps even a bit of fear.

I also noticed there was a pairing off between male and female sailors along the life rails watching the blaze. The number was not large, but I noticed. It was my job to notice. They were not breaking any of our rules, so. I said nothing. I felt a little bit like a babysitter with absolutely no control.

We worked at filling up down time with entertainment. This was standard at sea for maintaining morale. Hopefully, this would keep them from thinking about how far away they were from home. All Navy ships have movies every night while at sea. Most Navy ships have distractions like cookouts on the fantail, bingo nights, etc. *Yosemite* doubled down.

We worked at keeping them entertained as shown in these POD notes the day of the garbage dumping change:

15. Pizza, (Root) Beer, & Bingo Night: There will be pizza and soda served on the after mess decks in conjunction with Bingo Night. Bingo will begin at 2000. All bingo cards will be sold at 1930. Bingo cards will be sold for .50¢ per card. All proceeds will be used as prizes. Size prizes will be determined by the amount of proceeds, with a ceiling of $25.00 on the maximum prize.

17. Steel Beach Party: It's time for a party!! The ship will have a steel beach party and camera day on Sunday, 13 Nov 83. Appropriate (as defined by the executive officer) civilian attire will be authorized for the picnic, talent show and movie. The picnic will commence at 1530 on Steel Beach, followed by a talent show at 1730. Anyone interested in participating in the talent show should submit their name and type of talent to ENS Heer so they can be scheduled. After the talent show a movie will be shown on the flight deck.

It was hard work to keep our crew entertained, to motivate them to keep working at the impressive level they had been working, to keep their spaces clean, and act like good sailors. Coordination between the ship's alongside and our repair and support personnel was always a consideration. My performing in a manner that reflected the commanding officer remained foremost in my mind while overseeing the work and the entertainment.

Maureen, my outlet for expressing my feelings, got to read about those feelings:

Lady,

Back writing in green. Appropriate because i can't seem to get away from the job. It is really beginning to wear. I have even found it difficult to write to you. There are a lot of factors that are producing this malaise. I'll try to talk about them only briefly, but right now, i need to.

i don't believe it is the pressure of the cruise affecting me. i don't have that down-in-the-mouth, this-is-never-gonna'-end attitude. Shit.

i don't feel like writing again.

i got your wire. i was absolutely in heaven for a day. Thank god for you.

i will write when i am in a better mood. I love you and miss you terribly.

jim
Off Al Masirah, Oman
11 November 1983

With all of this and my being in the dumps, I could get angry but was unable to tell anyone else, except occasionally and minimally Doc Kerrigan. One evening after taps when Frank dropped into my office while I continued to work on updating the ship's regulations and instructions.

Previous regimes, probably since the ship was commissioned, would write an instruction based on current direction from above. Rather than just adapt the superior's regulation or instruction, they would layer the ship's version on top. The duplication was sometimes three or four times deep, and none had been deleted for years. The four-inch notebooks, at least 50 of them, were full of such nonsense. I wanted to throw them all out, burn them and start over, but I was concerned I might get rid of something of value, something that might burn the command later. To condense them to usable and make them understandable, simple, and readable was my goal. The deployment gave me that opportunity, over six months of evenings. I quit watching the evening movie in the wardroom in 1972 when I was the ASW officer on the *USS Luce (DLG 7);* I just had too much to do. I worked almost every evening through the deployment and when underway after the deployment. I estimate I got about half-way through the mess before I transferred.

This particular evening, I was angry at an occurrence that happened that day. A senior chief had told me he was sure that two of the women sailors were gay. When I asked him what evidence he had for this accusation, he told me he had observed them a couple of times walking down a passageway or on the weather decks with their arms around each other's shoulder laughing. I asked him if this meant all the guys being boisterous good old boys and having their arms around each other's shoulders meant they were gay.

The senior chief looked at me astonished and retorted, "That's different."

The double standard still existed. I was irritated I had to deal with that kind of foolishness when I had much more difficult and real problems facing me.

Frank agreed. That helped.

• • •

We attempted to keep the dependents and loved ones back home informed about their sailors. One such effort to do so was with the *Yosemite* "Familygram." We had sent one of these short newsletters to families in the states when we arrived at Diego Garcia in October. This first six-page missive included articles about our activities. One was of a bullfight in Palma de Mallorca. The significant portions of the transit, our route and port visits, outbound were included. A lengthy part explained and described the "Crossing the Line" ceremony. Also highlighted were awards for "Sailors of the Quarter," and congratulations for those sailors who had been promoted to chief petty officer. A paragraph was devoted to some noteworthy divisions and their accomplishments on the deployment. It ended with the captain's personal note to the recipients:

The getting here is over. We have begun our work of repairing and maintaining ships of the fleet. Your sailors already have established a reputation for doing outstanding work here in Diego Garcia.

Our schedule shows we will be providing services for many ships in the near future. I am sure that our crew will continue to maintain Yosemite's *reputation as one of the finest tenders on the east or west coast, and the best that's been in the Indian Ocean.*

We have some difficulty in mail reaching us. That predicament and our recent schedule change may have caused some difficulty for you or your sailor. Unfortunately, those of us who have deployed before can vouch that this type of inconvenience is more likely than not. I can only promise that I and my administrative staff will do everything possible to minimize the impact of such difficult situations.

In the meantime, we appreciate your support, and I can't stress enough how important your letters are to the morale of the crew. Thank you for that support and remember that you can be especially proud of your crewmember on the Yosemite.

Keep the letters, love, and prayers coming. Your support is what will carry us through this deployment.

Maintenance for the *USS Horne (CG 30)*

We were about to hitch the entertainment up a notch with the arrival of the *USS Horne (CG 30)*. As usual, this entertainment meant more work for this XO and proved to be challenging. *Horne* arrived for her availability on 15 November. They brought with them a USO group who had flown to the *USS Ranger*, performed there, and then rode the *Horne* for a day to be with us. They would perform for us and the ships that would be alongside for maintenance.

The entertainment was a rock group that leaned toward doing Bob Seger songs. I was certainly okay with that as Seger's "Fire Lake," "Her Strut," "Betty Lou's Getting' Out Tonight," "Still the Same," "Old Time Rock and Roll," "Hollywood Hills," and what I considered my hymn, "Against the Wind" were on the top of my playlists.

But there was this other problem. The name of the USO group was Belladonna with a female lead singer. Belladonna was a name used by many for marijuana. I didn't know the group sang Seger songs, but I was concerned how the group's name might be defined by the crew.

67 days deployed, 127 days to home

A big problem was brought to my attention after Belladonna's arrival.

I was in my cabin going through the endless pile of paperwork when I answered a call from our Supply Officer, CDR Tim Allega.

He said, "XO, I need your help."

He did.

Previously, when we found out Belladonna would be spending about ten days on board, it was immediately decided they would stay in officer's quarters and dine in the wardroom mess. We had enough staterooms to accommodate them, and the wardroom mess could feed them with no problem.

Our plan did not include the problem we had with the arrival

Belladonna performs in a USO show on *USS Horne's* flight deck.

of Belladonna. Women as part of the ship's complement was a new thing. We knew any reports of fraternization or worse would be serious blows to the continuation of the program. One of the rock solid rules throughout the fleet and certainly aboard *Yosemite* forbid fraternization. It simply was not allowed. Recognizing this rule should apply to everyone on board, we selected Noreen Leahy to share her stateroom with the female lead singer.

The issue was something we had not considered but learned about quickly once the group arrived aboard the *Horne,* 0800, Tuesday morning, 15 November. Tim explained to me Belladonna's lead singer was female, and she was married to the group's manager and lead guitar player.

Tim further explained that Belladonna, the lead singer herself, had blown a gasket. When Tim was attacked verbally by the lady concerning the berthing arrangement, he called the captain. CAPT Boyle, in his strict adherence to the fraternization rule, declared the couple could not share a stateroom. Hearing the captain's decision, Belladonna launched into another tirade. Tim had no response he thought would work.

He called for outside assistance: me.

I understood the captain's decision, and whether I agreed or not, I remembered my rule which I violated only once when the *Passumpsic* made her approach coming alongside. I would stand by his decision as if it were my own.

I felt like I was in a Monty Python movie, or perhaps Peter Sellers' "Dr. Strangelove." I straightened my khaki uniform, looked into my bathroom mirror, cocked my jaw, and said, "It's magic time," the statement Jack Lemon said right before he went on camera, every time.

When I arrived in the wardroom, the lady remained upset. I tried to calm her down and explained how important to the women on the ship that she go by the same rules as they did. I went into detail about the Women-at-Sea program. I continued that I understood how she must feel and told her about leaving my wife of ten days to report to the ship almost five months ago and I certainly understood why she would be upset being separated from her spouse. I added I hoped she understood and would help us out by not sharing a stateroom with her husband. Surprisingly, she did calm down and agreed. Headed back to my cabin, I not only breathed a sigh of relief, I silently thanked Maureen for her help.

Years later, Noreen remembers sharing her stateroom with Belladonna:

The USO show was another strong memory. The lead singer shared my stateroom because the Captain wouldn't let her share a stateroom with her husband...given our integrated crew, it was a really good move. She was so sweet and interested in my career. She even showed me the pants she could unzip from her navel to the small of her back to rip off during a show. The 24-year old me learned some interesting things in Belladonna's stay on board.

The group put on a great show that first afternoon. We put them on the Horne's flight deck and the crews of both ships really enjoyed it.

In that first show, Belladonna demonstrated the unique pants, ripping off the pants she would later show Noreen and performed the rest of the show in swimsuit type pants.

The next day, the *Horne* departed. After the evening mess and before I went to the captain's cabin to get his input for Eight O'clock Reports, LT Leahy and LTJG Baker knocked on my office door and asked to enter. They explained they had a problem and weren't sure how they should handle it. They went on to explain that shortly after the *Horne* departed,

Emily was given a letter by a crew member. The letter was from the *Horne's* weapons officer, a lieutenant, the one who had stayed close to her at the concert and during her visit to *Horne's* wardroom.

They gave me the letter. As I read, I realized it was a love letter. The lieutenant went on about how beautiful Emily was and how much he cared for her. One of his complements raved about Emily's blue eyes.

When I finished reading, they both asked me how to deal with such a rash letter. Almost simultaneously, they pointed out Emily's eyes were blue, not green.

I explained sailors can get very lonely on deployments, especially single officers. I surmised the lieutenant was probably just lonely and became lovesick. I recommended they just let it slide, adding when the lieutenant got back to San Diego, he would be fine.

Later, I shared our discussion with the captain, and knowing male sailors and officers from many deployments when no women were on the ship, and liberty was the hunting ground for many of the lovesick sailors, we understood both sides and laughed at how much had changed.

Maintenance for the *USS Lynde McCormick (DDG 8)*

The *Horne* completed its availability on 20 November and left the next morning, replaced by our good friend from the transit to Masirah, the *USS Lynde McCormick.* Belladonna put on two shows for the *McCormick* crew and ours.

LTJG Emily Baker, the Damage Control Assistant, also recalled the group:

I remember the boxing match and having a ring side seat. Boxing had never appealed to me and I was glad when it was over. I have a very strong memory of the Belladonna concert. It started after dark, and we had sailors from both ships lining every conceivable topside level to get a good view. The band sang "Eye of the Tiger" and we all just absorbed the deep primal beat: we were surrounded by darkness listening to the pounding lyrics of stalking prey in the night. To this day, 35 years later, hearing "Eye of the Tiger" still gives me goosebumps.

That was the first evening of the deployment that I forgot about my responsibilities for an hour and just lost myself in the music. I was very grateful for the USO program. I remember that band had to stay on board overnight (or two) and the female singer expected to get bunked with her husband. (At least, she said he was her husband but who knew?) Anyway, CAPT Boyle was unswayed and said no couples would co-habit on his ship and he split them up. I was impressed that CAPT Boyle stood by his crew that way and didn't have double standards for the military and the civilians.

CAPT Boyle had a strong moral compass that never deviated throughout the deployment, and an excellent example was refusing to let the female officers be exploited as "dates" for an evening on the Horne. *I do remember going over as part of a group from our wardroom. The mess specialists on the* Horne *had baked and decorated a really good looking sheet cake in our honor. It turned out though, that they had made the frosting with Crisco and we all ended up with grease slicks in our mouths! The officers from both wardrooms discretely pushed the frosting to the sides of our plates, pretending nothing was wrong, and carried on with socializing. It was a fun expedition and a nice break from routine (The cake itself was good, too, so all was not lost!)*

...There was a lieutenant who sat beside me for the entire Bella Donna concert and stuck by my side during that social hour.

• • •

The night before they departed, Monday, 22 November, Belladonna put on their last show, this one after another "boxer," where the *Lynde McCormick* and *Yosemite* sailors got into the ring for some fisticuffs. Belladonna had been on board for a week. The group dined with me every meal in the wardroom. As mess president, I sat at the head of the table. Belladonna sat to my immediate right and her husband was on the other side. The rest of the group was interspersed among the other officers at the table.

The three of us swapped stories and became friends. Belladonna was pleased I was such a Bob Seger fan, and she was particularly interested in my stories about how I met my wife and complimented the photos of her, especially when she and her husband visited my office and saw Maureen's portrait photo on my wall.

McCormick's captain and executive officer and CAPT Boyle and I had front row seats next to the boxing ring for the "boxer" and consequently ringside seats for Belladonna's last performance before leaving. When the group was nearing the conclusion before the penultimate song, Belladonna stepped to the microphone and spoke about how the group enjoyed their stay on *Yosemite* and how much she appreciated how the women were contributing to the Navy.

Then she thanked me personally for the ship's hospitality and dedicated the last song to Maureen and me. The song? Bob Seger's "Fire Down Below." I remember wondering how the crew would perceive this while knowing Belladonna had got it just right.

Once more, I felt myself in a strange position. I was in the vanguard to ensure the crew was considered as sailors, not men, not women. Fraternization and any show of endearment between crewmembers were totally *verboten* on the ship. Yet here was this woman in a rock group dedicating a song to me inferring about the love affair I had with my brand new wife.

I was pleased and I was embarrassed. The crew and the wardroom took great delight in my embarrassment. Maybe, I thought, just maybe it was a good release for all of them.

Belladonna left the next morning on the *Camden* headed back to the carrier *Ranger.* I put my embarrassment behind me and was back to work immediately after the concert.

77 *days deployed, 117 days to home*

I took time out to write Maureen and seek to correspond with her more frequently:

Boggs,

A late thought. A reserve going back to Dallas will mail this to you from stateside.

On the long tape with the cigarette ad, there's a shopping list if you can get and send. And a couple of other things: a shaving brush, a blank tape or two (so I can talk to you), and a couple of mailers like the one this came in.

i love you and miss you and will be thinking of us on Thanksgiving. Desperately wanting to touch you in oh, so many ways.

jim

Off Al Masirah, Oman

November 22, 1983

A much needed distraction yearned for by the crew even more than their enjoyment of Belladonna was impending: Thanksgiving.

Maintenance for *USS Camden (AOE 3)*

The captain had his own daily mess and in his cabin. We invited him to the wardroom mess for the big meal and he accepted. I was the president of the wardroom mess for the 44 officers. The chief petty officers had their own mess in chief's quarters, and the rest of the enlisted ate on the mess decks. The Supply Department's cooks and messmen were working hard to ensure the Thanksgiving meal was as close to a Thanksgiving back home as we could get.

But, as with all things military, if you do a good job, someone higher up will want to give you credit. *Yosemite* had established a remarkable record of accomplishing in three or four days, "restricted availabilities," which would take two to three weeks back in home port. We had conducted eight of those availabilities and received rave reviews from each ship. Considering the tender we relieved had not one maintenance availability while sitting for almost six months in Diego Garcia, it was a remarkable record.

So naturally, the admiral in charge of those eight ships wanted to come, see our operation, and thank us.

For Navy ships, an admiral's visit is not necessarily a good thing, certainly not good for the ship's XO. A visit from a flag officer means a tour of the ship, and this means all hands must ensure everything, everything is beautiful, and clean, and shipshape, and clean. Did I mention clean?

So I "sternly encouraged" all hands to clean, and clean, and clean as if their lives depended on it. Then, the Captain, department heads, and I checked all the spaces where the admiral might go to ensure things were shipshape. In fact, at 0745, a couple hours before the admiral was to arrive on board, the department heads and I walked the planned route the admiral would take on his tour just to make sure we didn't miss anything.

RADM Arthur arrived at 1000 as scheduled. He toured the ship, had lunch with CAPT Boyle in the CO's mess, and departed at 1300. He had nothing but good words for the ship and echoed the ships we had serviced for our outstanding work. It was a good way to go into Thanksgiving Day.
75 days deployed, 119 days to home

USS Ranger (CVA 61) approaching Yosemite for Battle Group Commander to visit via helicopter.

Typical home on Masirah built to be impermanent as required by sultan's edict.

And on that day, the Supply Department did a great job with Thanksgiving. Every mess had a Thanksgiving dinner to match the ones back home. Turkey and dressing with all of the sides. We even had our substitute for wine: Martinelli's sparkling cider instead of a white wine and their sparkling apple cranberry for a red.

I wondered how many of our sailors, especially those on a deployment for the first time, would forget the loneliness of being away from their families amidst the festivities. Even though I had many Thanksgivings away from home, I got a twinge of that lonely feeling once more. My first time was the worst. I felt sorry for those who were in that position that Turkey Day.

Chapter 13: Al Masirah, Oman: A Different World

November - December 1983
Maintenance for **USS Sample (FF 1048)**

The week after Thanksgiving, we selected a group of seven enlisted and six officers to disembark to the island and take a tour.

The Captain was not interested. His focus, as it was for the entire deployment, was on the ship and its performance. I also demurred. My job was to support the Captain. However, there was a part of me that considered going on the tour.

When we relieved the *Cape Cod* in Diego Garcia, her XO had given me a fact sheet on Masirah. I wanted to see if the conditions described in the information sheet were true. I was also a bit concerned about how our women officers, chiefs, and enlisted dressed in their uniforms, and from the dress required of women on the island, would be treated and wondered if my presence might be needed.

LT Sharon Carrasco, LTJG Linda Schlesinger, and Doc Kerrigan were selected to be the officers on the tour of this island of Masirah, Oman. Another enlisted group headed up by Chief Warrant Officer Ken Dawson also went ashore. They included Dental Technician 3rd Class (DT3) Yaques, Seaman (SN) Warren, SN Maki, Chief Storekeeper (SKC) Boone, Seaman Storekeeper, Striker (SKSN) Benedict, Chief Hull Maintenance Technician (HTC) Mapps, and Radioman Class 2 (RM2) Bernhardt. Both groups were a mixture of male and female.

When the tourists returned to the ship, they verified my Masirah fact sheet the *Cape Cod's* XO had given me was accurate.

Al Masirah is a rugged, mountainous, and sparsely populated island elongated almost 60 miles long from south by southwest to north by northeast and less than ten miles wide at its widest point. The currents are strong and quirky around the island and the coastline is rough and rocky, which has contributed to a number of ships going aground on its shoreline. As with all of Oman, the population is devoutly Muslim. Due to its remoteness and an unfortunate event at the turn of the twentieth century, the inhabitants led hard lives.

In 1904, the British ship, *Baron Inverdale*, ran aground. When the crew came ashore, believing the islanders would be friendly and hospitable like the inhabitants in other areas of the North Arabian Sea, they were massacred. It is rumored they were cooked and eaten by the natives.

The sultan of Oman apparently was not pleased with his subjects on the island for this act, and therefore decreed there would be no permanent housing for the island residents for 100 years. The version on my fact sheet further explained no residences could be made of permanent materials and could not exceed five feet in height. Our two touring parties took their cameras. When they returned, their photos and tales verified the sultan's edicts were in effect, at least where they went on the island.

The islanders' extreme interpretation of the Koran and adherence to their beliefs made living there even tougher on the women. All women had to wear a burka anytime they were outside. Instead of a veil, they wore an instrument usually made of leather that prevented anyone from seeing both eyes and the woman could look at someone with only one eye.

Our tourists couldn't verify several other assertions on the fact sheet. One was that when a woman reached menopause, she was no longer allowed in the home, such as it was, and had to live outside. The other was that if a man was unhappy with his marriage, he could gain a divorce (or perhaps "annulment" would be a better description) by holding his hands over his head, turning a circle and clapping three times.

Before our group had returned and debriefed the captain and me, I was dubious about the veracity of the fact sheet. From their descriptions, it appeared the fact sheet was pretty much on target.

Doc Kerrigan remembers the trip ashore:

...Masirah was a great visit for me. I was with Linda and Sharon. Somehow, we ended up at the home of the BBC radio people stationed there and not surprisingly I had a good Foster's lager buzz before noon. Afterwards, the guy gave us an impromptu tour

of the island. I remember seeing women in full covered garb just thinking this ain't Kansas. I didn't do any medical visits as far as I recall. We heloed in and out.

When I heard Frank's description, I knew I had made the right choice in not going because although he and I would have had a great time, and I would have downed too many Fosters: not a good idea for an XO.

LT Sharon Carrasco, our Safety Officer and who, with ENS Emily Baker were the two female officers who had transferred to the *Lynde McCormick* on our transit North, also gave an excellent account of her experience ashore:

Well, I could write my own book about Al Masirah...I will tell my story but understand that I was not alone...

There was a British man stationed on the UK compound on the island. He had come onboard Yosemite. *We got to talking about collecting seashells. He said his wife was a big collector. What followed was talk of a visit to his wife. A few of us flew to the British station* (by helicopter). *We went to his house, and his wife showed us her collection. There are some rare types that are only found in that area of the world. We then had something to eat and drink.*

Then we all went in a van to go outside the British compound. He drove us around the area. Yes, we saw a lot of incredible things like corrugated homes, camels, goats, and sheep wandering about. I saw a woman and her husband and little boy walking, I got out and asked to take their picture. All I knew were polite greetings and few words in Arabic. The man in particular was a character to behold as he had an old fashioned type rifle and extra ammunition with him. He got together for the photos, but he pushed wife and son away and wanted only his picture taken.

Next, we came across a woman alone. She was glad to pose for a picture...but she would not look in the direction of the British guy. She did look full on to me and the camera. Women covered their head and face except for their eyes...but even more they wore a stiff divider between their eyes so they could look, but a man could not see both of their eyes at once.

Top: A woman on Masirah in her burka.

Right: A man of Masirah

Below: Camel on Masirah

She posed and showed some of her wealth in the gold she wore.

Next, we stopped at a small house. There was a fence around the house. The man there worked with the British guy. He opened the gate and his family came to the gate. Since the woman was not covered and her hair showing, she did not come past the gate door.

Now here is the good part: I and the other women officers were wearing our khaki uniforms. So, our hair showed and our arms were bare from the short sleeves, and we were wearing slacks. It caused a scandal. You should remember. We were oblivious at the time.

Somewhere I have a copy of the letter from the State Department and signed by George Schultz, Ronald Reagan's Secretary of State, that refers to Al Masirah folks (men of course) being offended by our clothing.

LT Schlesinger's account of the visit is also interesting:

I recall that the expats (Brits) at Masirah welcomed females from the ship so that the expat wives could converse with English speaking women. My division, ship's stores (S3), did provide ample supply of American geedunk (geedunk is sailor talk for junk food) *to the Masirah folks (expats and local U.S. beach detachment) who craved candy bars, etc.*

The Captain and I heard the group's accounts of the island's culture. The *Cape Cod's* brief was verified.

We did receive George Shultz' admonition. He directed that any of our women officers or sailors who went ashore should wear skirts, no slacks, and have minimum bare skin showing. I felt like I was in a very strange movie or a dream.

• • •

Schultz' admonition required some new ways to strategize when it came to women going ashore. LT Leahy was our communications officer and therefore the "Top Secret" control officer. To transfer such sensitive and classified material, especially cryptography materials for secure communications, Noreen was the only officer or crewmember who had to personally carry such material. She describes what occurred to make such transfers work after George Schultz' edict:

I did, however, have to make trips (I believe I made two) to Masirah on a chopper to pick up crypto materials. Remember that we could not land helo's and anyone riding the chopper had to be hoisted aboard. Our flight deck was not certified to land helicopters.

My first trip was uneventful. I was hoisted aboard the chopper, flown to the landing strip at Masirah, where I signed for our delivery, chatted it up with a few good looking pilots and airmen, and returned to Yosemite.

Shortly thereafter, we received that message from the state department saying that if women were to go to Masirah, we could not wear pants. I remember distinctly that you and CAPT Boyle called me in and told me I had to wear a skirt to pick up the new delivery. I was the only one who could sign for the crypto material because of my Top Secret clearance. We had to figure a way for me to go because regulations would not allow a male replacement. I was TS Control Officer at the time. Anyway, you both politely asked me to wear a skirt. I respectfully declined to wear it, reminding you that I was going to be hoisted aboard a helicopter in order to fly to Masirah. Jim, I think it was you who thought I was concerned about someone looking up my skirt when I was hoisted and suggested I wear a pair of shorts under my skirt. This I remember clearly. I looked at you and said that I was not concerned about someone catching a glimpse of my panties, but I was very concerned about having to maneuver myself into a hovering helicopter in a dress. You laughed and then agreed it was probably not the safest thing. Anyway, we devised a plan. I wore my slacks, but when we landed, about eight or ten of the aforementioned airmen and the helo pilots made a circle around me and hid me from view. I signed for the package on the air strip. Then my protective circle escorted me back to the helo and no one was the wiser.

82 days deployed, 115 days to home

The *Yosemite's* officers and sailors were on the cutting edge of a transformation of the United States military, integrating women into ship's crews and wardrooms. We could not have been in a more starkly different world than Masirah. The British women craved to spend time with other women from western cultures and all the western folks on the island craved things like candy bars that they couldn't get there.

And yet in the middle of this craziness, political correctness was more important to our highest levels of government than supporting the very women and the ship that were not only implementing the country's policy but were at the vanguard of changing the military.

In my experience, I never had high regard for the State Department and foreign policy. I now had less regard and even that would take another hit before our deployment was over.

It mattered not as we had a ship that needed to meet its mission.

Maintenance for *USS Shields (FF 1065)*

After our idea about going home via an around-the-world route was rejected, our schedule for the trip home continued to list our Mediterranean liberty port as Malaga, Spain. Doc and I came up with a plan for our liberty there. We thought Maureen and Jan, Frank's wife, could travel together and meet us when the ship arrived in Malaga.

Great plan, we thought.

Chapter 14: Relatively Good News

December 1983

It was back to business, and there was plenty of business. Mike Jackson, our admin and legal officer joined the captain's and my discussions about our two major nemeses: Fireman Edmunds and Seaman Moore.

The former, the sailor who was caught while trying to desert, continued to be a problem. We decided when it was prudent, to transfer Edmunds to the Naval Base, Subic Bay (Luzon, Philippines) and let the JAG office there handle the general court martial. Somehow, Edmunds managed to be flown back to the States before the court martial and gained an audience with a senator from New York, which eventually required another response within 24 hours to a congressman's inquiry.

There were more headaches with Moore. I had recommended we give her an administrative discharge and get her out of the Navy (and my hair). She was very much against that, and her division, First (or Deck) division because she could no longer be in radio, was working to get her to agree to an administrative discharge. I was ecstatic when I learned crusty old seadog BMCS Johns had convinced her to sign the necessary paperwork. I began to go through the paperwork when Mike Jackson came into my office.

"It's not going to work, XO," he said.

"What's not going to work?" I asked, adding, "I hope you are not talking about Moore."

"I'm afraid so," Mike said, and explained, "Everything lined up and was legally correct, except for one thing: Senior Chief Johns didn't read her rights to her before she signed."

I knew we were going to have to begin the process all over.

I understood. Asking any sailor or officer regardless of rank, except for those who had been a CO or XO, to jump through all the legal hoops was problematic at best. I was not blaming BMCS Johns, but I was not looking forward to telling the Captain. It was my job.

As it happened many times, CAPT Boyle surprised me with his understanding. He, like me, was frustrated with not being able to get rid of Moore, but he did not blame the senior chief even though we were going to have to deal with Moore for longer than we wished. I had no idea as to just how long that would be. It turned out to be more than a year, long after we had returned to Mayport before Moore received her administrative discharge. And even that was not the end of my difficulties with Moore.

• • •

After being anchored off of Masirah for a little over a month, we learned that our schedule was changed: surprise. We did not request the change. Someone decided we needed a break. The new schedule has us steaming back to Diego Garcia for Christmas.

When the announcement of the change was made over the 1MC speaker system, there was sustained cheering. For this old sailor, it would be a nice break. Yet I was fine with staying where we were. But for all of these folks who had not deployed before and had been working hard almost every day, spending Christmas on a small atoll in the middle of the Indian Ocean was a wonderful thing compared to staying where we were, if the cheering was any clue.

And to be honest, returning to that lagoon was really okay for me as well.

• • •

Sometimes my frustrations would get to me where even my late night laments with Doc Kerrigan or Chaplain Poe did not fully express my woes, nor would I write of them in my letters to Maureen. Several did find their way as asides in my to-do action notebook:

No evolution is easy on this ship because every evolution is a major change.

It is a fact that the best sailor thinks when he is supposed to think and just as importantly, not think when he isn't supposed to think.

The Women At Sea program suffers from both the men and the women not being able to forget they are men and women.

• • •

The world of this executive officer was wearing thin. Yes, I would escape when the First Lieutenant, Doc, or the Chaplain dropped by in the evening, but such diversions were brief. There was really no one to whom I could express my true feelings. After all, I was the executive officer. The tensions of running a ship at the behest of the commanding officer, even though I had gained the greatest respect for him and considered him a friend as well, brought about my frustration. I knew I could only tactfully point out my difference in opinion. I could not do things my way. I was absolutely required to support him.

Maintenance for USS Fife (DD 991), second TAV

I vented my frustrations in long letters to Maureen, including one I wrote in snippets over ten days, concluding on 2 December. She was my escape to whom I could express my darkest and brightest moods.

I knew I had to sublimate my ideas to the captain's will. I knew the XO's position had to reflect the position of the captain even if I disagreed. I had experience with executive officers who did not support the captain of the ship, some even undermining the CO's position. On my previous ships, most XOs had attempted to support the CO. Some had succeeded. Several failed, some even intentionally. One of my former commanding officers was a "screamer," often giving orders that made no sense. He frequently behaved in a manner that was counter to good ship operations, sometimes dangerously. The XO made fun of him, making a bad situation worse. Fortunately, that CO rotated off the ship a short time after I reported aboard. The new commanding officer was one of the best I ever had. Our XO gave him full support. The difference was obvious and made the ship much more effective. After Roger Newman's counsel about supporting the CO, I vowed to do that regardless of how I felt about my Captain.

I also was lonely, possibly lonelier for Maureen than I had been for anyone before. I was having to deal with controlling a wardroom of 44 officers as diverse as ever existed, not to mention a crew of 900 who were more diverse and less controllable than even those officers. Perhaps I was under more stress than I realized in that long letter:

...Tomorrow, the admiral visits. i'll explain tomorrow. It's another big day. Geezus, how can many "big" days be so boring. Must sleep...November 23, 1983.

...Today with the admiral en route, scurrying about, hectic almost frantic pace...

Good visit. The admiral was impressed. i lunched with him and the CO. It makes no difference...another day to tick off our time in Masirah...

The CO's moods carry us all...his crew hangs on his mood, and i'm his implement to convey those moods: slow motion in nightmares. Maybe i'm paranoid. Enough. i'm solid...i'm just not comfortable in playing this role.

Perhaps I was just chomping on the bit to be in command. My hubris of considering myself a good Navy officer was driving my frustration even as my experience told me I must completely support the captain. I recognized my angst and chose to expose Maureen to how I felt:

...You know, i guess what really bothers me is that i know almost exactly what the CO wants, and i could make it happen, but he keeps getting in the way.

I also showed I missed her:

Moments of you hang lightly, joyfully in the air...What lake did you come from?

...Christmas will be when i'm particularly in need of Christmas. Goddammit, i want to be with you. I want to share that, our first Christmas, with you. Is it just my world of unreality here in the North Arabian Sea — the Navy calls it "NAS" — cloistered, inescapable that brings me to this brink of sentimentality? Could it be the start of the "mid-cruise blues?"

To her, I expressed how my frustrations were manifested:

"New World" (Symphony #9) and Dvořák settle me into Thanksgiving mid-afternoon. Last night, i dreamed of cigarette butts on the weather decks.

i'm letting this job get to me too much. i know it's happening;

i know the involvement is temporary; but i admit my flight toward insanity. The chemistry between the CO and me is not quite right... so i react, perhaps incorrectly. That creates my frustration. i know it is within my power to react properly, that i should be his parrot, and that would be best for the ship.

i know we both carry our responsibilities on our shoulders and if the XO disagrees, he cannot display that disagreement to anyone. That is the way of Navy ships on deployments.

And this old sea dog longed for his old Navy without women on board:

...my problem with women at sea is i can't deal with women sailors like i can with men. i can't tell women to "get fucked." i can't say, "You pansy ass, boot-licking shithead, get the hell out of my sight" when i'm pissed at one of them.

I was also feeling my age, at nearly-forty years old as an executive officer on a quest that was beginning to be more like Don Quixote tilting at windmills, but I could laugh about that.

...With all sorts of deep and serious problems floating about, today at noon produced a bit of an uplifting day. During a discussion with Mike Jackson, the admin officer, i voiced some concern about how young the executive officer of the ship tied up to us appeared. Mike said i shouldn't worry. When i asked what he meant, he said he'd overheard several of the enlisted women talk about how cute i was and what a "terrific heinie" i had. Apparently, several have been watching me run. i attribute this to them not having liberty for a while...

• • •

92 days deployed, 102 days to home

10 December, 0830, *Yosemite* weighs anchor and heads south for a Diego Garcia Christmas.

The crew's feelings could be best expressed by a poem an "anonymous crewmember" contributed to the ship's POD on 12 December:

6. The Ode to Masirah:
It was the 10th of December when we got underway.
We had been anchored off Masirah for many a long day.
The crew had become restless, and was ready to go.
The eve of our departure we had a big show.
The talent was varied, from singer to fight.
We thought surely it would last into the night.
We worked on the ship so somber and brave.
We worked through the night, we worked through the day.
The CO's of the ships of the West Coast are best.
They give out "BZ's" like none of the rest. (BZ-Bravo Zulu—
    "Job well done")
The services we provided were varied and many.
Because the ships alongside were constant and plenty.
We repaired all the ships from stem to the stern.
It could have been worse, this we soon learned.
The engineers worked hard, and also repair.
If not for a unit effort, we would have gotten no where.
As we leave Masirah, it's a sunshiny day.
It hasn't broken anyone's heart, no one wanted to stay!!!

• • •

When we began our trek south, I had to once more screen a passel of outgoing "Class Easy" messages. One shocked me. I wanted to find out more and perhaps get the sender (who shall remain anonymous for obvious reasons) to the chaplain for some guidance. But I was committed to silence. My job was to screen these outgoing personal messages to ensure no classified material was included (like our schedule). I was unable to take any action on the contents unless they violated security. I was also intrigued with this sailor's situation. I redacted the sailor's message and sent a copy to Maureen with my thoughts.

HI, HONEY, I'M FINE. WRONG TIME FOR YOU TO HAVE A BABY. NOT FAIR TO YOU. ME, OR THE BABY. SORRY. BUT FOR NOW I'LL HAVE TO GIVE YOU A NEGATIVE ANSWER. I'LL BE PROUD AND HONORED TO HAVE YOU AS THE MOTHER OF MY CHILD. BUT NOT NOW, PLEASE.

My note to Maureen:

This is a wire note i released for a young sailor without revealing it to anyone. I wonder what prompted it and what really was the question. i wonder how it was received. Another strange moment of thought pondering for the ole XO. How the hell was the recipient gonna get pregnant while she was in Florida and the sender was off of Masirah, Oman, and had been gone for three months?

• • •

On the day after we left our anchorage off Masirah, the *Yosemite* reached the time at sea to have its own "beernic." We had been at sea for 45 days and had more than five days before arriving in Diego Garcia. Other than the bragging rights of having a beer at sea legally, it was a low-key event. I wondered if any sailors did some bartering to get the two-beer allotment from sailors who did not drink. I remembered my father's Seabee buddy when he visited my hometown in the 1960's. Over dinner, he leaned over to me and said, "You know your father was one of the most well- liked guys in our battalion."

"No, I didn't know that," I replied.

"You see, he didn't drink and everybody liked him a lot when they handed out our beer or liquor rations, hoping he would give them his ration cards."

• • •

As XO, I was concerned about returning to the "Footprint of Freedom" (Diego Garcia). I did not share this concern with anyone, but having men and women sailors go on liberty together with access to booze and not under the ship's control after 51 days at sea was not a happy thought in my mind.

As required, we submitted our "Logistics Request" (LOGREQ) for entering port. This radio message outlines the support and any special requirements needed as well as asking permission to enter port. The reply assigns berths or anchorages, verifies the support and services requested, and notifies the ship of any other requirements or events of note.

Diego Garcia's reply to our LOGREQ late Sunday afternoon, 11 December, was not good news, at least not for me. I reported the "good news" to the crew in the following day's POD:

The reply to our logistics request for Diego Garcia has indicated we will be having a guest on Christmas Eve, and it won't be St. Nick (he may come later). USCINCPAC, *all four stars of him, will visit* Yosemite. *All of us should start thinking now about how we can improve the appearance of the ship and of ourselves. This can be an extremely positive experience for all of us. Be proud of the "Busy Lady."*

Reading my note later, I wonder how much of my sarcasm was realized by the crew. I couldn't believe it. Our crew had been given a reprieve for their Christmas, at least better than sitting at anchor off Masirah, Oman, only to be subjected to a four-star admiral's visit on Christmas Eve. I knew even before any planning proceeded, this would involve a personnel inspection of the entire crew and a ship's tour for the VIP. I certainly didn't want to spend my Christmas Eve with inspections and ship tours. I was absolutely sure no one in the crew wanted to do that either.

As soon as it was verified there would be a personnel inspection and a ship's tour, I learned of another requirement. CAPT Boyle informed me I would be joining him and the admiral for lunch in the captain's cabin. I did not think this sounded like fun, but I acknowledged the captain and thanked him.

• • •

My concern about what might happen on liberty would be shared with the CO and other members of the wardroom. I warned the crew in a POD note, 14 December, indirectly when an item about "liberty risks" was included. "Liberty Risk" was a category used to identify crewmembers who the command considered likely to become an unauthorized absence, likely to get into trouble ashore, or even desert. Those personnel identified in the category were not allowed to go ashore on liberty:

3. Liberty Risk List: The list has dwindled to almost no one due to superlative performance reports and words of praise filtering to the XO via the chain of command. However, we have been away from the evil temptations of alcohol, which tend to make some of us do things we wouldn't normally do. Have the fun you all justly deserve when we get to Diego Garcia, but don't go overboard on drinking. We don't like securing individual's liberty and would prefer to keep the liberty risk list as it is now. If you drink, do it in moderation so that you can remember the good time you had the night before rather than not be able to remember why or how you got yourself in trouble.

The day before we arrived back in Diego Garcia, 15 December:

20. Memorable or Not So Memorable: Very soon, some of us will be privileged to enjoy liberty at Diego Garcia. Due to our extended "vacation" at Masirah, our livers, at least some of them, have experienced temporary relief from the abuse some of us tend to do to them. Our liberty at "Fantasy Island" can be one filled with excitement and relaxation; or a not so memorable nightmare requiring by appointment only to meet with the XO and CO. (Think about it and take it easy.)

• • •

After Doc and I discussed our wives traveling to Malaga for the scheduled stop there on the way home, CAPT Boyle came up with the great idea of requesting our liberty port in the Mediterranean to be the Greek Island of Rhodes. When our superiors nixed Rhodes, Malaga, Spain remained on our schedule, Kerrigan and I continued to discuss our wives traveling together. It was a grand idea and would have been a dreamy way to cap off the deployment before we sailed back home. I brought up the possibility to Maureen in a letter written two nights before we returned to Diego Garcia:

...My recommendation if you want to come to Spain and it fits your schedule, tentatively plan but don't commit coins. The way the cruise is going, we might not hit Malaga (a prophetic observation) *or the Med, but it is more probable than not. I would love to see you, but i know i'll have to spend a relatively large portion of my time on ship's business. I mean it wouldn't be like having a honeymoon although i sure as hell would love to be with you as soon as possible.*

• • •

After my disappointment at having to be part of the Christmas Eve luncheon with the Admiral, I was surprised by the captain's concern for me. I realized that concern the night before we pulled into the harbor. As was our daily routine for the past 55 days, I would hold "8 O'clock Reports" in the evening with the department heads and other key personnel like the command master chief, and then I would go to the captain's cabin where he and I would discuss the events of the day and what lay ahead.

It was a short meeting, unusual as we often talked for a long time. As we concluded, CAPT Boyle paused and said, "Jim, I want you to take a break. You've been putting in a lot of hours with no real rest, so when we have liberty call, I want you to go ashore, have fun, and spend the night at the officer's admin."

I was pleased and thought the captain was wise to recognize I needed a break. It was not difficult to respond with "Aye, aye, sir," adding a heartfelt "Thank you."

• • •

Bob Mandell, the assistant Supply Officer, was our liaison with the island for supplies, vehicles, services for the ship, and many other things. He had worked out a deal that one of the older BOQ barracks, (currently vacant with the new quarters having been recently completed), would serve as the wardroom "admin." When ships went to a liberty port, it was common for the officers to rent or otherwise establish a place, such as a hotel suite, where all of the officers could come, stow their gear and shopping prizes while they went out, or to relax and have some drinks, and sleep there if desired.

I was not certain I would stay ashore for the night, sleeping in the "admin" Bob Mandell had acquired, but I was glad the Captain gave me the okay to take a break.

There was a benchmark occurring for those who kept a short timer's chain. For the officers and sailors who kept count of the days remaining to reach home port, *Yosemite* had gone over the hump. 15 December marked 97 days on deployment. New Year's Eve gave us 97 days left before we would pull into Mayport.

97 days deployed, 97 days to home

I continued to attempt to influence the crew to stay away from trouble. The last POD before entering port contained one more handwritten note:

One final word from the XO: Your image and that of Yosemite *disproportionately depends a great deal on your conduct ashore. Don't overindulge in alcohol; don't get into trouble; don't start a fight, and if one starts near you, get away from it fast and take a friend. Let's keep the Busy Lady proud of her reputation and her sailors.*

A new phase of our adventure was about to begin.

Chapter 15: Back to the Footprint

December 1983

We set the navigation detail with LT Leahy and I manning the chart table with the quartermasters at 0630. The sea and anchor detail was set at 0700. At 0800 as we passed the toes of the "Footprint of Freedom," we picked up the pilot and sent a ten-hand working party, postal clerks, special services managers, and athletic officers, by boat into the base to gather our mail and immediate supply needs, arrange special services and athletic events ashore, and gather other information to have for us upon anchoring.

Yosemite anchored in the middle of Diego Garcia's lagoon at 0900, but our workday was just beginning. We had a field day to clean the ship. We assembled a 40-hand working party to handle the large number of supplies coming from the base. The captain had a request captain's mast. Chaplain Poe held a Catholic Rosary service in the chapel. And I conducted an inspection of the entire ship before granting liberty at 1600.

Liberty expired for all hands by midnight, except for officers who were allowed to remain ashore for the night.

• • •

I remained aboard that evening, made sure all was shipshape that morning before taking a liberty boat ashore around 1100. Liberty problems had already occurred. But it wasn't from the crew. A problem with a couple of officers and the base Command Duty Officer had developed. I eventually called it the "old salt van gang" incident.

A number of the officers had gone ashore the previous night and stayed in the "wardroom admin." Bob Mandell, in his dealings for services had acquired a "lease" on the old BOQ barracks, old wooden buildings

Diego Garcia's old barracks used by *Yosemite* officers as an "ADMIN"

elevated from the ground to keep out critters and water. It was a large room with several old barracks bunks. A urinal and sink (with running water) were in a small head on one end. Outside and in the middle of several of these barracks was a communal open-air, walled-in shower building with a large open entrance (think the shower building in "MASH"). And Bob, in his wheeling and dealing, had acquired use of an old three-seat Navy van without air conditioning, but it was transportation nonetheless.

When the officers awoke in the "admin" the next morning, they cleaned up, ate breakfast at the BOQ when they decided to tour the island in the van. They loaded it up with a large ice cooler behind the front seat and put in a case or two of canned beer. They headed toward the Naval Air Facility. Bob Mandell was driving; George Sitton was riding shotgun; Ken Clausen was behind the driver; and John Knight was behind the passenger seat. Mandell was a supply officer and the other three were two former enlisted LDO's and a warrant officer, old school Navy men out to have a good time, especially after fifty-five days at sea.

After driving off of the main base area for about four miles they were on the narrow two-lane road approaching the runway area. John Knight reached over to the cooler, grabbed a beer, popped open the tab top and took a swig. He cussed when he realized the beer was hot and thinking it would be no good if he put it back in the cooler, he tossed the nearly full can out the window.

Unfortunately, they were passing a runner who was hugging the shoulder next to a ditch and a sizable berm beyond that. The beer can hit the jogger in the head knocking him into the ditch. More unfortunately, the base CDO, a young and naïve lieutenant junior grade, was in a sedan behind the van, saw the incident, turned on his siren and pulled over the van.

After hearing the story, I kept trying to imagine this near-innocent and righteous junior officer trying to chew out the tough-as-nails LDO's and warrants. It was not a pretty picture. They chased the young man away as he shouted he was reporting their misbehavior to the command.

I first heard what happened when LT Carrasco met me at liberty landing. She was excited and did not have all of the details, but she had heard enough to give me concern. After learning the jogger was not seriously injured, just a bit woozy and surprised, I wasn't concerned about my officers. However, I was concerned about how CAPT Boyle would receive the news when the base notified the ship of the incident.

I considered turning around and going back to the ship to serve as a middleman and dampen the news to the captain and serve as a shield for some of the most important officers in the wardroom. But the Captain's advice to relax came to mind, and I decided to find out more and wait until I was summoned back to the ship.

Soon afterwards, I met up with the "old salt van gang" as I came to call them. They told me exactly what happened. I attempted to act alarmed and concerned about the aftermath, but they knew I was laughing inside. After all, I had been an old liberty hound myself. The group showed me to the "admin," and I dropped off my gear there. They hopped in the van and went off to tour some more. But the beer in the cooler was cold now. I remained behind, figuring the executive officer should relax but definitely not get into trouble. Bad form.

• • •

After the "old salt van tour" departed, I went to the exchange. The exchange had pith helmets like the ones worn by the "Ramar of the Jungle" cast in the television series that ran for two years in the early 1950's. The helmets also were like the one my father had worn as a Seabee in New Guinea, Bougainville, and in the Philippines during World War II.

A number of the officers and crew of *Yosemite* purchased pith helmets as mementos. I bought two, one for myself and sent one to my brother. In February, I received a letter from Joe after he had received my gift that the previous day:

Jim,

Here I was having just written and mailed a letter to you when low and behold! What should arrive in the morning mail, but a box from the midst of nowhere and inside it was not only the much desired T-Shirt (I included a tee shirt with the "Footprint of Freedom" graphic printed on the front), *but the stuff dreams are made of. Suddenly I've acquired Cary Grant's accent, small black men with parrots on their shoulders are following me around asking, "What now, Bwana?" I swear I've seen dingy men with long curved knives lurking behind the trees behind the house. Somewhere I know Jon Hall* (the creator and star of "Ramar of the Jungle" television series) *is suffering from sunstroke and sultry octoroons in sarongs lounge near the edge of my consciousness whispering words of endearment. I have visions of Sydney Greenstreet fanning himself in the shade of Morocco. I MUST HAVE THE TROPICS!! I wore it most of the last night. Kate* (Joe's daughter) *loved it, but Carla* (Joe's wife) *is beginning to worry.*

It was six below when I woke up this morning (At the time, Joe was the minister of the Chestnut Street Gardner United Methodist Church in Gardner, Massachusetts) ...

Return quickly, but with caution for the lion sleeps lightly under the banyan tree. The natives are restless, and I fear a general uprising. Bring ammo and Douglas Fairbanks.

6 Below!

Your friend,

Ramar

Regardless of the current situation or my mood, when I received letters from Joe, or my shipmate and running partner while aboard the *USS Okinawa,* JD Waits, they made me smile.

• • •

Frank Kerrigan and Linda Schlesinger came ashore later and met up with me. The three of us decided to go on a run together. Frank and I changed into our running gear in the admin. Linda found a suitable barracks nearby to change, and we took off. We ran from the barracks area, which was on the northeast end or the toes of the "footprint" along the eastern strand toward the aviation facility and past. It was an easy run and felt so free after the constricted eleven-lap mile circuit we had to run on the ship. Although humid, the weather is not oppressive on the atoll, and we ran to the heel of the "footprint" and back to the barracks, somewhere over 13 miles. We felt good but needed showers. Frank and I took our showers in the communal shower. Then we took turns standing guard while Linda took her shower and dressed inside.

I laughed thinking about how old Navy men would not believe this arrangement.

After the shower, Frank went to the base gym for more exercise. Having played basketball at Michigan State, Frank was serious about his physical fitness. Linda and I walked over to the officer's club and went to the bar. We both ordered a margarita, and that was where my trouble began. Linda and I were having a wonderful conversation. We had another round of margaritas. We then decided to have supper at the bar, checked out the somewhat limited menu, and in the spirit of the margaritas, ordered a Mexican meal of tacos, rice and refried beans. I had a couple of more beers with the faux-Mex meal. I decided I needed to either go back to the "admin" and sleep until the next morning or catch the next liberty launch back to the ship.

Wise thinking, great idea. It went south. As I was paying my bill, Frank showed up after his extra workout and shower. Then George Sitton and a couple of the other officers showed up. They urged me to stay and one of them bought me another drink.

I don't know how many more I had that night, but I know it was several too many. Finally, I realized I was sick and found the head to prove it. I went back to the "admin" and crashed on one of the racks. I slept for about twelve hours. Waking up the next morning, I brushed my teeth, found some coffee, grabbed my things and caught the first liberty boat back to the ship.

I worried for the entire boat trip about how I was going to deal with the "old salt van gang" incident.

LT Noreen Leahy, who was the Command Duty Officer during the "van gang" event and my absence, greeted me as I crossed the brow. I asked if she had heard anything about the van. She informed me the base CDO, the LTJG who had been embarrassed by the "old salt van gang" had called the ship on the UHF radio and reported the incident believing appropriate action would be taken, justice would be served, the guilty "old salt van gang" would receive the appropriate discipline, and consequently, he would be avenged.

Noreen, wisely recognizing the situation as a tempest in a teapot, saw only negatives in reporting the incident to CAPT Boyle. I wrestled with my loyal obeisance to the Captain but agreed with Noreen's assessment. The "old salt van gang" incident was closed. CAPT Boyle did not know of the event until he reads this the first time. I did regret not telling him when I later recalled the incident. But I laughed anyway. After all, I, too, in my own way, was an old salt.

• • •

We quickly settled into a fairly regular routine. Liberty call was early for those not on duty that day. We continued our replenishment and resupply. Athletic events were everywhere. There were numerous intra-ship contests, competition with the base personnel and the British contingent. The crew was taking full advantage of the athletic facilities. Basketball, racquetball, weight-lifting, tennis, and softball were almost constant during liberty hours. Sailing and fishing were also popular. Runners were everywhere on the island. Of course, the officers club, chiefs club, acey-deucy club (for first and second class petty officers), and enlisted club were nearly always full. Even the merchant seaman's club for the crews of the USNS forward deployed fleet had plenty of visitors from the *Yosemite.*

The lines to call home at the base's Military Auxiliary Radio System (MARS) call center were long. And the base exchange overflowed with *Yosemite* personnel buying gifts for home and memorabilia of the "Footprint of Freedom."

There was another diversion, another USO group. This time, it was the Dallas Cowboy Cheerleaders. I kept imagining a Bob Hope show with many girls so the all-male troops in World War II and Vietnam, thinking how those men would have gone crazy if the Dallas Cowboy Cheerleaders had been part of the show. Then, I wondered how it would be received by a ship with women as part of the crew.

The shows were warmly received by the crew, both men and women.

• • •

Another change occurring in the first two days back in the lagoon was the transfer of our operations officer. LT Kathy Rondeau had proved her mettle. She had been competent and skillful, a good leader. The only assuaging aspect of her departure was LT Noreen Leahy had proven she would be just as reliable as Kathy.

Kathy's departure also had brought CAPT Boyle and I to consider something new. It was guidance to our female junior officers on career choices. The two of us discussed the subject often during our nightly meetings in his cabin after I had conducted Eight O'clock Reports.

As Kathy was preparing for her departure en route from Masirah back to Diego Garcia, the CO and I met with the women officers in the wardroom.

Kathy asked the two of us, the old guard, about what she should do next to further her career in the Navy. Although aware of the success we had had thus far with women at sea, CAPT Boyle and I both were conscious of the senior chain of command, all male, being resistant to women continuing to be on ships. We advised her and the other women officers to continue to go to sea as much as would be allowed. Our reasoning was any operational tour would be looked upon as a plus throughout a female officer's career.

We also advocated them getting a sub-specialty. A sub-specialty for an officer was a secondary expertise not associated with sea duty. For example, there are sub-specialties in computer programming, international relations, and later in my case, human relations and training. Having a sub-specialty would allow the women to continue on that path if the advancement for female officers at sea did not go further.

Upon arrival in DGAR (another Navy acronym for Diego Garcia), Kathy departed on her way back to a shore billet at her new duty station at Naval Air Station, Jacksonville.

After she left, she sent me a letter, which I received when we returned to our anchorage off Masirah. Here are excerpts from that letter:

...Thank you for all you did for me. You can never know how much you have helped me grow as a Surface Warfare Officer. That night we spoke about OOD quals - you said a lot of good things and I listened to your good advice. I agree with you about not worrying about what other people think or how other people got their quals. Also, I am proud to be a Surface Warfare Officer, and XO, if it had not been for the cruise, you, and the Captain, I wouldn't be so proud. Many times, I wrote (but never sent) letters requesting a designator change. But under your leadership and with your advice, I never sent any of those letters and don't know if I will. Thank you for your being professional. Not once did I feel hampered professionally because I'm a woman. I always felt treated like a surface warfare officer. I told you once that it was the first time I was fairly treated as such.

...I never said goodbye to you, XO, it was too hard for me to do...you were so good to me and taught me so much professionally and built up my self-confidence as a Surface Warfare Officer and a department head.

Kathy's letter not only made me feel good. It made the entire deployment feel worthwhile. I knew for sure we were doing the right thing.

• • •

Even with all of the activity, the Captain and I had obligations. CAPT Boyle went ashore Monday, 19 December, to pay an official visit to the Commanding Officer of the Naval Support Facility. That same day, I took the captain's gig over to the *USNS Jupiter (T-AKR 11)* for an official visit to the master of the USNS ship, perhaps the largest of the merchant ships in the lagoon. CAPT Boyle had made an official visit during our first stop in Diego Garcia. It was my time to make the call.

About a half-dozen of these ships were anchored in the harbor. They were filled with supplies, equipment, and vehicles for the military and forward deployed to Diego Garcia for provisioning our forces for a potential conflict in the Indian Ocean. If such a conflict broke out requiring U.S. military forces to respond, it would be impossible to provide such materials and vehicles in a timely manner from the United States or our bases in the Mediterranean or Western Pacific. Having them in Diego

Garcia would give our forces access to much needed equipment in a timely fashion for sustained operations.

The *Jupiter* was immense compared to the USNS ships I rode during my first XO tour. It was also more modern. The *USNS Geiger (T-AP 197)* and the *USNS Upshur (T-AP 198)* had been converted from cruise liners to cargo and troop transports before they were launched in the early 1950's. Although considerably older, those ships had also transferred dependents. Consequently, the main dining room and all the spaces above the main deck had retained the configuration of a cruise ship. My stateroom was roomy with a private head and well appointed, even with portholes for viewing the ocean. *Jupiter* was a working ship. I sat down with the master in his expansive stateroom and compared my experience with his. My earlier conversation with the master of the *Catawba* brought back ideas of life after the Navy.

If I did not select for command at sea, I had committed to returning to San Diego in order for Maureen to resume her career with her office interior firm. The idea of getting a third mate's license with the merchant marine and becoming a master was appealing. It would provide a secure and substantial income. It would allow me to be at sea and there would be a great deal of time at home.

The *Catawba*'s master had revealed a master of a USNS ship made $90,000 a year (this was 1983). But they were only at work, at sea, six months of the year. Not bad, I thought.

Then in my conversation with *Jupiter's* master, he told me the masters of the ships in Diego Garcia had worked out amongst themselves where they would be on the ships for four months and then at home for four months. He also told me the ships would sit in Diego Garcia except for one day each month, when they would get underway, steam around together and return to their anchorages the next day.

Admiral Crowe, Commander-in-Chief, Pacific Fleet, addressing *Yosemite's* crew on Christmas Eve in Diego Garcia, 1983.

It sounded good to me except for my time being away from Maureen and Blythe. After all, I had already spent over three months of our three-and-half month's marriage away from Maureen, and I hadn't seen my daughter at Christmas, which I always tried to make happen. I didn't like that. Besides, it was all conjecture on my part until I heard about my screening for command. Even still, it was a nice official visit.

• • •

Back on *Yosemite* in what I had hoped would be a stand down from all the requirements of an XO, I went into high gear preparing for the CINCPAC to join us for Christmas Eve. I was not pleased, but as executive officers are supposed to do, I cinched up my belt and went to work. It was another opportunity for *Yosemite* to shine, and I was the shoeshine boy. While the enlisted were having a day-early Christmas Eve party, the ship was spiffing up for the Admiral Crowe.

The big day came and was certainly not as bad as I anticipated. The admiral was well aware of the inconvenience of his coming aboard on Christmas Eve. He made a short presentation to the crew, lauding their efforts and explaining how important *Yosemite* was in meeting strategic requirements.

His tour of the ship was short and went off without a hitch. At lunch with the captain, Admiral Crowe, when he found out I was from Tennessee revealed he was from Kentucky. The two of us had a delightful conversation about the South. He was as equally engaging and down to earth with CAPT Boyle.

His time on board was just over an hour. As with nearly all ship visits from dignitaries, especially flag officers, the preparations greatly exceed the time of the actual event. For me, this became a nice distraction from not being home for Christmas Eve, certainly nothing like I had envisioned.

108 days deployed, 86 days to home

Christmas was a celebration, a big celebration, at least as big a celebration as 900 officers and sailors could have in a lagoon in an atoll in the middle of the Indian Ocean. Christmas trees, although all artificial, were everywhere. The wardroom had a huge one. Christmas lights and decorations were in every living space and most offices. The Christmas dinner in all the messes was even more spectacular than the Thanksgiving dinners, if possible. I am sure we dulled the loneliness from being away from home for the crew as much as we could. I was too busy to be too lonely, and Christmas with my new bride was an unknown to be realized when we were together for our first Christmas the next year. I did miss being with my daughter Blythe as the day wore down.

• • •

Christmas was over and it was time to begin thinking about the upcoming sail and port visit to Mombasa. This was when we learned the liberty in Mombasa would be cut short when another port was added, Mogadishu, Somalia. The commander of the Seventh Fleet (Western Pacific and Indian Ocean) had visited Somalia several months before. He had promised some assistance for the Somali navy, including maintenance and repair of some vessels. When he saw *Yosemite's* schedule taking us to Mombasa, he realized we could be the means by which he could fulfill his promise.

There was a slight problem.

Scuttlebutt on the deck plates had indicated Somalia and Ethiopia would swap allegiances to the super powers back and forth. If Ethiopia was allied with the Western powers, Somalia would align with the Communist bloc. If either changed their alliance, the other would bounce as well, but to the other side. During our deployment, Ethiopia was in concert with the Communists. When the switch occurred, Russia moved out of Somalia and left a number of their patrol boats behind. Seventh Fleet was sending us there to repair those boats.

The Somalia and Ethiopia situation was tenuous and sensitive. There were likely some issues of which we were not aware, but the State Department had put out an edict US Navy ships would not visit Somalia

When the problem was pointed out to higher command, Commander, Task Force 73, our operation commander ordered us to continue as scheduled, but to omit any mention of the port visit to Somalia in any correspondence that would go beyond our task force.

I was only curious about the two ports on our schedule, not terribly interested. I would forego both to get home faster.

Regardless, our schedule was modified one more time. We would depart Diego Garcia on Thursday, 5 January 1984; visit Mombasa, 11-15 January; transit to Mogadishu, 16 January; depart for return to Masirah, 19 January; and arrive back to Oman to continue maintenance of ships in

Battle Group Alfa, 24 January through 16 February when the *USS Prairie (AD 15)* would relieve us.

Another schedule change had occurred. Our request to have the Greek island Rhodes as our liberty port was initially accepted. Rhodes was cancelled. Malaga, Spain remained our designated Mediterranean liberty port.

• • •

There was a good bit of time left in the lagoon in the island paradise of Diego Garcia. I always had something to promote my concern. Christmas was over and next up was New Year's Eve. To me, this celebration had potential problems all over it. In a handwritten note, I warned the crew in the POD the day after Christmas even while giving them some good news:

Liberty hours will be extended on New Year's Eve. No trouble will be tolerated anytime but especially that night. The liberty hours will be announced Tuesday. All hands will have a much better time if none overdo it.

And after announcing those liberty expiration times, I hand wrote another warning in the New Year's Eve POD:

Remember, liberty expires at Fleet Landing for E6 and below at 0100 and for officers and CPO's at 0130.
	Don't overindulge if you wish to go ashore in Mombasa!

Even after the big and essentially good celebration of the New Year ended, I was on guard and warning the crew against misbehavior as a note in the New Year's Day POD:

4. Fraternization: The following USS Yosemite *regulation is provided for the information of all hands: Fraternization between crewmembers of the opposite sex is prohibited on board and on the pier controlled by* Yosemite. *There will be no public displays of affection, no physical contact, or other type of conduct except that which is normally expected in a military environment. Off ship, public displays of affection between members in uniform is prohibited.*

I added a hand-written warning:

Includes fleet landing and liberty boats!

Sometimes, I thought, I must be thought of as being like a schoolmarm, or perhaps a sports promoter. *Yosemite* played every kind of sport possible on the island, divisions against divisions, departments against departments, and ship teams against all comers: the base teams and the British detachment teams. With the British, it went a step further with an Olympiad type of one-day competition. We were doing our best to keep the crew entertained and busy.

· · ·

While all this was going on, I was orchestrating the plans for the turnover of information and material to the *Prairie*, the ship that would relieve *Yosemite* in two months. The captain and I had discussed giving the turnover to the *Prairie* extensive attention. Turnovers when the tenders sat in Diego Garcia had been short and sweet. But *Yosemite* had forged new ground, and both the CO and I wanted to maximize the information we could give to the *Prairie* so her learning curve would not be so steep. Both of us mentioned to Ed Wicklander, the Repair Officer, how the turnover for the Repair was critical. Ed, a professional through and through, understood and worked hard on his end.

· · ·

We also had to get ready for sea, and this would require taking on extra sheets of metal for possible repair work for the Somalis.

In addition to taking on supplies and readying the ship for sea, there were other duties to be met. The captain had a farewell lunch with the Commanding Officer of the Naval Support Facility. I once again met with the commanding officer of the British detachment, ending up with a game of darts and ale in their small club.

Medical and Admin worked together to prepare for dangers in Mombasa with the POD note that ran for several days:

Malaria Note: Medical Intelligence reports from the Mombasa area lists this geographic location as a high risk center for malaria. The

Medical Department will start malaria prevention medication by handing out medication in the chow line once weekly. Tourists and non-residential personnel in this area are considered to be at high risk!!!! Don't become a statistic. Take you malaria medication.

And:

Rabies Note: Rabies is considered prevalent in the nation of Kenya, as well as other third world countries. Rabies vaccines for animals are virtually non-existent...Don't pet or play with animals on liberty. There is no cure for the virus that causes rabies.

• • •

There was also good news. On Thursday, 29 January, the first note in the POD was a notice from our administrative senior, Commander, Naval Surface Forces, Atlantic Fleet:

1. Fleet Support Excellence Award: (From COMNAVSURFLANT) The Fleet Support (FSO) Excellence Award is presented to the NAVSURFLANT ship which demonstrated superior performance in the Fleet Support Mission area during the previous competitive cycle. COMNAVSURFLANT takes great pleasure in announcing USS Yosemite (AD-19) *and* USS Suribachi (AD-21) *as the winners for the competitive cycle APR 82 – SEP 83. Yosemite's performance in maintaining the readiness of NAVSURFLANT units has been exemplary. Wherever she was located, she eagerly solicited work from other units and provided numerous services to groups while participating in North Atlantic Treaty Organization, Multi-national and U.S. operations and exercises in both Second and Six fleets has been superb...To the officers and men and women of* Yosemite *and* Suribachi, *congratulations for this most significant achievement. Presentation of the plaque and commendation will be addressed SEPCOR (by separate correspondence).*

As XO, even though I had not been aboard except for the last month of the award period, I was beaming, not only for the ship proving her mettle, but that the notice included "men and women" in the award. To make an exclamation point, I added in a handwritten note:

This means Yosemite *was cited as the number one tender in the Atlantic Fleet. BZ: Busy Lady. We're all proud of you and us!*

There was one more ship-wide evolution to conduct before departing the "Footprint of Freedom." On Tuesday, 4 January, the ship held its PFT for stragglers who had missed the first annual test during the first Diego Garcia stop in October.

The turn of the year had me feeling good about how I was performing as executive officer. It also appeared to me the crew and officers were performing as they should. I expressed my optimism in a letter to Maureen the night we left Diego Garcia:

...Things appear to be clearing up. All my really big projects are basically done. My primary aim is to get everything running smoothly prior to our reaching Mayport. If all documents, procedures, etc. are in automatic, then i only have two problems. One is to keep the old man (CO in Navy terms) from sweating too much. The second is to get the department heads and division officers away from playing politics and worrying more about carrying out ship's policy.

The Special Sea and Anchor Detail was set at 0700, and the *USS Yosemite* weighed anchor and got underway at 0800, Thursday, 5 January 1984.

The final phase of her stay in the Indian Ocean had begun.

118 days deployed, 76 days to home

Chapter 16: Transit to Mombasa

January 1984

For this old sea dog, it felt good to get underway even though it felt strange to me. I missed standing watches as OOD. On all of my other tours as a member of ship's company, I stood bridge and CIC watches in three-section or four-section watches and occasionally port and starboard. After my first ship, nearly all of my watch standing was as the OOD on the bridge. It is a chore to stand three four-hour watches in addition to taking care of your work-hours job as a division officer or department head. But being in charge of a ship as the OOD where everyone on the ship, especially the commanding officer, trusts one to keep the ship safe and execute its mission is a thrilling responsibility. Being one with the ship and sea was one of the best feelings I have ever known. Even as I write, I feel the yearning to stand those bridge watches. That, however, is not the role of an executive officer.

As executive officer, getting underway and back at sea also felt good, but for other reasons. At sea, the CO and his or her alter ego, XO, is in control of what happens. No one was going anywhere, and outside interference was minimal – of course, the chain of command could order us to change many things through radio messages. There was a feeling of freedom from the problems with shore establishments, liberty headaches, and constant requirements to visit or be visited by VIPs, and other interruptions. But not at sea. As mentioned earlier, it was always a relief for me to hear "All lines clear. Underway."

• • •

For the crew and most of the wardroom, Mombasa would be a welcomed liberty port, the first since Palma de Mallorca almost four months earlier. For me, the potential problems of the crew going wild after such a long time loomed.

I expressed my concerns many times through POD notes throughout the six-day sail. As I had contemplated what the crew needed in terms of direction, I realized I was not hammering them with notes about water conservation, gear adrift, and "battening down the hatches" so to speak. We had a crew who had spent well over two months at sea, and such admonitions were no longer necessary. But visiting a real liberty port for almost a week was not a pleasant prospect for the executive officer responsible for good order and discipline.

POD Warnings:

13. Mombasa: As we leave the Footprint of Freedom, it is now time to start thinking soberly about Mombasa. Yosemite's record in Diego Garcia for conduct was commendable with a couple of notable exceptions. If you are an exception in Mombasa, you could be in serious trouble like in a Kenyan jail. You don't argue with police or you may be in a cell when Yosemite *heads over the horizon.*

14. Mombasa I: There is a possibility you may be approached in Mombasa by a drug dealer. Let someone in authority know it... FAST. And don't think about using. Besides being dangerous to your health, it can be indirectly more hazardous (like sitting in that Kenyan jail cell a lot, lot longer). Yosemite *will make every effort possible to ensure that all hands are complying with the CNO's Zero Drug Tolerance Program.*

The next day, the POD addressed another potential problem:

8. Epicurean Delights while in Mombasa: Generally, health care and sanitation standards in 3rd World countries are not up to American standards. Many ships pulling into the Mombasa area have experienced problems with consumption of food and water, and sickness derived from it. The following Do's and Don'ts should be followed:

Do's:
1) Eat and drink in obviously good hotels, restaurant, and clubs.

2) Drink only bottled beverages and use ice only when in an apparently OK restaurant or club.

Don'ts
1) Eat or drink from sidewalk vendors food or drinks.
2) Eat or drink with local persons unless in an apparently suitable club or restaurant.

And even though *Yosemite* had a co-ed crew, many of them were old school male sailors, and there was a large number of young men who were about to experience opportunities never easily available in the states. My vehicle for warning the crew was apparent on the first full day underway:

9. But Doc, she was beautiful, intelligent, and spoke perfect English: Once upon a time in a land far, far away...there was a beautiful maiden with lots and lots of money in her pocket.

Please, if you indulge in a past time other than a safari or market place visit, use the proper precautions and report to sick bay at the first sign of an infection.

On the weekend before we were to arrive in Mombasa, we received yet another schedule change. Instead of Mogadishu, the capital, we were redirected for the second port visit to Chismayo (currently spelled "Kismayo") on the southern coast of the country. This was because the type of repair assistance Seventh Fleet had promised was for the Russian built patrol boats, and they were all ported in Chismayo.

The Osa and Komar patrol boats the Soviets had abandoned in Somalia were well-known to me. These two classes carried guided missiles capable of delivering nuclear warheads. Those officers who had served on combatants were drilled on the capabilities and firepower of these Russian craft and were trained in tactics to combat them if required. Although the craft in Somalia did not have nuclear weapons, a missile firing patrol boat could be an effective asset for a third world navy. These were the boats in Chismayo we would be helping to repair.

I was intrigued by this new task assigned to us. Working on boats built by the USSR was an ironic twist to me.

• • •

During the last few days of our transit from Masirah to Mombasa, my frustrations with dealing with officers who thought they knew more than they did were beginning to boil over. They were beginning to lean on me, wanting me to do what they thought was best. I was accessible, and they knew it. After nearly four months at sea as the executive officer, the constant flow of folks entering my office or catching me in a passageway with their problems was beginning to get to me. I vented my spleen to Maureen:

...i mean here it is 11:20 p.m. when most humans are either in or thinking about going to bed. i'm working. i'm working because my day has been spent counseling, inspecting, running (or at least overseeing) ship-wide drills, briefing the CO, and doing thousands of other things except the paperwork on my desk, which continually piles higher while i'm away. So i'm sitting here at this ungodly hour, writing my ass off about care packages to Kenya and what kind of community project we can volunteer for if and when we get there, so all of the wonderful friendly people of Kenya will fall in love with the good ole US of A for us painting some goddamn cinder-block orphanage while my sailors are out drinking beer, whoring around, and my officers are down at the resort drinking some exotic drink undoubtedly in a glass with a mother-fucking elephant etched on the side, watching the rich Germans wander around half-nude while i'm worrying if my sailors pissed off the orphanage managers by not cleaning up, and if my other sailors got put in jail for some dumb shit trick any 20-year old sailor might try with the right amount of booze inside, and i'm thinking about all of that wishing i were writing you love poems instead and then this jerk, this good officer is so concerned about his troops, comes in and wants to talk to me — remember this is 11:20 p.m. and i've got more goddamn paperwork on my desk than crossed the shelves for toilet paper in a supermarket in a year — and this clown is going on watch to sit on his ass in a dark little room to make sure that any ship within five miles of us is in this is reported to another, more responsible officer on the bridge who has his own radar scope and both know that the probability of a ship being within five hundred miles of us in this god- forsaken part of the ocean just north of the equator some

thousand miles south of India where no one in his right mind would be anyway — he wants to talk to me because when he was feeding his face after a four or five hour nap getting ready to sit on his ass for four arduous hours, he read the plan of the day that i wrote (or had written) and he came in to tell me he was stressed greatly at something in the POD. And i'm sure i've overlooked some great heinous injustice in a statement i had rapidly read as innocuous as i edited that offensive POD. But then he tells me he is distressed that we are limiting overseas liquor purchases to four bottles per person (a U.S. Customs restriction) when one might buy "fifth" bottles and be entitled to five, which would be an exact gallon, which is Custom's free maximum amount. Then when i am about to explode in frustration at such a minor bullshit concern, he continues that he is further greatly distressed that the purchases must risk the possible loss of $10 worth of customs-free hooch and suggests Welfare and Recreation funds (over 10% profit for the ship's store sales are used to fund crew activities) be used to cover the potential loss, and i quickly pointed out that would make the ship liable for about $16,000 if just half the ship bought booze, and i start to give him what for but stop and try to explain the reasoning behind the decisions and tell him i don't give a shit without telling him i really don't give a shit. But he gets up and says, "oh, I can tell you are not open, when you are not going to change your mind, no matter what i say, your mind is made up. And he leaves, and i want to yell, "No shit!" but i don't.

And then i sit here feeling guilty that i didn't act receptive…that i failed to make him understand how insignificant his concerns were and how time-wasting it was to discuss it further. And then i think, "Why the hell do you feel guilty? You should have told that stupid son-of-a-bitch to go to hell." But i didn't and i won't, and i will still feel guilty, at least a little bit.

And so, the days go past, my watching all the insanity, mine and theirs and sometimes both, go on by their own volition, beyond anyone's control and that allows me a laugh or two.

And i love you.

• • •

Deck department on the forecastle, Admin Department on the ceremonial deck, Captain and LT George Sitton with pilot on open bridge as *Yosemite* enters Mombasa.

As we prepared for entering port, I realized I would be taking the sailor who had pledged the most money to the Combined Federal Campaign to dinner one evening for his long- delayed prize. I was not looking forward to that evening.

I also thought the crew would be impressed with some revised data and let them know in another handwritten POD note on Sunday, 8 January, *Yosemite* had traveled 14,331 miles since departing Mayport, 9 September.

An executive officer's work is never done. Yet a major step was accomplished when on Sunday, January 8, we announced this in the POD:

18. AD19 INST 3120.1A, Standard Organization and Regulations Manual (SORM) has been published and is ready for pickup in the ship's office. Due to the anticipation of numerous changes forthcoming, each department will be issued only two copies of the SORM. Department heads are asked to review the SORM and if any changes are required, submit them to the ship's office via the executive officer no later than 1 FEB 84. (A ship's SORM is the bible for a Navy organization, especially a ship that provides all hands a guide to the way the ship operates internally and what the rules are for that operation)

I considered the publishing of the SORM a major goal accomplished. I didn't believe our officers or crews paid attention to a pretty essential document because it had been so woefully out of date. I hope the revised and updated version would make it understandable and useful to all of us as a guideline in how we went about doing our jobs.

I also knew it was not going to be used by everyone, but we had a viable document for the way we operated. Of course, that phalanx of gibberish instructions in the bookshelf behind my desk in those oversized notebooks remained. I had streamlined many of them but realized I would not ever reach the goal of making them all extant and applicable.

I often wondered if it mattered. But I had set out on my mission and vowed to keep at it.

And we had two liberty ports ahead of us, something we hadn't had since Palma de Mallorca.

124 days deployed, 70 days to home

Chapter 17: A Wild Safari Ride

January 1984: Mombasa and Long Awaited Liberty
0730, 11 January 1984: Yosemite moors pier- side in Mombasa, Kenya.

It was yet another different world. Mombasa was the only major city in the country, advanced in many ways, but tribal, and over-populated. It was a city with both overwhelming poverty and great wealth. It was primarily Muslim and trouble with terrorism was on the rise. It also was the gateway to some of the most incredible destinations in the world, the Serengeti and Mount Kilimanjaro. The port was a bustling, busy international haven for ships of all nations regardless of affiliation to NATO, the Communist Bloc, or neutral. It was a perfect scenario for a spy novel with the potential for intrigue and shadowy goings-on.

It loomed as one huge problem and potential disaster, especially with such a naïve crew, and one that had not seen a real liberty port in four months. And I was well aware relationships between male and female sailors had developed since leaving Mayport in early September. I was much concerned a pregnancy or two might develop, which would cause us major problems. But I was too busy to ponder all of those possibilities.

Yosemite was moored at a commercial international pier. We began to refuel at 1400. The U.S. attaché came aboard with a list of visits, both for the CO and me to make ashore and for VIPs to visit the ship.

CDR Allega, LCDR Mandell, LT Sitton and LTJG Jackson, under the watchful eye of the captain and myself, met with the local folks providing services. We would take on some supplies, but the big tickets were to address our pier space as the port was crowded and shifting berths or anchoring was possible. We also had to contract with Luciana Bacilli, the Kenyan responsible for ship husbanding for pier and garbage services and Saoud Bacilli, for painting of the ship's exterior. George Sitton had saved used manila and nylon line in the boatswain's locker, which he used to barter for painting the ship. The captain, George, the other officers and chiefs who had been on ships in Hong Kong, and I were reminded of the bartering system for painting the ships. Mary Soo, with a crew of mostly women, would paint the ships in that port, and the trade was usually for brass from expended powder casings from the big guns.

Bacilli did not have women in his painting crews. This wasn't Hong Kong and Bacilli wasn't Mary Soo. Mary Soo's painters did a good job, but the painting was done quickly with a lot of proper preparations being skipped. George, CAPT Boyle, and I were all wary of the quality of painting we would receive, and we knew it was not likely going to be the quality of Mary Soo's work. We also knew if a ship's sides were to be painted properly, the preparation and painting would be done by sailors in a ship's deck department.

However, sailors painting out the ship in a liberty port was not feasible. With the allotted in-port stay, there simply wasn't enough time to do it right, and to do so would deprive crewmembers of the precious liberty they had over the six months. But *Yosemite* definitely needed painting and hopefully, the job would last until we got back to Mayport.

I knew the painting would not be satisfactory for the command. CAPT Boyle, as the former head examiner for the Navy's Atlantic Fleet Propulsion Examining Board (PEB), did not take shortcuts on any project. He was rightfully a stickler for doing work properly. I knew he would be checking out the progress, and if he found it lacking, quite correctly, demand corrective action.

I also knew the deck department under George would be chomping at the bit to get ashore and likely to be less observant and demanding of the paint crew about meeting the Captain's standards. The problem of checking for proper preparation and application would fall to the duty section, and other than some of the hard-nosed old salts like Gunner Knight, they had no experience in overseeing painting of a ship and none in managing a foreign contractor to do the job correctly.

It did not bode well.

· · ·

There was little time for me to dwell on that. The visitors, planners, and greeters kept coming. Perhaps the best news, although I did not recognize it then, was "Paddy Purchase." This outfit was the tour planner. Although I was surprised by the number of the crew who went on tours in Palma, I was about to be knocked off my feet. More than half of the crew signed up for tours in Mombasa. This was new to me. On my previous, male- only ships, tours at liberty ports rarely reached twenty percent. In my previous nine deployments, I had been on exactly one tour.

The large number of sailors on tours meant most of the crew would be sightseeing, not down in the red light districts, and not getting drunk (I'm sure many of the crew imbibed, but the numbers were small compared to the male only sailors looking for "Fiddler's Green" as on my previous deployments). Considering my past experience, having women as part of the crew was a positive. This one was unexpected. I was envious of those who had signed up for two and three day tours to Mount Kilimanjaro or the Serengeti. Executive officers could not and should not be away from the ship that long. Conversely, I was thrilled that many of our crew would be thus occupied.

The consul for Mombasa, Robert E. Gribbin, was given a tour of the ship. Through Mr. Gribbin, the captain was scheduled to meet the mayor and I was volunteered to meet with the chief of the Mombasa police. Later, after Griffin had observed the capabilities *Yosemite* displayed in the machine shop, he returned on Friday with the mayor and a phalanx of city managers. They brought along a drive shaft of a Mercedes Benz truck. Pointing out the drive shaft had been hopelessly bent, they asked if we could make a replacement. Mr. Gribbin was enthusiastic and pointed out to us how it would greatly enhance the United States relationships with Kenya.

Our machine shop was superb. The capabilities were amazing. But making a Mercedes Benz drive shaft was not one of those capabilities. The entourage left disappointed.

• • •

I was mildly disappointed that the consul for Kenya, stationed in Nairobi, had not come down to see the ship. The U.S. consul for Kenya was Gerald Thomas, a retired rear admiral.

Admiral Thomas was a captain and the commodore of Destroyer Squadron 9 in 1974 out of the Long Beach Naval Station. I was the chief engineer of the *USS Hollister (DD-788),* also homeported in Long Beach. Our ship, the wardroom and several of our crew were directed to attend the "Executive" version of UPWARDS, the program to bring racial awareness to the Navy and promote equality. CAPT Thomas, his staff, and the commodore and staff of a minesweeper squadron attended the same one-day program.

In the mingling of the participants before the 25 or so of us were seated in a large circle, one of the other department heads pointed out my Southern accent to CAPT Thomas, implying I was racially prejudiced. The commodore told me of this occurrence afterwards. I don't know if the other department head thought it was a joke, if he was serious, or why he would say such a thing.

At the beginning, the facilitators directed each attendee to stand and state their name, expressly directing us to announce our first and last names only, to not use our rank or rate. When it was the commodore's turn, he stood up and said, "My name is Captain Thomas." The facilitator's two first class petty officers thought it wise to let it go. I loved it.

Later in the session in one of the exercises, CAPT Thomas and I ended up in the middle of the circle (I don't know how the exercise put us there by ourselves). What followed was the captain and I addressing all sorts of racial profiling and shooting down misconceptions, even those of the Caucasian and black facilitators. By the end of the day, he and I had become good friends.

I really would have liked to see him in Mombasa. But I'm sure a consul's work was a continuous time consuming job.

It struck me I somehow had been in the forefront of another equal opportunity effort. And now I was XO of a ship with women as part of the crew and the wardroom.

• • •

One of the first to board was YNCS Carl Wheeling, who was the head of the Navy detachment the Kenyan United States Liaison Officer (KUSLO) in Mombasa, and our source of the most important information. He proved invaluable to us as our main line of communication to all important contacts in Mombasa. I was surprised the actual liaison officer, LCDR Warren Lobs, could not come down from Nairobi to greet us.

More important to me on that first day's parade of meeting various officials was meeting the hotel czar, Dave Carl. He was also from the U.S. Consulate and provided information about places to go and things to see in Mombasa. He gave me the information on the Nyali Beach Hotel, which became the gathering spot as well as off-ship lodging for officers and enlisted although there were other excellent hotels along the beach where some *Yosemite* personnel stayed. The beaches at Mombasa were superb. A large number of the hotels catered to Germans who were the primary group of Europeans to vacation there. Those hotels were the ones most like beach hotels back in the states. The beach, I knew, would be one of the main attractions to the women.

Colonel Buhla Kemenitti of the Kenyan military also gave us information about other hotels available in Mombasa. He also informed us the Mombasa polio clinic for children needed painting. I recognized this would be something that would attract a number of the women in the crew. We placed a note in the POD to see if we could get 12 volunteers to paint the clinic.

Along with those came the tours. Paddy Purchase was the outfit who provided tour information. There were many tours of varying lengths to many places and many variations on the tours to the Serengeti. Everyone was signing up.

As we completed the deployment in late March, I was given the statistics for tours. We had 75 percent tour usage over the course of the deployment. Of all the ships I rode on in the Pacific, Atlantic, and Indian Oceans, I have never seen more than 25 percent tour usage, and it was usually significantly lower.

It was in Mombasa I confirmed what I first realized on our liberty port of Palma. The men in the crew followed the women in the crew. Instead of hitting all the bars (and yes, a number of the male crew, especially old salts, did that), hanging out in the red- light districts, getting into trouble, and causing all sorts of problems, the *Yosemite* males chose to hang out with the women. They went to the beach. They went to nice hotels. They went on tours. And yes, they even were in the group of twelve who painted the children's polio clinic.

These kinds of things can make an XO very happy. Although we had some "problem children" on liberty, we did not have an international incident throughout the entire deployment. This was a first for me.

• • •

One officer was not involved in most of the normal liberty pursuits. Noreen Leahy's husband, who was the Main Propulsion Assistant on a

Knox class FFG, took leave and flew to Mombasa for *Yosemite's* week of liberty there. Noreen took her leave upon arrival. The two got a room at one of the nice hotels on the beach. Although they occasionally mingled with other members of the wardroom, the couple spent most of their time on a second honeymoon.

I was glad the young couple had pulled it off. Noreen had been critical in supporting me as navigator. Oh, all right, she was really the navigator except for the official title after about the first week of the deployment. She also was an extremely capable CDO and OOD and was an enthusiastic supporter of many of the ship's activities. She contributed greatly to the ship's *esprit de corps*. She deserved a break.

I was also a bit jealous and wished Maureen and I could be the other newlywed couple with a second honeymoon in Africa. However, I accepted my primary reason for being there was to serve as the XO, and Maureen's presence would have conflicted with performing my job in the manner I should.

• • •

The first night, a bunch of the officers met at a recommended restaurant for dinner. It was a nice meal, but I did wonder about the quality for digestion. After all of my adventures, I had a pretty strong stomach, but this meal was a little suspicious. However, I was fine afterwards and the next day. There were others who dined at good restaurants throughout Mombasa who did not fare so well.

My Thursday was full of activity. First, I went to the heart of the city and visited the Mombasa Chief of Police at his headquarters. My meeting with the chief was pretty standard. We chatted over a cup of tea. He bragged about his police force and how crime had decreased. He refrained from providing any warnings I could forward to the crew as to places not to go and what not to do. I gave him a ship's plaque, and he gave me an engraved and highly polished wood cane. I gave it to the admin office on return to the ship for a ship's display; I did not wish to take gifts from any one in my role as executive officer of a U.S. Navy ship.

While I was visiting the police, the captain was having his official visit with Mombasa's mayor. We both returned aboard in time to host a VIP lunch in the Flag Mess. Our guests included the American Consul Mr.

Gibbins, the mayor and his deputy, the Kenyan Navy commander, and the chief of police.

• • •

That afternoon, as navigator, I had the delightful duty of gathering information about our upcoming port visit to Chismayo, Somalia. Our Navy contact, Senior Chief Wheeling, had arranged for a privately owned tugboat master to come aboard and brief me on the conditions in Chismayo's harbor. It was early afternoon when he brought his tugboat alongside, tied up, and joined me on *Yosemite's* bridge.

Kevin Patience, a British expatriate, came straight out of a Joseph Conrad short story. He was big, blonde, and bombastic. He was ruddy in complexion, looked as old as the hills and sported a full, white beard. We took a liking to each other immediately. He had been plying the waters off Nairobi, Kenya, Somalia, and Nigeria for years. He was an old salt in the truest sense of the word.

We discussed Chismayo. CAPT Boyle and I were concerned about entering the port. The harbor entry was narrow. The entrance required a passage to the northwest. The channel between the quay walls appeared difficult enough on its own. When we factored in the strong prevailing currents from the north and the limitations on *Yosemite's* power and maneuverability, the possibilities of grounding gave us apprehension. Kevin confirmed all we feared.

After my meeting with Mister Patience, we notified all involved with our pending visit to Chismayo, *Yosemite* would anchor out in the seaway rather than moor at a pier in the Chismayo harbor.

Kevin and I continued our chat. I asked about Chismayo, the city, any sights or entertainment, and what the people were like. He wasn't very positive about Somalia except he spoke proudly of his "woman" who was a Somalian. I asked him about her, and he told me she was his tugboat crew, his cook, and was good in bed.

• • •

That evening was the night I had been dreading for about four months. It was time to pay up. The fireman who had contributed $600 to the CFC was due to be rewarded. It was time for me to take him to dinner. YNC Lucy Gwinner had made reservations at an upscale restaurant in downtown

Mombasa. Chaplain Poe, aware of my concerns, volunteered to join us. I was breathing a bit easier. Then, LTJG Mike Jackson also volunteered to accompany us. I was more relieved.

My concerns were unfounded. The prize winner was pleased he had been awarded the dinner for his Combined Federal Campaign contribution. He was not looking to gripe about anything. It turned out to be a very nice evening. The fireman was excited and seemingly enjoyed the evening Afterwards, even though the dinner had been pleasant, I took a deep sigh of relief and went to a bar for a whiskey, vowing to not make that mistake again.

All was going well except CAPT Boyle was rightfully concerned about the ship painting by the locals. George Sitton, the First Lieutenant and the guy in charge of the painting, along with Bob Mandell, the assistant supply officer, had worked out the contract. George was responsible for the ship's appearance. He was not particularly concerned. He just wanted the ship to be painted and look respectable until we returned to the states where it could be done properly. As stated earlier, the captain did not appreciate any job not being done correctly. Mary Soo and her ladies in Hong Kong were known for their gun decking and radioing (Navy slang for not doing the job right and recording it was done correctly; it's a little more complicated than that, but you would have to be in the Navy to get the subtle differences). Bacilli of Mombasa was not likely as thorough as Mary Soo of Hong Kong.

The inexperienced CDO's had not yet had to deal with a third party who spoke a different language who was painting a ship. The captain was not pleased his duty officers weren't more diligent and demanding in checking the painting. I was torn in several different directions. I wanted the job to be done correctly, but I wasn't as concerned as the captain. I had been a first lieutenant as a department head in charge of exterior painting during three tours. I understood George's idea of getting it done from an appearance standpoint and then getting it done right when back home. I also sympathized with the officers and crew wanting to maximize this rare opportunity for liberty.

On a past tour as a member of the Amphibious Squadron 5 staff, I had raised quite a ruckus when then Vice President George H.W. Bush visited the Navy base in Subic Bay, Luzon, Philippines. Admirals and captains ordered all of the ships in port to paint everything, cover rust, to violate all of the rules for proper painting of ships to look good for the president.

Kenyan workers painting exterior of *Yosemite* in Mombasa

I argued Vice President Bush would have been appalled if he knew we were doing that just to look good. Consequently, I agreed with the captain in principle and supported him completely on this one, even though I was certainly conflicted.

CAPT Boyle was not conflicted. He had planned on taking one of the safari tours for several days but cancelled it due to his concern about the ship being painted properly.

Consequently, I felt compelled to stay aboard and serve as a buffer between the captain and the CDO's. I knew I could soften the approach with the junior officers and still have the paint job be closer to what it should be. After considerable consternation and two wonderful offers, I decided to go ashore the next two days and return early to be on the ship the following mornings to ensure all was going well. There were also a lot of other things requiring my attention, and I wanted to be on board if a liberty crisis arose.

• • •

I remained anxious about the women on liberty as I had been for the entire deployment. Although they were having a positive impact on liberty in general, drawing many of the male sailors away from trouble, they were also in a liberty world much different than one in the states. There were a lot of bad actors in foreign liberty ports and our female sailors could be targets for such vermin. I recognized my concerns came from an upbringing that put women on a pedestal and considered them vulnerable. I worried how the locals might treat women, and I wanted to be available if any of our female crew members needed help.

• • •

The ship was getting attention from other U.S. citizens. A couple in the Peace Corps visited the ship. At the end of their ship tour, they asked if I would like to visit them at their home. I was pleased they would ask me and readily accepted.

With their pre-school daughter in tow, they picked me up in the early afternoon and took me to their home. They lived in a rural area with lots of palm trees and within yards of the beach. They served delicious vegetable and fruit appetizers. Afterwards, we took a walk on the beach. The four of us were the only ones on the beach within eyesight in either direction. The wife told me it was the beach filmed in "Out of Africa" where Robert Redford's character Denys flies his airplane down the coast.

I was enthralled and thought about what a great place to be to do good things.

• • •

They returned me to the ship in time for me to travel out to the Nyali Beach Hotel and meet other officers. We sat out by the pool and were entertained by native dancing while we drank Tusker's beer. George Sitton, Frank Kerrigan, Bob Mandell, and Ken Clausen had joined the group after a round of golf. Frank and George laughed about the round. Young boys had served as their caddies, not only carrying the group's clubs, but two of the youngsters carried large coolers with iced down beer on the top of their heads. I was sorry I missed it.

The next evening, the captain and I went out to dinner.

• • •

Friday evening produced one of my greatest regrets of the entire deployment. The only other Navy personnel in Mombasa besides Senior

Chief Wheeling was LCDR Joe Taylor. Joe was the Seabee officer in charge of the Navy's survey of the harbor. The intent was to determine how to dredge the harbor to a depth that would allow Navy carriers to anchor, opening another liberty port for the carriers in the Indian Ocean.

Joe invited Ken Dawson and me to dinner at his home. We arrived and were amazed at the place. Joe had bought the home rather than rent. It was on about five acres of nicely kept land. The front of the house was the living room and dining room. The walls slid back, and we dined al fresco in the dining room and settled in living room chairs for an after dinner cup of coffee.

The CEC officer knew he was going to be stationed in Mombasa for at least two and possibly four years. He found this house for sale because no one else would buy it even though the price had plummeted. He then told us how the previous owners were a well-to-do Japanese couple. The husband had a thriving business in the city. But their valet, apparently upset with some perceived offense, had killed the two with a machete and then dumped their bodies in the home's cistern. Potential buyers backed away, believing the place was haunted.

Joe introduced his eleven-year old son. He then came up with a wonderful idea. He asked if I would like to spend the night at his home and join his son and him on an outing. The plan was to get up around four and drive his Range Rover out to take in the Serengeti's wildlife. Joe described earlier trips where they ran with rhinos and giraffes and saw lions, elephants, and many other wild animals.

This sounded like a wonderful opportunity and would go a long way to make up for not being able to go on the tour to Mount Kenya and William Holden's resort. I was envious of our officers and crew who had taken the three-day tour to that destination.

I considered the possibility and really wanted to agree. But I was the executive officer, and there were lots of things requiring attention, not the least of which was the paint job. I felt I would be shirking my duty to make the paint job go better and ease the captain's concerns. I knew if I asked CAPT Boyle for permission to go with Joe and his son, the CO would encourage me to go.

Reluctantly, and of my own volition, I declined.

After thirty-plus years, I remain regretful I did not see the Serengeti with Joe and his son, but I am placated by knowing I did the right thing returning to the ship. I am sure CAPT Boyle remains disappointed he was unable to go on his safari. That's the nature of the beast of being a CO or XO.

The painting was completed on Saturday. As I knew he would be, the captain was not happy with the result, but the ship did look better and hopefully the paint job would last until March when we returned to Mayport.

• • •

The rest of the day was spent in preparation to get underway. On Sunday, we departed Mombasa and headed north for Chismayo, Somalia.

In spite of my frustration, the liberty port of Mombasa was a huge success. There were no significant incidents that would have marred our stay. The crew was finally able to let off some steam with excellent tours and sights to see. In the POD when we departed, I entered this hand-written note:

> *Good show to all hands on performance in Mombasa. Early reports* (from the U.S. Embassy) *praise* Yosemite's *crew on conduct ashore. BZ on having good fun!*

In my mind, it was yet another example of how the women had been a positive impact on the ship.

• • •

One of my best moments during Mombasa liberty was a MARS telephone call to Maureen. Then, we got underway, the dining in Mombasa finally took its toll. Intestinal problems reared their ugly head and in between handling all of my tasks, I spent significant time "commode hugging." I wrote of my problems to Maureen:

> *My Dearest Soul,*
>
> *Damn, i was all psyched up from talking to you. i was ready to generate all sorts of work. Then today, i started to catch the Masai Mamba. It's an indigenous dance of Mombasa, named after the Masai warriors known for their height and fierce independence and less known for the flies that can cover their person. The Masai*

Mamba was created by some early traveler whose name is lost in posterity but whose tracks to the loo are imprinted on every hotel floor. Our wardroom has almost succumbed en masse. I thought I had escaped.

And Christ, we have two days of Chismayo, Somalia starting tomorrow, and the main fare at the one hotel is goat, and the only salvation is that electricity runs only in daylight hours, although there is not enough for air conditioning, which means that if we dine after sunset — we will be invited with no refusals for XO's allowed — to at least one fine meal where one cannot see how well it's cooked in the oil lamp glow, and maybe not even able to tell what it really is.

The meal with Somali dignitaries was changed from the hotel to a plantation. Little did I realize my letter was prophetic regarding my next meal ashore.

130 days deployed, 45 days to home

Chapter 18: *Back Into Another Time in Another World*

January 1984: Chismayo, Somalia

Once again, *Yosemite* was headed into unknown territory. We knew we had to minimize our communication about our destination. The State Department had forbidden U.S. ships from visiting Somalia. But Seventh Fleet, Admiral Jimmy Hogg, had visited the country before the State Department edict and had promised to help them with the repair and maintenance of the Osa and Komar patrol craft the Russians had left behind after Ethiopia and Somalia had switched allegiances. Apparently, the two countries were never aligned with the same powers.

We kept our Navy chain of command informed of our trip, but we endeavored to not go beyond Navy superiors.

After the daylong journey of roughly 300 nautical miles, *Yosemite* anchored in the seaway about a mile east of Chismayo's harbor entrance at 0800 on Monday, 16 January. We had a complete picture of the harbor entrance and confirmed the size and speed of the fetch of the "Somali Current" (fetch is an area of ocean over which the wind blows in an essentially constant direction, thus generating waves). In the winter, this particular "fetch" runs from Oman to the southwest for some 1500 nautical miles, increasing the size and speed of the current. The current would have made entering the harbor for *Yosemite* an extremely dangerous maneuver. We had chosen wisely to anchor out.

• • •

The military liaison for Somalia, an Army major, whose name has been lost in antiquity, came aboard as soon as we had lowered the accommodation ladder. His information was not encouraging.

Shortly afterward, Ed Wicklander took a team ashore to survey what was required to get the former Russian patrol boats running. George Sitton, Frank Kerrigan, and a few other officers and enlisted went ashore at liberty call.

When all returned that evening. George reported the one hotel was rudimentary and did not have air conditioning and the electric power was intermittent. He also told me that the only beer available was Tusker's, and it was only served hot. I decided then I would stay on board. I did not consider that kind of liberty worth the hour ride in a small boat in the seas where we anchored.

Chismayo was more like a rural town in the previous century. The hotel was an excellent example. The city was labeled as a commercial center, but the only apparent means of commerce was agriculture, and that was pretty dismal compared to US agriculture.

• • •

Upon his return to the ship, Ed's report was almost comical. Somali enlisted sailors did not show up for work unless they wanted to be there and that was usually around noon. All of the enlisted left around four. The officers were doing all of the work. His report on the Osa and Komar boats was dreadful. He didn't know if his repair personnel could get them up and running in our limited time there. Ed told the captain and me he had witnessed one of the officers working in the engine compartment on one of the boats. The man could not find fuel oil for the fuel tank. Therefore, he took an old coffee can, dipped it into the bilge where there was almost as much oil as there was water and put that mixture in the fuel tank.

The entire trip to Chismayo felt like a fool's errand. Ed said his team would do what they could, but the boats were a pretty hopeless case.

• • •

The next morning, *Yosemite* moved anchorage. The initial anchorage was too deep and the anchor was not holding on the bottom. The problem was amplified by the current. When the shift in anchorage was accomplished, we were waiting for a working party from the Somali Navy to come out and pick up a large amount of sheet metal. When Ed realized we did not have enough time to get the boats in working order and a significant problem was rust and deterioration of the hull and metal supports on the boats, he promised to give them the sheet metal so they could continue to work on the boats.

Ed remained aboard while his team went in for more assistance to the Somali's. He, along with supply officers, would supervise the transfer of the sheet metal.

We did not see a barge or any other craft until around 1000. When it was approaching, Ed went to bring the working party aboard for the transfer of the sheet metal. But the boat was a tugboat, fitting since we had cancelled liberty for the day due to rough seas and a tugboat was a craft that could handle those seas. There was no barge.

But when the tug tied up, Somali Navy officers came aboard. Ed couldn't make out why they were there instead of the working party. Finally, he decided they were there to see the ship. So being the good guy that he was, Ed took the dozen officers on a long tour of the ship. When he had concluded the tour, he took them up to the wardroom and the mess cooks were serving them snacks and coffee before the ship's officers came for the noon mess.

That is when the bridge received a frantic call from the shore. It was the U.S, Army Major, the liaison officer, wanting to know what happened to the tugboat and the working party aboard who were supposed to be transferring the sheet metal.

When he found out the officers' real purpose, it was a sheepish CDR Ed Wicklander who directed them to the sheet metal and completed the transfer to the tugboat.

• • •

The port visit to Chismayo had been strange so far, but it was about to get even stranger.

The liaison officer had contacted us that morning to inform us that the government officials had invited fifteen15 officers to an afternoon meal on a banana plantation along with 15 Somali VIP's and Navy officers. We asked for volunteers from the wardroom and immediately filled up thirteen spots. The CO and I were already committed. It was, in our opinion, a way to further cement the relationship between the U.S. Navy and the Somalis.

Accompanying us would be the first lieutenant LT George Sitton, the medical officer LT Frank Kerrigan; Chaplain LT Ernest Poe; Operation

Left: Deck seamen readying the captain's gig for use

Below: Getting captain's gig underway

Department officer ENS Susan Talley; Food Service Officer LTJG Jim Smith; dental officers CDR Bruce Janek, LCDR Nate Williams, LT Phyllis Varnado, and LT Jack Campbell; Supply Department Officer CDR Tim Allega; Administrative Officer LTJG Mike Jackson; DCA LTJG Emily Baker; and Safety Officer LT Sharon Carrasco.

Around 0800, the liaison officer came aboard. I escorted him from the quarterdeck to the captain's cabin. The captain and I had already dressed in our summer whites. We discussed how there were two vehicles, a bus and van for the officers. The captain would be joining the Somali Chief of Naval Operations in his sedan for the trip to the plantation. Due to worsening seas, the Captain and I agreed I should return to the quarterdeck to determine if it was safe to board the gig from the accommodation ladder.

I told the captain I would check the lowered accommodation ladder while George Sitton was lowering the Captain's gig into the water. George would drive the gig around to the starboard side where he and I would determine if it was safe for the Captain, the liaison officer, and the other invited guests to board the gig.

I went to the quarterdeck. The seas had worsened. I foolishly decided I would board the gig to determine if it was safe, explaining this plan to George by radio as he had taken over as coxswain. Tying the gig up to the accommodation ladder was both impractical and unsafe. George brought the gig as close to the accommodation ladder's lower platform as he could get it. But it was difficult, even for someone with the skill and experience of George to hold it close. I slowly went down the first 15 or 16 steps of the ladder, clinging tightly to the side rails as the ladder bounced up, down, and sideways. I was about four steps up from the landing platform where the waves were splashing against the rungs. George brought the gig to within a couple of feet. The seas were bouncing and the accommodation ladder and the gig were not in sync.

I leaped from the fourth step about three or four feet into the gig. George powered the gig away from the accommodation ladder and the ship. We circled and George and I discussed the situation. I knew I had to make the decision if the others should board or not. And perhaps somewhat smugly, I thought why not, if I did, so could they. George agreed. I called the quarterdeck on the radio and told them to tell the Captain it was safe, but everyone should be careful.

Fortunately, everyone made it safely. It was a rough ride into the harbor, but we made it. The quay where we tied up was a large area with some storage buildings. There were three vehicles waiting for us with Somali Navy officers in their distinctive khaki uniforms waving us toward our transportation. One vehicle was a late model van. Another was a small bus that resembled a school bus from back in the states. The final vehicle was a worn looking, early 70's Nissan. The liaison officer explained the captain would be riding with the Somali Chief of Naval Operations in the sedan and the other guests would divide up for riding in the other two vehicles. Everyone moved toward their assigned vehicles, and I headed for the bus, thinking how much fun the ride would be with our wardroom officers.

As I walked toward the bus, the captain called me back to the CNO's sedan.

As I leaned in, CAPT Boyle directed, "Jim, you are going to ride with us." Realizing I had no choice and the captain probably would benefit from some moral support, I resignedly took the shotgun seat. As the bus and van completed loading, we drove off.

Emily Baker Black described the trip for the officers who were in the van and the bus:

The ship was anchored just south of the equator and the plantation was north of the equator. We rode in vans from the boat landing to the plantation. On the way, we passed a monument marking the equator, and we got out to pose for a group photo.

Sharon Carrasco Friendly also described the experience:

Oh, I was there. It was something not to forget. I took the photo of a camel that day. There were two vehicles used to get us there, a van/suv type and a bus. I was on one going and the other one going back, don't remember which. Both stopped for pictures at the equator.

In the CNO's sedan ahead of the bus and van, I observed the surroundings. Except for the mud huts with thatched roofs and the number of people, mostly women in gaily colored robes walking barefoot along

Yosemite officers with Somali escorts and drivers at the equator.

the side of the road with huge bundles of things on top of their heads, I was reminded of the desolation of West Texas. It was not a beckoning environment, to say the least.

We were at a turn when the driver had to brake for one of the women who was walking too far out into the roadway. There was a grinding of brakes all too familiar to me from the days of my youth when I didn't have the money to replace worn brake pads. The driver explained the brakes really needed to be replaced, but he had learned how to drive safely with them in their current poor condition. I was no longer paying much attention to the view but attempting to be a lookout for possible road problems requiring brakes.

We found one. Somewhere just after we crossed the equator, a camel loomed before us. This camel had its legs spread out across the road while munching on leaves of an overhanging tree. Our driver hit the brakes and ineffective grinding commenced. Fortunately, this poor excuse for a Chief of Naval Officer's limousine had a standard transmission. Downshifting and brake grinding allowed us to stop about five feet from the camel. The driver stuck his hand out the window (no problem, as the CNO's limousine did not have air conditioning and the windows were all down) and waved the beast off with a shout.

Fortunately, we did not meet any other native women or camels on the road for the remainder of our trip of just over two hours. As we neared our destination, we turned off the main road, and the vegetation became very lush. The banana trees were everywhere. There were cultivated plots with vegetables and the wild vegetation crowded out all else until we came to a clearing.

We were directed to park in an area where several other vehicles were already in position. The bus and van carrying our other officers arrived soon after we parked. They had stopped at the equator and had their picture taken standing on the marker. Admittedly, I was jealous. This was a much better experience than nearly whacking a camel.

At the end of the clearing, there was a huge banyan tree. On our left side as we approached, about thirty folding chairs had been set up in an oval underneath the huge tree. We sat down alongside our Somali counterparts. Servants in sarong-like wraps and colorful shirts brought each of us a coconut. They sliced off the tops and handed them to us with a straw. This was, we learned, our pre-meal cocktails. It wasn't like a martini, but not all that bad.

After some small talk, which I'm pretty sure no one really understood, we were escorted to another area covered by the banyan tree's shade where a table for thirty was set. I looked over my shoulder and saw a large number of rugs or mats laid out under the the tree's shade. Someone informed me that was where the owner and his friends would rest after dinner. It looked like a pleasant place for a nap.

Then the dinner began. I was sitting next to the owner of the plantation, a pleasant man who spoke enough English so that we could communicate. I'm guessing he was in his early to mid-seventies. I was startled when he proudly told me he had gotten married the previous Saturday. He continued by proudly boasting the bride was eighteen. Before I figured out if I should congratulate him or not, he amplified my startled condition by bragging that she was his eighteenth bride.

Somehow, we managed to get off this topic when he mentioned how proud he was of his new house, the center of the banana plantation. He confided his house was the only one in southern Somalia with an indoor bathroom.

Somewhat amazed by all of this news was the focus of our conversation, I nevertheless filed the information about the bathroom in my mind.

The dinner was quiet and the shade of the banyan tree made it bearable in the heat. There were people everywhere. There were unlimited servers, and we could feel the people in the gardens and banana tree orchards around the scene who were curious about these U.S. Navy officers all dressed up in their summer dress whites complete with white shoes.

The first course was a salad. I was rather a bit surprised that the salad included goat meat among the other greener ingredients. Water was served with the meal. As we finished our salads, the cadre of servers picked up our dishes and departed. It was several minutes before the next course was delivered. This was repeated for five more courses: the waiter conglomerate would serve, wait until we had finished the course and collect the plates. Then after ten or fifteen minutes, they would return with the next course. The final course was the only one without goat meat in one fashion or another. The dessert was flan.

Somewhere around the fourth course, I needed to go to the bathroom. Recalling that vital information about an indoor bathroom in the house, I excused myself and headed in that direction. The place was teeming with people. I assumed they were plantation workers and their families. As I neared the house, I came upon an area that was about fifty or sixty square feet of dirt. In the middle was a pit about four to five feet deep with a

Captain Boyle speaking at
Somali banquet

diameter around a dozen feet. There was a fire in the middle and workers stood in the pit around the fire cooking with long handled tools. This didn't look like a Grade A restaurant. I became concerned. Then I spotted several buckets with a garden hose. I realized there wasn't enough china to serve seven courses for thirty people. After each course, the servers brought the china and utensils back to the buckets where they were cleaned with the garden hose, dried off and used for the next course.

I immediately began to worry about our officers and wondered how many would go down with our repast and the boat ride back to the ship.

But I had some personal business to attend to and quickly headed to the house. A servant motioned me to the left side of the house where the bathroom was located. I stepped into the room and immediately realized the owner had not lied. He did, in fact, have an indoor toilet. Unfortunately, as the odor told me, there was no plumbing. Everything just went into the hole. It was an indoor outhouse.

I returned to the dining table for the last course with goat and, finally, dessert. I actually had enjoyed the meat but from the start had been leery of the vegetables and fruits. The flan dessert did not taste good, so I only had a few bites.

After we concluded our meals, we thanked our hosts, shook hands and loaded up the three vehicles to cross the equator once more. I presume the hosts were headed for the mats of the banyan tree for an afternoon nap.

The ride back was uneventful, not a camel in sight, no braking dramas. I later learned the bus and van had stopped at the equator marker for photos.

When we arrived back at the pier, the captain's gig was waiting. The seas had worsened as night approached. We had not even gotten out of the harbor before officers began to hug the rail, dinner was coming up in a revengeful way. As we approached the ship, we discussed our options for boarding with the command duty officer. Using the accommodation ladder was out of the question. The seas from the fetch of the Somali current were too rough. Finally, the ship lowered cargo nets over the portside. To get on board using cargo nets is physically demanding. I was familiar with the procedure from my time as first lieutenant aboard the *USS Anchorage (LSD 36)*. There, these "cargo nets" were called "debark nets" which the marines used to debark from the ship into or board from landing craft. For us, the climb up the nets was about 15 feet. It was far from safe, but much safer than any other means of boarding.

George pulled the captain's gig close. Following Navy protocol, the Captain was the first to board. I decided I would go last. George and the gig crew would then remain in the boat while it was raised into its chocks. I wasn't too concerned about the Captain or Doc Kerrigan and a couple of the other women officers having a problem with ascending the nets. But I was concerned as the others took on the task. Some were overweight and a few more weren't very athletic. Eventually, they all made the ascent. But it wasn't pretty.

Finally, I climbed onto the gunnel of the gig, climbed onto the cargo nets, and made my way up to the main deck. A number of the sicker officers had already gone to their staterooms while George and the crew were being hauled aboard. Our summer whites were soiled almost to the point of being ruined. And several of the party had stained uniforms from being sick on the journey.

We were a motley- looking bunch. But we were safely aboard, just worse for wear. And our time in Chismayo was over.

131 days deployed, 63 days to home

Chapter 19: The Goat Kicks Back

January 1984 - Headed Back to Masirah, Oman

The next morning, Sea and Anchor detail was set at 0500. The only three officers who made their stations for getting underway and bidding adieu to Somalia of those who had attended the banquet were the captain, LT Sitton, and me. The other dozen officers were in their staterooms unpleasantly revisiting the banquet.

It was also my 40th birthday. There was no celebration, and I didn't want one. It was a time when I missed Maureen more than usual. A letter from my brother, received while we were in Kenya helped. He included a poem for my birthday.

Two Views on Turning Forty (one whimsical, the other maybe not)
I – On the Bridge
Will you be alone on the bridge
when the moment comes?
Surrounded by the winking lights
on the night watch, the scopes that
tell you it's out there
the horizon etched in nothingness,
abstract as another's death,
the indigo sky meeting and reflected
by the dark ocean, so only
the externals, the stars, tell you where you are.

One wrong move and it's a plunge
into the depths of that darkness
Which is shallow compared to the depths

of You.
Can all those lights and signals guide
you there? It is a technical question
I realize, answering how, not why or who.
We're tacking too close to theology there.

The externals tell you about entering a new
age, new year, new decade. I've never
believed them. Only you know when you are.
History is just a record kept to tell us
about the others. We all cross the bridge,
but a span in time, and make it Ours.
When you sit there in the dark watching the lights
straining to know the horizon, capsuled in steel,
knowing the tropic heat will come like a cat
to steal your breath, remember, all moments
are the same and age like History and illusion.
It is the sequestered heart that brings you home.
Remember on your bridge to ask the right questions,
and
laugh the coming day.

I – Meditations on Five
You've always been my big brother,
I guess I can have no other;
So, as you turn this age forty
You must recall a rare sortie
or two when we were youthful
beyond the bounds of taste, if truthful.
They say we all come to middle age,
so remember, that life is surely a stage.
Strut and preen, recall the cock
Who every day the sun does mock.
This aging stuff is a lot of jive.
You're forty? Hell, I'm thirty-five.
Joe Jewell, 1984

I treasure that poem, even as I write.

The evening after we began our transit, both the captain and George Sitton became ill from our adventure. Fortunately, their discomfort lasted less than a day. I had become the only one left standing. I had not felt really well since the boat trip return, but it was more of an annoyance. I could still function just fine.

Yosemite lifted anchor and headed east southeast before turning north en route to Oman. But we had some things to attend to before we became too involved in the transit.

As noted earlier, we had gone to Somalia on the orders of Commander, Seventh Fleet. This was not in compliance with the Department of State standing directive for all U.S. government entities to not enter Somalia. We had reported our efforts to our superior, Commander, Task Force 73. In turn, they had sent a draft message to us they planned to send out to the chain of command, including the State Department.

When I saw the draft, I immediately went to the CO's cabin and pointed out a message like that would notify the State Department of *Yosemite*, CTF 73, and Seventh Fleet of being in collusion to violate the State Department's directive concerning Somalia. CAPT Boyle concurred, and we immediately sent out a response advising our boss not to send the message. He sent back a message thanking us for catching the oversight.

From that, several officers and I were joking around in the wardroom and decided to have fun with CDR Ed Wicklander, our Repair Officer who had dealt with the Somali Navy and their ill-fated patrol boats. I'm not actually sure who came up with the idea. George Sitton and Noreen Leahy were in on it I'm sure, and probably Emily Baker and Linda Schlesinger were involved. We told the captain of our plot, and he agreed it would be fun. Noreen and I worked on a fake radio message.

Noreen, Susan Talley, and the radio crew printed the message to be just like the real thing. It referenced an intelligence report where Ed was purportedly the source of information about the poor condition of the USSR Osa and Komar boats his department had attempted to repair. As related earlier, *Yosemite* had been directed to visit the port by the Commander of Seventh Fleet in spite of the State Department policy.

The text (with my edits) read:

Secretary of State, Washington and Department of Defense extremely concerned with inflammatory and possibly damaging statements made by Yosemite Repair Officer concerning Chismayo, Somalia.

Due to serious implications on US-Somalian relations, direct officer concerned to report in 10 days to the Secretary of State headquarters office in Washington DC for debrief.

Ed was fooled. He was very worried and even began to consider what he had to pack for the trip. We let him stew for about half a day before we let him in on the joke. Being Ed, an incredible repair officer and perfect for his job, he was also a good sport, and took the joke on him with no anger.

133 days deployed, 61 days to home

The morning after getting underway, we held our second "Crossing the Line" ceremony. It obviously was much smaller with only the sailors who had reported aboard since we arrived in Diego Garcia back in mid-October were pollywogs. All went smoothly.

• • •

Later that evening, our security watch discovered a sailor outside the safety lines appearing ready to jump. He told the security watch and the other personnel nearby he wanted to commit suicide. The sailor was talked back inside the lines to safety. We kept a watch on him until we anchored off Masirah, had him medevaced to Diego Garcia, and then on to the Navy Hospital at the Naval Base in Subic, Luzon, Philippines.

The sailor was placed in the psychiatric ward and evaluated by a recently commissioned psychiatrist. Shortly afterward, we received a radio message from the hospital. The psychiatrist informed us the sailor would be returned to duty, that the attempted suicide was only a gesture.

The Captain and I were shocked they could consider the sailor should be returned to sea duty. I wrote a reply strongly opposed to the decision and noted a "suicide gesture" on a ship at sea was most likely to be more than a gesture.

CAPT Boyle released the message with his approval.

The next day, we received a reply from the hospital's commanding officer. He apologized for the diagnosis, repealed it, and informed us the sailor would not be returned to the *Yosemite* or any other sea duty.

The hospital CO added he was considering assigning the new psychiatrist to some sea duty in order for him to learn first-hand about being at sea with suicide gestures.

We breathed a sigh of relief and laughed considering what kind of lecture the CO had given to the young psychiatrist.

• • •

The day before the second "Crossing the Line" antics, 20 January, I began to feel weak. My digestive system went haywire. I developed a fever. I went down hard. Looking back, I suspect I had resisted backing off to keep things going while the others had reeled from the feast in Somalia abetted by seasickness — Doctor Kerrigan could not specifically identify the cause. We were pretty sure the illness came from parasites or bacteria.

Resisting the illness made it worse when it finally came upon me full bore. I spent two days in bed with a raging fever when I wasn't traveling between my rack and the john.

It was so bad the doctor and the captain conferred about my condition and considered having me medevaced to Diego Garcia as we neared our Masirah anchorage. Fortunately, I began to recover and was back up and operating, albeit weakly, by the time we rendezvoused with the *USS Knox (FF 1052)* and participated in the exercises between the two ships. We also conducted a VERTREP for receiving supplies by helicopter drops from the *USS Mars (AFS 1)* before *Yosemite* anchored off Masirah, Oman.

I had lost 15 pounds, weighing less than I had since high school. Although weak and a little woozy, it was good the day had been so busy. It felt good to be back in battery.

My down time became a standing joke in the wardroom, especially with George Sitton and Doc Kerrigan.

When we returned to Mayport, I had not gained my weight back. Upon arrival, Maureen was shocked when I debarked from the ship to meet her for the first time in 198 days.

I was detached in early April 1985. At my "hail and farewell" party, I received a number of joke gifts. Doc Kerrigan, who had become my regular golfing partner while his wife, Janet, who was also a Navy doctor, became close to Maureen, gave me a prescription to take to my new duty station. The prescription was attached to one side cut from a

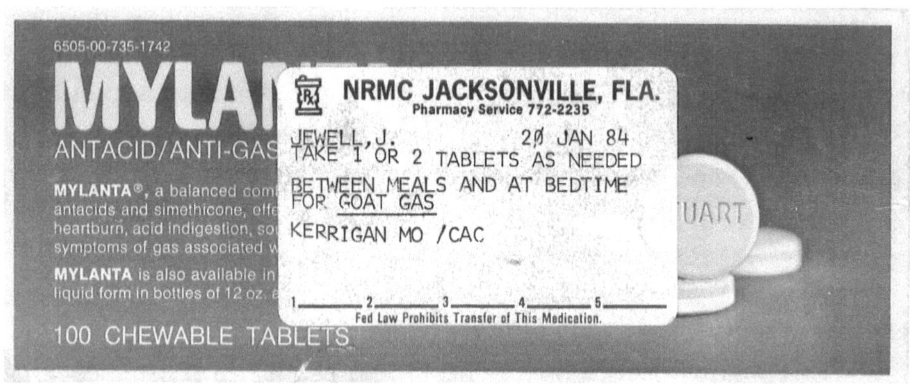

The mock prescription for Mylanta to cure XO's "goat sickness."

Mylanta box and read:

NRMC, Jacksonville

    For: Jewell, J., 20 January 1984

    Take 1 or 2 tablets as needed between meals and at bedtime
for goat gas.

    Kerrigan, MO.

Frank had poured a lot of stuff in me those four days. I wish they had worked. To this day, I shy away from eating anything with goat in it.

• • •

I was back in operation by Friday, 24 January. I was met with a full day. *Reveille* was early at 0530 for an underway vertical replenishment with the *USS Mars (AFS 1)* followed immediately with underway exercises with the *USS Knox (FF 1052),* including "Leap Frogs" where two ships keep coming alongside each other, then pulling away to repeat the ship handling drill, flag hoist drills, running a manila highline between the two ships, and a light line transfer.

I was glad our "liberty port visits " were over, perhaps even a bit glad we were going to be back to that desolate anchorage off Masirah, Oman. **137 days deployed, 57 days to home**

Chapter 20: Off Oman, One More Time

January - February 1984 - The Last Days at Work

Maintenance for the *USS Knox (FF 1052)*

After the underway exercises with the *Knox, Yosemite* anchored in a familiar spot, off the island of Masirah, Oman just outside the 12-mile limit. Shortly after she anchored, the *Knox* moored alongside for her maintenance availability.

Maintenance for the *USS Lawrence (DDG 4)*

As it had been during our first time off of Masirah, we immediately went into non-stop motion. The next day, the *USS Lawrence (DDG 4)* anchored nearby, and a *Yosemite* maintenance team went over by boat for repair services. As if we had never left, the Tuesday and Saturday VERTREPs for resupply resumed.

Another daily event also was reinstituted. The nightly trash burns from the steel box hanging from a crane resumed to be a thing to behold and entertain the crew.

Showing I was glad the goat sickness had left me with a sense of humor, I posted a hand-written note in the Friday Plan of the Day:

Welcome back to Masirah, which means "stay flexible." Note: there may be a raffle for the next XO's ticket to a goat dinner.

• • •

The day after we anchored, we received our final bad news of schedule change. Our liberty port of Malaga, Spain was cancelled. We were going to spend our Mediterranean liberty in Naples.

My only real excitement had been the idea of seeing another Greek

Island, but with the Mediterranean stop having been changed, the idea of actually seeing Malaga was intriguing to me even without Maureen joining me. Sixth Fleet changed our Mediterranean stop in the continuing roulette wheel of change.

The reason was pedestrian with no consideration of the best liberty for the crew. The admiral in command of the Mediterranean Battle Group had his "Admiral's Barge" break down. The boat was left for repair when the carrier completed its deployment and headed back to Norfolk. They needed someone to pick up the "barge" and bring it back to the states. *Yosemite's* dream liberty stop in Rhodes was denied, the wonderful alternate of Malaga was cancelled, and we were rerouted to Naples. *Yosemite* was the duty gopher.

I informed Maureen later that night:

...Things are going well here. Oh yes, big news is that we're going to Naples, not Malaga when we cross the Med. i'm a little disappointed in that i've spent a whole lot of time in Naples. We'll be there February 29 through March 4 as it's scheduled now. Need anything Italian?

153 days deployed, 41 days to home

As much as I wondered how the crew was handling time away from their loved ones, thinking this old seadog had the experience to not be affected, my letters and poems to Maureen suggested otherwise, like this one sent 9 February 1984:

Thoughts of Maureen, Far Away
whoa, i think, where are you going?
i look to see me pell-melling down the road, hell bent for
destruction i run
laughing
until i think whoa.
Sparkling pellets of moon on the water
straight line walking to my place at the rail of my ship home
after all saner men have gone to bed
i stare at the pellets
feel her in the wind

see her in the deep black of the water
hear her in the silence of the night
laughing inside bubbling
when i think of her.
Black night land of sand where dust in the air above the water coats
this hostile world of fanatic backward men
that make the screaming preachers back home look liberal
i stand beyond them on my ship, staring into this strange land's eyes
though choking with dust that does not reach its worst until
another monsoon season blows from the land
through the sparkling pellets of the moon
into the deepest recesses of its foul dark mind.
stopped. whoa, bubbling laughter again
for i have my thoughts of her.

• • •

Another major occurrence happened the day after we anchored. Noreen Leahy and the doc, Frank Kerrigan, met with the Captain and me. As noted earlier, Jim Leahy had taken leave and flew to Mombasa while *Yosemite* was in port there. It was the Leahy's second honeymoon, this one in a German hotel on the Nyali coast. Back at anchor off of Masirah, Noreen realized she was pregnant.

Had she been enlisted, we had regulations to guide us. I'm not sure if we would have found it prudent to transfer a pregnant enlisted sailor considering our circumstances, but we had direction and would have had to request a variation on those directions when we learned of the pregnancy.

But after searching the regulations and instructions, I could find no regulations concerning female officers who became pregnant while stationed aboard a ship. I drafted a radio message after conferring with the captain to the Bureau of Personnel's Women at Sea Coordinator requesting guidance and pointing out we were anchored off of Masirah, that we had a medical officer on board who could provide needed care, and that Noreen held some critical functions as Operations Officer. The last of the message strongly recommended she remain on board.

 Shortly afterwards, we received the reply we should transfer Noreen immediately. I shall not note here what I thought of that direction. We conferred with Noreen and the doctor. Then I drafted a stronger message,

Top: LT Noreen Leahy taking bearing on gyro repeater.

Right: Captain Boyle, seated, and his executive officer observing another vertical replenishment on the port bridge wing.

pointing out that transferring Noreen would require her to be helo- lifted off the ship, stay at the Omani Air Force Base until she could catch a Navy C-40 to Diego Garcia, and then taking at least three flights if not more, lasting at least three days to return to stateside. I further pointed out that was a great deal more dangerous than having her remain on board with a doctor, a family practice physician for the next two months.

I included that LT Leahy also was critical to meeting the ship's mission. I pointed out she was the operations officer, one of our most reliable qualified Officers-of-the-Deck, our Top Secret Control Officer, and as assistant navigator, performed nearly all of the navigation duties.

I was proud of that message.

We received no response.

As we closed in on our departure date from Masirah and the transit back home, the captain and I considered what we should do. Our chain of command had directed us to transfer Noreen off the ship. We truly believed it was much safer for Noreen to remain on board for the remainder of the deployment. Although we had argued she was indispensable for the ship's operations, our overriding concern was what was best for our pregnant officer. Doc Kerrigan agreed it was best for her to remain on board.

In a brave move, we did something rarely done in the Navy. We sent an Advise Action Taken (ADTAKE) message to an admiral, the head detailer in charge of the Women At Sea program, copying our chain of command. The term normally is a rebuke from a senior to someone junior for not getting a message response or a required scheduled action submitted on time. The captain and I held our breaths while waiting for the reply.

When the *USS Prairie (AD 15)* anchored nearby to relieve us on February 16, we had not had any response.

• • •

This second time off Masirah was easier for the most part. We had settled into an appropriate anchorage. We had worked out the routine of the repair department's port and starboard work schedule (six hours on, six hours off, six days a week). The trash issue was known and resolved, not only taking care of the problem but giving the crew another source of entertainment. We were much more comfortable with ships maneuvering to come alongside for their maintenance periods. We even had gotten used to the Tuesday and Saturday supply replenishments from the Service Force ships via VERTREPS.

And probably more than any of the other reasons, everyone knew we were over the hump. The short timer chains were a source of inspiration: In the Navy, a short timer's chain was a way for a sailor to count down to his discharge date. This was in vogue during the days the draft existed. It also was used to mark the number of days left on a deployment. On this deployment, there was a preponderance of personal calendars having a number added to each calendar date indicating the number of days remaining to arriving home and then crossed off as that date passed to the next day.

Being inventive in entertainment and morale, *Yosemite* and *Knox* came up with a "punt" race. For those who might not be aware, a "punt" in the Navy is not related to an American football game. A punt is a very small boat with only human power for propulsion. It is frequently used to paint the sides of the ship. My handwritten note describes the outcome:

BM3 White & SN Mitchell won the punt race against the Knox *yesterday. BZ for the show of strength.*

The *USS Lawrence (DDG 4)* remained anchored nearby. The seas were too rough to attempt coming alongside to starboard when *Knox* was tied up on the other side. This was unscheduled maintenance after *Lawrence* suffered a casualty to some engineering equipment. The repair department selected an ad hoc repair team to transit to the anchored ship by boat to effect the repairs. The work took three days to complete.

Maintenance for the *USS Kirk (FF 1087)*

Typical of the flexibility required, on Sunday, 29 January, the *Knox* got underway to be replaced by the *USS Kirk (FF 1087)*.

Maintenance for the *USS Sterett (CG 31)*

Next in line was the *USS Sterett (CG 31)*. Her availability resulted in a different problem, one that had not occurred in any of our other maintenance periods for Battle Group Alfa. *Sterett* was not able to come alongside for two days due to rough seas, created by the winter monsoons. Although previously the *Lawrence* also had anchored instead of mooring alongside *Yosemite, Lawrence's* maneuvering was complicated by another ship moored to *Yosemite*. But for the *Sterett,* it was solely because the seas had worsened. She arrived Monday, 6 February, and did not come alongside until the following Wednesday. For those two days, *Yosemite* launched boats and took maintenance and repair teams to the anchored guided missile cruiser.

When the *Sterett* arrived, the commanding officer made a request to CAPT Boyle, which he and I had heard before. He offered to have our women officers come over to his wardroom for dinner. CAPT Boyle's reply was the same as it had been before. "You may ask our officers to come over for dinner, but it cannot be just female officers." Several male and female officers took the offer and had a good time.

· · ·

Roughly a week back at Masirah, we received a radio message from the intelligence community. The possibility raised by the message was not a pleasant prospect. Intelligence had found an Iranian source that indicated the Iranian government could be considering an attack on *Yosemite* while she was at anchor at Masirah. The report indicated the attack would come from Iranian patrol craft most likely out of Bandar Abbas. These craft would travel along the coast for about 500 miles to attack our ship.

The Captain and I discussed how we should prepare. In my mind, I questioned how patrol craft could make a voyage of that distance without being detected by the battle group and intercepted by the *Ranger's* aircraft or one of the combatants. I also knew we couldn't count on such interception and we should be prepared. We stood up extra watches to be alert for strange craft coming over the horizon. We performed some extra training for our 20 mm, Mk 68 gun crews. We then assigned the Mk 68 gun crews and ad hoc .50 caliber gun teams around the weather decks from sunset to sunrise for defense if such an attack actually occurred.

I walked around the decks at night to check on the deployment of the teams. I wondered just how effective they might be and was concerned they accidentally shoot themselves or someone else on the ship. I wasn't convinced they could shoot a moving target. My fears were not justified, but the amount of training, especially for the .50 cal's was extremely limited.

Fortunately, there was no Iranian attack. But we were on edge for several days.

151 days deployed, 43 days to home

Tuesday, 7 February, our normal vertical VERTREP was moved to Wednesday due to the operational schedule of the *Mars*. The cargo received was larger than usual, and we had a number of crew who were being transferred. The operation took nearly all of the daylight hours. The following Saturday before our usual bi-weekly VERTREP and yet another one the following day, I placed this handwritten note in the POD:

Warning: All times related to VERTREPS are pure guesswork by the XO!

Maintenance for the *USS Hammond (FF 1067)*

On Saturday, 11 February, the *USS Hammond (FF 1067)* came alongside. She was our last customer for a restricted availability before we headed home.

• • •

In 1983, the Navy called their one-star flag officers "Commodores." Previously, they had been called "Rear Admiral," the same as the two-star admirals. Navy one-star admirals are now called "Rear Admiral, lower half." So, *Yosemite* was about to be visited by a classic one-star "Commodore." Our task force commander, Commodore Butcher, would be arriving the day the *USS Prairie*, our sister tender and relief would anchor nearby.

The two ships would have a day of turnover, much more extensive than when *Yosemite* arrived in Diego Garcia four months earlier and discovered that turnover from the *Cape Cod* would be brief as they provided no significant maintenance services, sitting in the lagoon for their entire deployment except for transits and liberty port visits. Each department head had generated turnover packages, which I reviewed and approved two days before. We also conducted a turnover presentation "murder board" (where we rehearsed our presentation and critiqued it before the actual presentation: this can sometime be brutal and consequently acquired the nickname).

At 1600 on Wednesday, 15 February, Rear Admiral (lower half) Butcher, Commander of Task Force 73, our superior in the operational chain of command was lowered by helo to *Yosemite's* flight deck. He was formally "piped aboard" including "side boys," a Navy tradition.

I liked him immediately. He was old school and showed it. I was included when the admiral was introduced to CAPT Boyle in the CO's cabin. Commodore Butcher made it a point to thank us for catching the staff's update to higher authority in a radio message where the captain and I alerted them that any mention of our stop in Somalia was not a politically wise action.

The thing I remember most was when he met with the officers in the wardroom after the evening mess. He addressed many factors and was mildly in favor of the Women At Sea program. During the Q&A afterwards, one of the junior officers asked Butcher what he did that got him selected to the flag level. The admiral replied, "I stayed around long enough that all of the flags who didn't like me either retired or died."

Even now, I laugh when I think about his answer.

• • •

But we were going home. All else was secondary. We had transferred all of the material to *Prairie* that would help them during their time in Masirah. The department heads and other key personnel had briefed their counterparts. We had our last VERTREP, this one with the *USS Mars (AFS 1),* for the supplies needed for the transit to the Mediterranean.

The final confirmation that we were headed home was when we transferred the second metal cage we had constructed to burn our trash and garbage, i.e., the "burn box" about a half hour before weighing anchor.

The POD had an entry that morning with a notice about the "burn box:"

11. On 17 FEB 1984, Deck Department and R Division Shipfitter Shop will muster with the Garbage Control Officer on the Flight Deck for a solemn ceremony to commit to the deep a faithful friend (the Burn Box) to the deep. No snickering, please.

Immediately below, I hand-wrote a clarification:

Cancelled due to Prairie's *desire for a souvenir from* Yosemite*!*

At 0900 without the above-mentioned "Burn Box", the *USS Yosemite,* "The Busy Lady," her officers, and crew were on the way back to Mayport, Florida.

162 days deployed, 32 days to home

Chapter 21: The Sail West:
Crossing the Mediterranean

February - March 1984

I was ready to get back to the States. Hopefully, Maureen would be able to be there when we pulled into the base pier, but I knew her job might keep her in San Diego. I also knew it would not be long before we were together. All stops in between were just things I needed to get through. I had been on enough deployments where I was conditioned to not get too excited. I knew we had a long way to go.

. . .

The Executive Officer must attend to good order and discipline. With that, I penned a handwritten note in the POD for the morning we weighed anchor and had great news on the results from a unit drug analysis sweep. I wrote:

Good show at Masirah again. Now let's all get ready for the transit. Ensure you and your space are secured for sea. Rougher seas predicted headed home. Don't forget personnel inspection – blues – before Naples. And it's time to put that final effort into making the ship A-Number one for standing into Mayport. Proud of the Busy Lady.

And the results of the unit sweep are all in! The entire crew tested negative in the unit sweep. That's something of which we can all be proud. A super BZ!

For several days, the POD ran a notice for signing up for tours in Naples. One was a day tour to Pompei, the Amalfi Coast, and Sorrento. I added "Recommended by the XO."

In 1972, I took that one tour in all of my deployments, earlier mentioned in my tour assessment in Mombasa. I had just gotten back on active duty by the skin of my teeth and a recommendation from Max Lasell, the commanding officer of my first ship, the *USS Hawkins (DD 873)*. I met my ship, the *USS Luce (DLG 7)* in Korfu, Greece. When the *Luce* pulled into Naples over Thanksgiving weekend, I took that one tour. It was a wonderful experience. Sorrento was a shopper's paradise. The guide took us to a cameo manufacturer, and I bought several, one for Kathie, my wife at the time, one for my mother, and several for other ladies in our family. Then, we rode that bus over the narrow roads, cliffs, and incredible views of the Amalfi Coast. We stopped at the crest and had lunch, a salad with Italian white wine in a perfect romantic setting. The three hours in Pompei had me silently walking the streets in awe of their civilization and the incredible disaster that befell the citizens over 2,000 years before.

I wanted to encourage the crew to go on that one. They did in droves and apparently found it as enchanting as I had a dozen years earlier.

• • •

21 February 1983, we "chopped" to the Mediterranean operational chain of command, a.k.a. Commander, Sixth Fleet, as we transited the straits of Bab al-Mendab and into the Red Sea.

It was at this point, we finally received word from the Bureau of Personnel on our request to retain LT Noreen Leahy on board for the duration of the deployment. It declared we should retain Noreen on board for the rest of the transit, but immediately transfer her to TAD upon our arrival in Mayport. Of course, it was a bit late in that we really had no other options except to transfer her in Naples or Rota, our last two stops and those choices made no sense at all. But we finally had the authority to do the right thing. We were happy we had clearance to do the right thing, but both the Captain and I were saddened we would lose her upon arrival.

Noreen was a champ. Although she suffered morning sickness in the first trimester, she performed all of her duties, including most of the navigation duties throughout the transit. She continued to perform superbly in all of her duties. She remains one of the finest and best officers with whom I served in my 22 plus years.

• • •

Readiness for going to sea was my focus, and it showed with another hand written POD note:

In case you haven't looked out lately, the seas are rough. There are gale force winds in the Red Sea, 30 to 40 knots with gusts to 50. It's all from astern now, so the ship is riding well. However, if it shifts to the quarter which it will when the course change is required this morning, it's going to be rough riding. What I'm trying to say is, Secure For Sea or someone is going to get seriously hurt.

• • •

The transit through the Red Sea was relatively uneventful except for remaining on the alert for terrorist attacks. Again, we were not in a very hospitable environment for U.S. ships, and the waters were restricted. I continued my deployment-long tirade against careless acts causing more work, especially when we were headed to Naples and home, where *Yosemite* should be in tip-top condition. One hand-written POD note harangued the thoughtless:

There are some personnel aboard who lack common sense or common courtesy or both. They are those that walked all over the deck wash even though the word was passed and the areas were clearly marked. Nearly all of the crew is working hard to ensure Yosemite *looks her finest. It is unfortunate that a few unthinking clods can mar the work of so many. Have you looked at the bottom of your shoes lately? Clods have deck grey on their soles. Are you a clod? The XO's looking for you.*

We took extra precaution to not pinpoint our location to potential terrorists. I emphasized this in another hand-written note:

Communications on MARS is poor to non-existent. Due to that fact and the not-too-super-friendly area of the world we're in right now (and in restricted waters), the MARS station will not be operating until the ship is in the Mediterranean except for emergency calls.

But compared to what was next, the Gulf of Aden, Red Sea transit was a piece of cake.

• • •

I was busier than usual. I had begun collecting award recommendations from the department heads for their personnel during the deployment. As expected, once they began to appear in my "In" basket, they required some pretty severe editing. I was writing the drafts for all of the department heads. The captain and I would continue with this task until a couple of days before we arrived back in Mayport.

• • •

Somehow, the captain and I determined I should make a Closed Circuit Television (CCTV) brief to the crew on Naples, especially in regard to the liberty there. We would be Mediterranean Moored (MED Moored) in the harbor as I had been on several stops there previously. Naples provided the gateway to many wonderful sights, including Pompei, the Amalfi coast, Sorrento, and, of course, Rome. I considered Naples itself more of an attraction for the older generation of male sailors. Later that day, I appeared on CCTV after the evening mess, and educated, or at least entertained, the crew on liberty in Naples.

I was familiar with the renowned sailor town, having spent a number of liberty port visits there. I had a wristwatch ripped off my arm by a group of innocent-looking children in an upscale shopping district. Fleet Landing was surrounded by every kind of slick sales pitch available. Cheap watches, jewelry, really just about anything, were pitched to sailors coming ashore, and they were nearly all fake. And nearby, lining the streets were ladies of the night, unmistakable even if they didn't approach you with offers, which they often did. And just past fleet landing were all sorts of night clubs with women escorts who would dance with you and sit in a booth being served a sugary concoction, which turned out to be a twenty-dollar drink on your tab. Older, experienced sailors found it better to find a safer bar to drink with buddies or alone and then go out in the streets and find a bunch of young Italian men playing socer and join them in a game in the middle of the night. Younger sailors were eager to explore less savory and more dangerous places, including those off limits.

Some sailors learned the hard way to stay away from such places. Some sailors didn't learn.

Of course, before this tour, that was the norm in every port frequently visited by the Navy ships I rode.

I made my presentation, pointing out the off-limits areas and warned every one of the scams at fleet landing and elsewhere. I did warn of the clubs and the ladies of the night but was tactful and used polite language. But mostly, I emphasized the tours as I had and continued to emphasize in the Plans of the Day.

I did not tell the crew of my stop in Naples in 1972. While in transit to the *USS Luce (DLG 7)*, which I later joined in Korfu, Greece, I ventured into an off-limits area with fellow travelers, including a Naval Enlisted Scientific Education Program (NESEP) ensigns. Selected high performing sailors attended college for free and became officers by attending OCS during their summers in college. The other travelers were two chiefs. One of the chiefs boasted of a great restaurant from his earlier port visits. We walked up a series of steps as wide as a four-lane road. About three-quarters of the way up the hill, the chief announced we were there. We walked through a small, windowed door into a white on white room with four tables. We were motioned to the table for four in the middle of the room. Motioned is the proper description of our seating as none of the restaurant workers spoke English, and our chief could only speak sailor Italian. But we were able to order four spaghetti with meatball plates, Italian bread, salad, and a bottle of red wine. It did not take long to be served. The wine had no label and was hand corked.

It was an incredibly delicious and wonderful meal, and the wine was terrific.

The other thing I remember was a black and white television at the top of a corner wall. The 1972 Summer Olympics was on, in Italian, of course. We watched the track and field events before the "Munich Massacre" occurred when Palestinian Black September terrorists killed 8 members of the Israeli Olympic team. I learned of the massacre when I reported aboard the *Luce* two days later. Despite those sad events, I still remember that dinner as wonderful.

After joining the *Luce* in Korfu on that time in the Med, the ship participated in a Mediterranean Ocean wide NATO exercise during which we anchored in the Gulf of Izmir for a port visit. After Izmir, the *Luce* was scheduled for a port visit to Genoa, Italy. But before we arrived, the port call was changed from Genoa to Naples. The Navy was apparently denying me stops in much desired Mediterranean ports.

While the *Luce* was in Naples, I went on the only MWR sponsored tour in my Navy career. I thought again of Torre del Greco where I bought cameos for my then wife and mother. Then our bus climbed through the narrow road with incredible views of cliffs and the Tyrrhenian Sea of the Amalfi coast. The trip was breathtaking from both the views and the bus spending a great deal of time hanging out over the cliff road before we reached our main objective of Pompei. That amazing ancient city captivated me. As others went on the guided tours, I walked through the streets listening to the ancients, trying to imagine the life there before it was plunged into darkness and death.

It pleased me our officers and crew would have the opportunity to repeat my trip. I knew my time in Naples would be limited. *Yosemite* was going home, and this XO's focus was on getting there.

• • •

Sometimes, the irony of the ship's events and activities juxtaposed in the Plans of the Day made me chuckle. In the 24 February edition, these three schedule entries produced such a chuckle:

1700 – Set the Special Sea and Anchor Detail
1800 – Anchor Suez Roads / Prepare for Suez transit
1930 – Bible Study

169 days deployed, 25 days to home

The next morning at 0600, the transit of the canal began with a problem, a big problem. Amongst hundreds of ships of all sizes and condition, we weighed anchor and moved to get in line for boarding the pilot. We remembered the transit in the other direction almost five months earlier and were not looking forward to refusing extra Egyptians attempting to join the pilot on board. The expensive pilot, although required to be on board for transiting the canal, was only useful for translating the canal's management passed to us. Otherwise, he would not be needed for the transit, and he would cause problems.

But we first had to maneuver to board that pilot.

Unfortunately, another ship, a large freighter, decided it was her turn to get in line. Although the captain, and I in my role as navigator, and George Sitton felt we were correct in the order of entry, the canal operations control disagreed. George showed his rather formidable ship-handling talents. Even that would not have avoided a collision had not the engineers answered the "all flank emergency" command to main control. We avoided the collision, allowing the freighter to go ahead of us. We maneuvered through the morass of ships at anchor, finally falling in line behind the freighter.

The pilot somehow managed to get several of his people on board, but they were immediately sequestered and remained there as they had been on the south transit. This pilot proved just as bad as the previous one. He spent a great deal of time in the wardroom eating and drinking coffee, attempted to buy all types of goods, including cigarettes in volume from the ship's store, and made suggestive approaches on several of our women officers. He spent most of his time sitting in the captain's chair on the bridge, doing nothing.

The transit north was significantly worse than the earlier southern transit. The primary reason was sand and poor visibility. The ships in the single line were about 500 yards apart from bow to stern. While that distance might look like a long way to those who have never conned a large WWII vintage steam ship, it is dangerously close. Communication with the other ships was practically non-existent. The pilot's sole value as far as we were concerned was taking his information from canal operations and letting us know if we needed to slow down because of ship traffic ahead.

Because of the conditions, the captain decided there would only be three officers to pilot the ship through the canal on this transit. LT Sitton had the conn for the bulk of the 18-hour transit. The captain took control several times for a few hours and remained on the open bridge with George throughout except for getting a couple of hours sleep during the night and also when we anchored in the Great Bitter Lake, roughly halfway between the entry and exit points. The third to pilot the ship was me.

The captain's primary concern was the safety of the ship and not wanting to put pressure on the less experienced Officers of the Deck during such a difficult transit. I understood and was actually pleased he thought I was the third capable officer up to such a task. I did feel sorry for the junior officers, especially the women. At least two of them had shown they were capable of such a stern test. But safety as determined by the Captain ruled the day as it should.

On the evening watch (2000-2400), I took the conn from George. The open bridge was exposed completely to the weather. The wind-borne sand whipped against anyone who was out there. Consequently, we limited those who normally stood watch there and moved everyone inside, except the captain, the conning officer, the lookouts, and one phone talker. Everyone wore as much protective clothing and gear as possible. During the day, we wore sunglasses, but for a reason I cannot recall, unless we simply did not have them on board or felt goggles would hamper our vision, we did not wear goggles at night.

Once we left the canal and entered the Mediterranean, CAPT Boyle and George took Navy showers. I showered right after I had piloted the ship for about two hours, my only time on the open bridge except to advise the captain or when he or I wished to exchange information. The sand had penetrated our clothing. We felt like it was all over us even after the showers. The two of them got some much-needed rack time, and after I had given them that brief relief from the open bridge, I went to bed for the night. The following morning, we all awoke with eyes burning. It was as if sand grains were underneath our eyelids. My eye problems, even with the limited amount of time on the open bridge, lasted over half a day. CAPT Boyle and George had burning eyes and difficulty seeing for two days.

But we successfully completed the canal transit Monday morning, 27 February, depositing the pilot and his accomplices on the pilot boat. I noted the transit effort to the crew by handwriting this note in the POD:

A special well done to all personnel who contributed to the effort during the Suez Canal transit. It was a long and tedious ordeal that required a lot of flexibility in one of the most dangerous situations a ship can be in. The engineers who responded magnificently when power was needed to escape from the first false start at the entrance. The helmsmen and the remainder of the bridge watch teams and CIC watch standers that never missed a beat in recommendations and support. Supply and the MAA's (Master at Arms) in diplomatic control of some unwanted riders. There are numerous groups not mentioned that should be, but it was a fine effort by all hands. Glad it's over, whew!

Now let's get to Naples and home!

• • •

The thoughts of getting home had become a driving force for all of us. Praise of our performance just made it better. Sunday, 26 February, the day after the personnel inspection, our Suez transit was ameliorated somewhat with the Bravo Zulu (job well done) from the Commander of Seventh Fleet, which we published in the POD:

18. BZ from COMSEVENTH FLEET: To maximize fleet repair service for IO (Indian Ocean) *CVBG's* (Carrier Battle Groups) Yosemite *most effectively provided much needed support at Masirah Island, expending over 80,000 man hours of superb repair work for 12 ships as well as providing over 70,000 man hours of invaluable medical, dental, and supply services. The quality of work, exceptional dedication, efficiency, and ultimate flexibility were demonstrated by adjusting to the dynamic Indian Ocean operating schedule and continuing to provide first class service to the fleet, often with only minimal advanced planning (e.g., repairs to the* Ranger's *fire damage, repairs to the* Lawrence's *boiler and main engines, and repairs to* Mispillion's *deck equipment).* Yosemite's *innovative solutions to unique problems encountered at Masirah were exceptional.* Yosemite's *professional performance in a remote and arduous location has been flawless. Well done. – VADM Hogg*

Our ship, our officers, our crew, men and women, had proven their mettle and that the Navy's Women At Sea program could work, even better than what anyone expected.

• • •

On the next day, Tuesday, 28 February, *Yosemite* readied for its liberty port the Navy way: she held a ship wide personnel inspection. I sat down with CAPT Boyle to discuss which senior officer would inspect which departments as usual. The captain gave me specific direction on which inspector should be assigned to inspect which departments.

"Jim, I'll inspect any of the departments you think is best except I don't want to inspect the Medical Department.

Yosemite "med moored" in Naples.

Curious, I asked why.

"I don't wish to have Frank present his department. The way he salutes, I'm afraid he is going to put his eye out with his thumb," concluding, "One of the worst salutes I've ever seen."

The next day, I inspected the Medical Department and almost lost it when Frank, who had become my good friend and confidant, saluted. I agreed with the CO, it was a pretty bad salute. I didn't tell the doc why I was laughing until later.

• • •

In the afternoon, *Yosemite* transited the Strait of Messina, the waterway between the toe of Italy's boot and the island of Sicily. At the northern end, the narrowest point in the passage is just over a mile wide. Many claim the northern end of the Strait of Messina near the town of Scilla was the location of the passage in Homer's *Odyssey.* Odysseus ordered his crew to plug their ears so they could not hear the Sirens' calls. The calls lured seamen to jump over the side and try to swim to the sirens, only to die in the rough waters and jagged rocks of the shoreline. He also ordered his men to tie him to the mast so he could hear the Sirens and not either sail his ship into the rocks or try to swim toward the enchanting song and die on the rocks.

We set Sea Detail for the passage, a conservative but safe move. This was not because of the Sirens but because the passage of the straits was narrow and dangerous.

LT Leahy and I, navigating together, stood on the starboard bridge wing as we steamed through the straits. Noreen pointed to the mainland village of Reggio Calabria and told me her grandmother was born there and emigrated to the United States at the age of four. She added she still had family there.

173 days deployed, 21 days to home

Wednesday, 29 February 1984, *Yosemite* had early *reveille* and set the Navigation detail at 0730. We executed a "Mediterranean Moor" near Fleet Landing. As mentioned earlier, I was more focused on doing all that was necessary to make the voyage back to Mayport be as effective as possible. Having been in Napoli several times, I knew the kind of trouble sailors could find. Even though *Yosemite* had the best record for liberty ports of any ship I had been aboard, this was a sailor's town and our last major liberty port. I wanted to be available if any trouble did arise.

That morning's POD notes warned of potential problems:

12. Naples Info:

A) Off Limits: North of Via Roma. For Your Health. Sailors have been shot in this area.

B) Drugs: Entrapment is used. The authorities are rough on any failure to cooperate. They carry bilingual cards and guns.

C) Black Market: Ration cards are in effect at NAVSUPPACT Exchange. Procedures are 1. Personnel planning to purchase any high value stereo/video/camera items must first report to the ration control desk in the NEX customer service area to establish a "ration control" card. Cards, which will remain on file at the NEX, will bear a statement, requiring the signature of the purchaser, that items are to be removed from the country and for personal use or a bona fide gift. 2. During subsequent purchase transaction, customers will be provided with their copy of the NEX sales receipt and directed to the ration control desk. A ration card entry will be made and sales slip validated. The customer will return to the sales counter; the salesperson will verify the validation and release the purchase to the customer.

D) Drinking: Alcohol can be consumed at NAVSUPPACT in the following areas only: EM club, crater house, NEX snack bar, steak house in the main admin building and within the fenced area around the hot dog stand. No alcoholic beverages in any other area is allowed.

E) Shoplifting: Don't. Security has increased and you will be surveilled at the NEX.

I added in one of my hand-written notes:

Don't ruin a happy homecoming. Trouble in Naples could lead to not going ashore when the ship reaches Mayport. Is it worth the chance? Don't over indulge! Stay out of trouble! Enjoy Italy the right way so you can enjoy your return to Mayport!

I went out to dinner one night with Ken Dawson, the master craftsman on board, John Dillingham, the electronics czar, and Frank Fortson, the assistant Repair Officer. The restaurant was just a short walk from fleet landing: very Italian, very good. Someone ordered pizza and the waiter was confounded. They didn't have pizza and the waiter claimed it was an American invention.

The only other trip was to the officer's club where I called Maureen and Blythe, my daughter.

My concerns about unruly behavior never materialized. The crew was ready to relax and go home, not get the ship into great condition for an impressive return to home port. I had to remind them with another ubiquitous handwritten note in the POD:

The ship is not at holiday routine. All personnel in the duty section and any other personnel required to get the job done will be working. Reveille will be held. Let's not slack off while aboard. Rough weather will probably curtail our beautification efforts soon. Plan ahead and beat the bad weather.

177 Days deployed, 17 days to home

On Sunday, 4 March, my note proved prophetic with another note:

The weather is not the best. A recall is still possible if the weather worsens. If you are going ashore, remain alert and get back to the ship as quickly as possible if a recall occurs.

Chapter 22: One More Port Before Home

March 1984 - The Eastern Mediterranean, Gibraltar, and Rota

The admiral's barge was aboard. Liberty had expired Sunday night. *Yosemite* got underway, headed to a brief stop at the naval base in Rota, Spain where we had stopped on our inbound transit and would be the last port before heading across the pond and home.

Naples had been a great success. There were no significant liberty incidents. The red- light district was underpopulated during *Yosemite's* stay. Use of the one and two-day tours to Rome, Pompei and Amalfi, Pompei and Vesuvius, as well as a ski trip were filled. Having witnessed this in our previous liberty ports, I continued to be amazed.

We also left Naples with yet another "Bravo Zulu" as I informed the ship in another POD note:

From COMNAVSURFLANT: "The Repair Services provided by Yosemite *and the statistics contained in Ref A* (the COMSEVENTH Fleet BZ) *most impressive. The exceptional performance of you and your crew is noted with pleasure. Well done!*

After we got underway, at noon, the Captain went on CCTV and read the best news yet about our performance. Admiral James Hogg, the Commander of the Seventh Fleet had forwarded the commendation to CAPT Boyle. A copy of the commendation was included in the next day's POD:

The Commander Seventh Fleet takes pleasure in commending:
BATTLE GROUP ECHO
for service as set forth in the following:

CITATION

"For sustained superior performance while assigned to Battle Force SEVENTH Fleet, from September 1983 to February 1984, during an exceptionally arduous deployment to the Western Pacific and Indian Ocean. Battle Group ECHO clearly demonstrated the resolve of the United States to deter aggression in critical and troubled areas of the world. Steadfastly maintaining an exceptionally high state of operational readiness while deployed to the Northern Arabian Sea in response to increasing tension in the Middle East, Battle Group ECHO's aggressive AAW, ASUW, and ASW posture was reflected in its successful completion of exercises and prompt reaction to real world contingency operations. Overcoming adversity when USS RANGER suffered a serious fire in the engineering spaces, the Battle Group remained on station, meeting all commitments, while working round-the-clock to restore full propulsion capability to USS RANGER. Although the deployment was characterized by extremely arduous duty and personal sacrifice, the ships, aircraft squadrons, and personnel of Battle Group ECHO maintained a well-integrated capacity to respond to any threat or contingency. Through their diligence, resourcefulness, professional competition and unstinting devotion to duty, the officers and personnel of Battle Group ECHO reflected great credit upon themselves and upheld the highest traditions of the United States Naval Service.

My buttons were ready to burst. I had never heard of or experienced a tender or other repair ship being considered part of a battle group. Many of the accolades in the commendation were directly or indirectly related to *Yosemite's* repair and maintenance services provided to all of the ships of Battle Group ECHO, including our assistance with our teams during the *Ranger* fire.

I felt it was a marvelous achievement. I knew it could not be quantified, but there was no doubt in my mind that having women in the ship's complement (officers and enlisted) had positively impacted our performance.

I was also thinking about home. I didn't want the officers and crew from being delayed in meeting their loved ones or liberty being delayed because of someone's lack of attention. My hand-written POD note addressed one potential problem:

Attached custom forms will be explained on 1200 CCTV today. Follow the sample attached to this POD.

Incorrect, incomplete, or missing custom forms could prevent the entire ship from going on liberty in a timely fashion after arrival Mayport. Don't be responsible for delaying the entire crew.

I could have added, "And if anyone delays the XO from seeing his wife after six months, there could be big trouble." I didn't.

Throughout the deployment, I had thoughts about my job.

I held out some faint hope the Navy would realize I would be a superb commanding officer. This executive officer tour was the last wicket I had to pass through to qualify. It would be up to the next "Command at Sea" selection board. That faint possibility was the sole reason I took this job. I also knew the board would consider the XO of a tender in the same way I did when I initially resisted the assignment. Without the description of my contribution to what *Yosemite* accomplished on this historic (at least in my mind) deployment, the members of the board would think of tenders sitting in their home port, turning around once a year being their only sea time, and I acknowledged the board members view of being number two with women as part of the ship's complement was much more likely to be negative than positive. There remained a slight chance I might get command of a combatant, my goal when I returned to active duty a dozen years earlier. That had been my dream and driver ever since.

But I pushed my speculation aside. There was still work to do for this executive officer. Some of that work was pedestrian administration. The purpose was to get us back to Mayport with no major problems. I recognized keeping the crew in line and adhering to regulations was critical as were bolstering the morale during the last leg of our journey. My handwritten POD notes had become my avenue to communicate with the crew, or at least I thought they were:

BZ to MARS operators. Monday night, the MARS station completed its one thousandth call. The work of these volunteers has been of great benefit to the entire crew. Thanks a lot for a job well done.

The reason for stopping in Rota is to prepare to go home, not liberty. Ensure your job and spaces are taken care of before hitting the beach.

Remember all hands are required to have a full seabag. If you are missing some required articles, the XO strongly suggests getting them in ROTA. Losing civilian clothes privileges when returning to home port is no fun. That's a full sea bag!

At 1600, 8 March, 1984, *USS Yosemite (AD- 19)* moored at U.S. Naval Base, Rota, Spain, the last stop.

The last port stop was focused on preparing for the trip across the pond. I added to the daily schedule to make that point:

The Uniform for entering port will be winter blue.

Liberty uniform will be announced after the boarding party briefs the XO.

Liberty Call will be passed after it is ensured all necessary action for loading stores are completed.

181 days deployed, 13 days to home

Friday, before the Atlantic transit, was a full day. But Doc Kerrigan and Linda Schlesinger asked me to meet them at the casino in Cadiz, a historic city and one of the oldest in Europe about ten miles south of Rota. I got the captain's permission after all of my work had been completed and met them there. It was a good evening and a proper way to say goodbye to the Indian Ocean and Mediterranean Sea.

Chapter 23: West Across the Pond

March 1984: en route Mayport, Florida

At 0800 on Saturday, 9 March, Yosemite set sail for home. My POD note was probably as much for me, if not more, than it was for the crew:

The last push is here. It is time to put the finishing touches on getting the ship in its finest dress for entering port in Mayport. It is also time to start thinking about the different way the ship will be operating and the way we will all be living. Think about it.

The second night of the voyage home, I went on CCTV again, this time to lecture the crew on productive work time when back in home port. I had a liquid chalk board beside me and conducted a math lesson.

I began with writing "40" on the chalkboard, the number of hours in a work week. I subtracted 15 minutes for call to quarters each day, or two hours and thirty minutes, bringing the subtotal to "37½." Then I explained we spent 1 hour each day for work center, division, and department meetings, i.e., five hours. Subtracting that, the subtotal was then "32½." I pointed out getting out the equipment and preparing to start work and cleaning up and storing equipment at the end of the work took about an hour amounting to 5 hours per week. Subtracting that, I wrote "27½" on the board.

I pointed out it took about 15 minutes after leaving the workstation for the day to change into civilian clothes and leave the ship at liberty call. Subtracting that 1 hour and 15 minutes, I pointed out the productive work time was down to "26¼" and wrote that on the board.

I calculated the noon mess was an hour and half or 7½ hours weekly, writing "18¾"down on the chalkboard. I wrote down "2½" for the hours required for the morning and afternoon breaks during the workday, bringing the sum to "16¼."

Pointing out the actual amount of time required for weekly training was much greater, I subtracted another 1 hour for that training. The subtotal was "15¼." Nearing the end of my analysis of productive work time, I explained nearly every sailor had to get a haircut, or go to the salon, exchange, take care of personal business, and so on, which would take at least 2 hours each week.

That brought the total to "13½" hours, which I recorded in very large letters, circled and underlined and then added three exclamation points.

I then urged the crew that once we were back in Mayport on a regular schedule, we should be conscious of how little time we had to do our work.

I didn't have a clue as to how the crew reacted to my analyis , but I was chuckling as I left the CCTV studio.

When I reported to the captain before taps, I was pretty sure he also was chuckling at my production.

The presentation was shown three times on CCTV.

• • •

We had a great amount of work to do on the way back. Mine was more than doubled. In addition to the daily requirements and ensuring all was taken care of before we arrived, I had to proofread and edit all of the award recommendations submitted by the departments. I also wrote the captain's award recommendations as well as those of the department heads. A number of the department heads were nominated for the Navy Commendation Medal. I recommended to the CO we nominate him for the Legion of Merit. In turn, the Captain told me I also should be recommended for the Legion of Merit as well. I was very pleased he thought that well of me.

But when it came to writing the award recommendation, I had belief in my writing skills. And I was the best writer on the ship. Several of my radio messages to higher authority had acknowledged my skill. However, I did not feel it was right for me to write my own award. CAPT Boyle understood and assigned the Supply Officer, Tim Allega, to write my recommendation.

To this day, I often wonder if I had chosen correctly. Had I written my award recommendation would I have been awarded the Legion of Merit?

Then, if that had happened, would I have been given more consideration for Command at Sea by the selection board? What was the likelihood that I would have been selected? But I knew that would have given me a better chance. Also, I realize that it also would have been unusual for the executive officer to be awarded the same level of commendation as the CO, regardless of how well the recommendation was written. My life turned out just fine even so.

I do sometimes think about it.

I didn't think about it then because I was just too busy.

• • •

Even though our arrival would be 21 March, Naval Station Mayport had notified us summer uniforms were the proper uniforms. This turned out to require the captain and me to make a difficult decision the morning of our arrival.

En route, we conducted zone inspections for the ship's material condition. We held another personnel inspection in service dress white, the uniform we would be wearing standing in to Mayport.

We were passing out plaudits for many of the crew who had contributed greatly to our success. We let the crew know some of the statistics we had rolled up as of Thursday, 17 March, St. Patrick's Day:

Fuel Oil Received: 3,638,168 Gallons
Fuel Burned: 3,978,048 Gallons (Underway 2,799,828 gallons; In
     Port 1,178,220 gallons)
Feedwater Distilled for Boilers: 4,218,470 Gallons...
Fresh Water Distilled for Crew Use: 6,600,597 Gallons
Fresh Water Used Daily Per Person: Approximately 37 Gallons
Fresh Water Transferred to Other Ships: 45,633 Gallons
Feed Water Transferred to Other Ships: 194,428 Gallons
Ship's Boilers have steamed a total of 13,238.3 Hours

As a former Chief Engineer, I felt proud of our engineering department to add this accolade: "All of the above was accomplished with no major casualties or oil spills." And this was accomplished by a 400-pound steam plant that began steaming when the Yosemite was commissioned in March 1944, forty years earlier.

• • •

One issue the captain and I discussed was emphasizing to the crew how they had to limit their involvement with politics. During my time at sea, there was very little time or information to discuss politics (another great thing about going to sea). Our return was in the year of a presidential election (Reagan was running for his second term against Walter Mondale), and we decided we should remind the crew of the restrictions in POD note, published 11th March:

15. Legal Note: POLITICAL ACTIVITY BY MILITARY MEMBERS. Military personnel must be aware of restrictions on participation in political activities. Navy policy precludes direct or indirect participation by naval commands, and limits participation of individual members. Naval Military Personnel Manual, Article 6210240 states restrictions on activities of active duty members. These restrictions permit members to vote and to encourage others to vote but prohibit essentially all activities connected with partisan political candidates and organizations. For example, members may not perform clerical or other duties for a partisan political committee, nor may they participate in political campaigns. The line between permitted and prohibited activities may be fine. For example, bumper stickers are permitted, but large signs on automobiles are prohibited.

Public Affairs Regulations, Section 0602 governs participation in and cooperation with political activities by Navy commands. Military personnel, facilities, and material may not be used to support political organizations, nor can they be used directly or indirectly to endorse, selectively benefit, or appear to endorse, benefit or favor any private person or group. US Navy Uniform Regulations prohibits wearing of the uniform while attending or participating in any activity which furthers personal or partisan political views, unless authorized in advance by competent authority. Bottom line is, voting is encouraged, but reviewing pertinent directives is advised before taking part in any partisan political activities.

• • •

Throughout the transit across the Atlantic, the CO and I discussed the manner in which we would enter port. We wished to demonstrate how successful the deployment had been and have a symbol to represent all of the praise the ship had received about her performance. Early on, the Captain hit on a great idea. When submarines returned from their sorties during World War II, they showcased their success by tying a broom to their mast as they entered port, indicating they had made a "clean sweep." I thought the idea of doing that was really a great idea.

The day before we were to enter port, I was getting ready to have crewmembers tie a broom to the mast as we set Sea Detail the next day. In our meeting in the afternoon, CAPT Boyle rescinded his idea. His reasoning was the broom hanging on the mast was a submarine tradition, and *Yosemite* was certainly not a submarine. Besides, he explained *Yosemite* should enter port like she had performed: no fancy ideas, just the best tender in the Navy.

My respect for my captain grew once again.

• • •

Yet another accolade came from higher command, 18th March. I posted it for the crew:

From: COMNAVSURFLANT (Commander, Naval Surface Forces, Atlantic)

Subject: WELCOME HOME

As Yosemite returns home from a most successful deployment, we in SURFLANT extend a hearty well done to all hands. In servicing the I.O. and MED deployers, you performed a vital role in supporting US National interests in this remote part of the world. You met the challenges of a demanding deployment with that extra touch of excellence characteristic of the Yosemite reputation. Every crew member can take great pride in the contributions made in maintaining the readiness posture of the ships in an austere environment. WELCOME HOME and may each of you enjoy a joyous reunion with your families and loved ones. WELL DONE.

I was giddy. But I was also XO, and I was concerned the crew might get big heads and relax on their laurels. I added:

The above message is a little bit more than ships normally receive from the type commander when they return home after a long deployment. It demonstrates the extent of Yosemite's success during the six and one-half months. It, along with the other accolades received, indicates the degree of pride each and every member of the wardroom and crew should have for his or her contribution to that reputation.

It has been a long deployment. The liberty ports were few and far between. The work was long and hard and conducted in the most remote of locations. Mail continually was delayed beyond what it is normally and often not there at all. But the crew, most of whom had never been exposed to such arduous conditions before, not only responded well, but went beyond the NORM. Morale went up and the pride the crew took in the repair effort, the performance of the ship itself, and her material condition fed upon itself. Yosemite returns to Mayport in the best material condition and state of preservation she has been in for a long time. Her superior performance is reflected in every task from sweepers to deck evolutions to communications to hair cutting to clothes cleaning to food preparation to DC equipment maintenance to running the main propulsion plant to mail order, and every other facet of shipboard life on a tender. Each and every one of us has changed during the deployment, and for most, it has been a change of growth and improvement. The change will require each and every one of us to adjust to the environment we left six and one-half months ago. Like us, that environment also has changed. But Yosemite crew members now have something special: the knowledge they are a cut above, that they can meet challenges not normally encountered and succeed beyond what is expected.

Returning to homeport is not the time to slack off. Everyone on the waterfront will be closely watching to see if Yosemite is really as good as all of those messages said she was. The crew will have to prove Yosemite deserved those accolades with continued superior performance in all areas. That means that each and every one of us will have to perform a little bit better. Off ship hours will increase, and there always will be more items to require attention while in homeport. The key has already been addressed in previous POD notes. Every crew member must put in a full and productive workday, that's from turn-to to knock-off, and occasionally, it will extend past knock-off. Every crew member must stand the twenty-four hours of his or her duty day ensuring that every facet of their duty from sweepers to working parties to watch standing is covered and covered well.

And that type of performance will be necessary from 21 March on. It won't be too difficult a task, especially considering what we have just accomplished. It will actually be easy if, like line handling or wagon pulling, everyone takes an even strain. So let's continue to keep Yosemite's reputation at the top of the heap. Be proud of yourself, be proud of the "Busy Lady" and perform accordingly…

• • •

The last night at sea, I held 8 0'Clock Reports outside my cabin with the department heads and special personnel like the Command Master Chief. Concluding that, I reported to the Captain, (our normal routine), to brief him on any items that came up, receive his instructions for the next day, this time a big one for coming home, and discuss what we considered important aspects of the ship and our personnel. I started to rise when CAPT Boyle directed me to remain, noting that he wanted to tell me something.

He said, "Jim, I know Maureen has come from San Diego to be there when the ship docks. I also know this will be her first experience as a Navy wife. I want you and her to know I will not hold her to the usual expectations for an executive officer's wife. She should participate in ship functions as much as she would like but not feel obligated to participate if she is uncomfortable in that role. I will not hold either of you to that old standard, nor will whatever she chooses have any reflection on my assessment of your performance."

CAPT Boyle once again had gone beyond my expectations. It was truly a thoughtful and noble gesture. One I will never forget.

• • •

The last day at sea, the morning mess, breakfast, was held longer, 0600-0900. When I met with the captain before quarters, we discussed the weather. The uniform would be service dress white, but it was cold, and the winds were strong and biting. We decided to add Navy pea coats to the

Yosemite entering Mayport.

officers and crew who would be standing at quarters for entering port. It certainly was an unusual combination, but necessary and after I checked out the crew, I decided the combination looked okay.

We were at Sea Detail and quarters for entering port for an hour.

A tugboat brought out the harbor pilot who had boarded just outside the St. John's River channel. Two tugs escorted *Yosemite* into the Mayport Basin and provided their power while the ship maneuvered to moor along the quay wall.

I was glad Mayport had the shortest sea detail I had ever seen in the Navy. It was a mile from the channel entrance to our berth.

At noon, *Yosemite* was home, tied to the quay wall for the first time since 9 September 1983. She had traveled 26,217 miles. She had been the "Busy Lady." It was time for enjoying the moment.

I was busy yet distracted. I wanted to spot Maureen amongst the large crowd of families and friends who had come to welcome their officers and sailors home. But I didn't want to gawk and needed to check on the crew and take care of any problems that might arise. Finally, standing on the port bridge wing, I saw her. She was standing with Mary Ellen, the captain's wife, and a number of the officers' wives, including Dina Weaver, the Command Master Chief's wife and ship's ombudsman. They were all close to the brow.

We quickly cleared customs. Shortly thereafter, the wives were escorted aboard before liberty call was passed.

The responsibilities of being the executive officer faded. I was with my wife, the one whom I had married 30 July 1983 and ten days later left her in San Diego with only a brief rendezvous when she visited Jacksonville over the Labor Day weekend: Ten days of honeymoon and three days of wedding bliss over 204 days. I would go to the ship briefly on Saturday, but we would be together until Monday when she would fly back to San Diego.

Man, it was good to be home.

194 days deployed, 0 days to home

Chapter 24: The Next Phase

March 1984: Home At Last

Maureen arrived two days before *Yosemite's* arrival (My daughter Blythe did not come for my homecoming; she was in school in Austin, Texas where she lived with her mother). Maureen stayed with my cousin Bill Prichard and his wife, Florence until the ship tied up at Naval Station Mayport. We stayed with them for two more days before Maureen went back to work in San Diego.

Our plan was up in the air as Maureen's company's annual profit sharing was in June. She wanted to remain at work in order to receive her share. When she went back to work, she and her boss, Jim Herr, agreed on a plan. Each week, she would leave work on Thursday afternoon and catch a red eye from San Diego through Chicago or Atlanta, arriving in Jacksonville at 6:00 a.m. Friday morning. I would pick her up, drop her off at our first home, and go to the ship for the rest of the workday. After the weekend, I would drive her to the airport for a 6:00 a.m. flight back to San Diego, arriving at noon when she would go directly to her office from the airport.

She began the routine in April. After about six weeks, we agreed the routine was driving her bonkers and was not worth the profit sharing, whatever it might be in June. She moved to Jacksonville full time.

In June, she found out there was not enough profit that year for any money to be paid out in profit sharing.

• • •

I had worked out a deal with one of the instructors at Destroyer School, Jim Sullivan, during my prospective executive officer course to rent his house in Ponte Vedra Beach. The house and its location were perfect for a newly married couple. It was an easy commute to and from the base. It was also about a half mile from the beach and five minutes away from the three Sawgrass golf courses.

• • •

After our return to Mayport on Wednesday, we learned Commander, Group 12 had scheduled our wardroom as the site for a briefing. The junior officer detailer would arrive from Washington on Friday morning to brief all the surface line officers based in Mayport. We learned the junior officer detailer was also the coordinator for the Women at Sea program.

The last guidance we had been given concerning LTJG Leahy was once we reached home port; Noreen was to be transferred for temporary duty (TAD) to a shore facility. There was no direction as to which shore establishment that would be.

I was unhappy Noreen was leaving because she had become an invaluable officer over the course of the deployment. The captain was not pleased either. I was also a bit angry at the system because it was clear to me her continuing as operations officer would be no more dangerous to her pregnancy on our ship tied to a pier than in a shore duty billet. I also believed she would be better off on *Yosemite* because our qualified medical officer, Frank Kerrigan, who had attended to Noreen throughout her pregnancy, was the best choice to continue tending to her and his aid would be very close to her, unlike a shore command.

CAPT Boyle and I agreed we should talk to this LCDR coordinator before his briefing to the JOs.

On Friday morning when he arrived, I escorted the junior officer detailer straight to the Captain's cabin. We asked him when we sent our radio message to BUPERS concerning LTJG's pregnancy, who were the personnel who made the decision to transfer her out of Masirah, a dangerous journey for a pregnant woman.

The detailer said the flag officer heading the surface personnel office sat with several medical officers, several JAG attorneys, and the detailer himself. I asked him why no one considered adding an officer who had been a commanding officer or an executive officer who had women as part of his command on the ad hoc decision team. He did not have an answer.

I asked him if the decision to transfer Noreen remained extant. He was firm in his reply in the affirmative. I told him we would transfer her when we got direction as to what command would be her TAD duty station.

We did not get any further instruction about the impending transfer, and I guess it dropped through the cracks, either intentionally or unintentionally by the coordinator.

Upon our arrival in Mayport, Noreen took leave to be with her husband Jim for the eight days before he would deploy on his ship. Toward the end of those eight days while she was at their home with her parents, Noreen suffered a miscarriage. The doctor in attendance assured her the miscarriage was in no way related to her being on the ship. She now has two children, one of whom graduated from the U.S. Naval Academy like her, and one grandchild. She earned her doctorate in education and just retired as the vice-superintendent of a school district on Long Island, New York. She and her husband Jim have a home in Newport, Rhode Island.

• • •

I found it ironic the Navy had declared ships returning from deployments would be free from material and administrative oversight for six months. Yet *Yosemite* already was scheduled for 26 inspections and "assist teams" of every sort coming on board in the first three months after our return. The "Busy Lady" was getting slammed. Later when I was a facilitator for a senior officer seminar for leadership, I read one of a dozen competencies for the superior leaders was the attitude that inspections and assist visits, regardless of disruption of regular work and as time-consuming they were, could be of benefit, could improve the command's performance. As I looked at *Yosemite* being overwhelmed with these visits, I certainly didn't think of them as helpful. I will not record here what I really thought of them.

• • •

In the spring, *Yosemite* was selected as the best tender or repair ship in the Atlantic Fleet. She was named the best repair and maintenance command, ship or shore, in the Fleet. She received the Battle "E" for effectiveness in meeting her mission. CAPT Boyle received his Legion of Merit, well deserved. My nomination for a Legion of Merit was downgraded to the Navy Commendation Medal, a significant honor in my mind.

• • •

After we returned, there were several more bad moments with my two "problem children", a black woman and a white male that required me to make more responses to Congress and other officials. But we got through those. These two sailors were what I called "organizational terrorists," creating innumerable headaches, and often dangerous. Gender and color were not contributing factors.

The next year was as successful as the deployment, including a couple of months at sea and travelling to Charleston to provide repair and maintenance services there. We participated in a large exercise in the Caribbean as an "Orange" force.

Maureen and I spent our first year of marriage together, a wonderful year meeting new Navy and civilian friends while Frank Kerrigan and I played a lot of golf together.

As expected, I was not selected for command at sea and before the end of the year, I considered my options for what would be my last tour. I could continue to chase the elusive command at sea, discussing with a number of people in the promotion and assignment business. CAPT Boyle was a former shipmate of the head of the BUPERS, who reviewed my record and assessed I had no chance of being selected. With no options to drive ships remaining, I thought of what I would like for my next duty station. I decided it was time for me to have my "twilight" tour and retire when my active duty obligation was complete. I asked my detailer to find a good, productive billet in San Diego. Maureen had taken a year out of her successful career in San Diego to be with me. It was time to give her a chance to resume that career in her native San Diego.

My detailer called me several days later and asked me to confirm I would go to the Naval Amphibious School, Coronado to be a facilitator in the Prospective Commanding Officer, Prospective Executive Officer "Leadership, Management, Education and Training (LMET) week-long course. I agreed.

CAPT Boyle and I chuckled over that prospect. I was amazed that a commander who had not been chosen for command would be assigned to teach executive officers, and especially commanding officers leadership. I also told the captain I might be the first Naval officer to recommend his billet be cut as well as the course he was assigned to teach.

It was a great job. I worked with Dave Carey, a POW for five and one half years in Vietnam. The course was changed to a two-day seminar in command excellence for senior officers (LCDR and above). It was much better than the previous course for arming attendees with a better understanding of leadership. Dave was and remains an incredible man and friend. I learned a great deal from him and many of the people with whom I worked and the seminar attendees.

After Dave retired, I became the director for LMET training for the Pacific Coast and Pacific Rim. I later became the director for "Command Management and Equal Opportunity" for the Pacific Fleet. My primary job was the lead facilitator for the Command Excellence Seminar, in which Dave and I had added mobile seminars to those in the schoolhouse.

This last job gave me the opportunity to compare how *Yosemite*, during my tour, matched up with the outstanding commands and outstanding Navy leaders in the two studies used in the seminar. Except for my not appreciating the inspections and assist visits as beneficial, the Busy Lady matched up well.

I completed my active duty service (retired, sort of) from the Navy, 30 November 1989. Our daughter Sarah was born later that evening, 17 years after her sister Blythe was born. I became "Mister Mom." It was a drastic change of careers.

• • •

My two-year tour aboard *USS Yosemite* was one of the most rewarding during my 22 plus years of Naval service. I had been an old school mariner who loved the older ships, the hard times at sea, and yes, the deployments with all male crews who were incredible at doing their jobs and wild on liberty.

I learned there are better ways.

The women on *Yosemite* taught me that. As the *Yosemite's* XO, I learned a lot about myself and about effective operation of ships at sea.

My job was about the same as it would have been with an all-male crew. One difference was the liberty port visits. On *Yosemite*, those liberty stops were not the problem they were on my other nine ships. Our sailors were much better behaved ashore. They didn't cause problems. Issues created on liberty were rare.

About 90 to 95 percent of the crew went about their jobs, performed well, and caused little problems. The other 5 to 10 percent were prone to get into trouble and about 1 percent of those were completely dysfunctional, creating problems way out of proportion to the rest of the crew. This was true with all of my other ships as well as *Yosemite*. Those same percentages applied to the men and women on *Yosemite*. The problems were a bit different and had to be handled in a different way, but the number of problems was about the same.

Captain Francis J. Boyle, Commanding Officer of the *USS Yosemite* (AD 19), 1983-1986.

My favorite tour of my career was as First Lieutenant on the Landing Ship Dock *USS Anchorage (LSD 36)*. It was an incredible experience and the very essence of being a Surface Warfare Officer on a capital ship.

But the *Yosemite* proved to me I was not only a mariner, but I could motivate people, both male and female, to meet our mission.

And I grew. During the deployment, I often groused about the Captain in letters to Maureen. I wanted things done my way, not his, but I also knew for the ship to be its best, the executive officer must support the commanding officer in all aspects of being on a Navy ship. By the time we returned to Mayport, my respect grew for CAPT Francis J. Boyle. He made tough decisions and demanded excellence. He was thorough in his analysis of situations, looked at the impact of decisions immediately and in the future. The Navy and the ship were always the top priorities in his thinking and his actions. My grousing had been part of my growth as a Naval officer.

• • •

When my cousin Bill Prichard saw the *Yosemite* was open for touring in the late 1980's, he took his son Brendan to Mayport and was escorted around the ship's spaces by a petty officer. When Bill told the petty officer I had been the executive officer in 1983 and 1984. The petty officer, who had been on the ship when I was XO, said to Bill and Brendan, "I wish he were still the XO."

That was one of the best compliments I received during my Naval career.

Yosemite was special, and a good way to close out my time at sea.

Thank you, CAPT Boyle, officers, chiefs, and crew of that old tender. She was not only the "Busy Lady," she was a proud, beautiful lady and an effective asset for the US Navy.

And *Yosemite* proved that women, both officers and enlisted, could be effective and a contributing force on ships at sea.

The key was the focus on meeting the ship's mission, getting the job done. All else fell into place.

After her decommissioning in 1994, *Yosemite* was sunk in a "SINKEX" in 2003 as a target ship for Navy weapons. When I learned of her fate, I posted this on my website:

USS Yosemite (AD 19): Good Ship Gone (2003)

The Navy radio message, the means of communicating throughout my Navy career, was the bearer of the news, forwarded by the Commanding Officer in the new mode of communication: e-mail.

The news came, as expected, from that Commanding Officer, a man who has Navy blue for blood in his veins. I did not call him "CO" or the aviator term "skipper" – he would have chopped off my head with that insult. I called him "Captain." Without fail. I now call him Frank and a friend.

The Yosemite *was special. I confess I had to learn to love her. I went to her to serve as executive officer in 1983 for the sole purpose of attaining the necessary qualifications to screen for command at sea. I did not like tenders: they did not go to sea enough. They did not land amphibious troops and equipment; they did not fire guns and missiles; they did not hunt submarines. They did not scream around at twenty-seven knots with the spume of a rooster-tail off the stern and the wake as wide as a four-lane highway extending to the horizon. They did not belch landing craft out of the stern of a well deck in rolling seas.*

But Yosemite *had been there when I first met the Navy in 1963.*

She was the flagship of Cruiser Destroyer Force, Atlantic Fleet, tied up at Pier One in Newport, Rhode Island. I was a midshipman on my way out of NROTC because I didn't have good study habits nor good sense at nineteen. She appeared massive and imperturbable as I walked passed her on my way to my destroyer and an eight-week cruise.

She was in Newport when I came back from deployment on my first ship after being commissioned from OCS in 1968. Her deserved reputation was such that we would figure out ways to get our repair work to her, rather than to take it to our "parent" tender.

And she was my last ship, the penultimate tour for me and the last step toward my never achieved goal of command.

She could wheeze out sixteen knots with her four hundred pound boilers, but we steamed at ten knots most of the time. The fact sheet lists her top speed as nineteen knots but that was several tons and numerous years before I became her "XO."

She steamed like a champion for my tour. We deployed for six and a half months just a month after I reported aboard. She was the first ship with women as part of the crew who spent extended periods out of port (Most before had transited from port to port and provided repair and maintenance services pier side or moored). She provided repair availabilities for destroyers and cruisers while anchored off Masirah, Oman, and she accomplished in four days what normally took two weeks back in the states. She did that for fifty-five days, took a break and then did it again for forty-five days. She had a crew of 900, including 106 women, and a wardroom of 44, six of whom were female, and gave me a completely different perspective of women at sea: the Captain said it best when he announced, "We don't have women on this ship. We don't have men on this ship. We have sailors on this ship, and we are going to operate that way."

She was given a letter of commendation for being a member of the Indian Ocean Battle Group, an unheard of honor for a repair ship.

She steamed as a member of the Orange force in a Caribbean exercise, something tenders do not normally do.

She was in the middle of the eye of a developing hurricane, eventually escaping to the northeast before the winds and seas reached full hurricane strength.

She was proclaimed the best repair organization in the Atlantic Fleet.

Her crew was an amalgamation of old sailors, repair personnel who had seldom spent any time at sea, and young wide-eyed men and women, learning how to be sailors. The first lieutenant was the best boatswainmate I knew in twenty years, even though he had outgrown the title. The doc was so new he didn't know how to salute or how to dress in Navy uniforms. He has become the godfather of my daughter and one of my closest friends. And there was this special woman, the operations officer, a lieutenant, who was one of the best officers with whom I served. And there were many others who had an impact on my life.

Yosemite *was commissioned in 1944, the year I was born. She was decommissioned in 1994. Fifty years, a half century of service.*

It is fitting that she went down the way she did. She spent her life supporting the fleet. She was sunk supporting the fleet, providing one last service.

And she and Davy Jones will sleep well together.

Epilogue: The XO's Final Cut

One thing I tried to do throughout my Navy career and for most of my life has been to look back on any significant period of time or major event, not to find blame, but to learn how to be more effective in the future.

The things I learned about myself on the Busy Lady could fill about ten more books. But here are a few of them:

First and foremost, I proved to myself I was a pretty decent Surface Warfare Officer, or as I prefer to call it, a mariner.

I learned yet more things about how to be an effective commanding officer from CAPT Francis J. Boyle. He showed me one has to detach oneself from personal needs and wants to focus completely on the job at hand, that is, being the most

Commander James Rye Jewell, Jr., Executive Officer of the *USS Yosemite* (AD 19), 1983-1985.

effective commanding officer possible, paying heed to the ultimate responsibility of that position, simultaneously meeting the ship's mission and representing justice in its truest form.

I also learned of my misconceptions about people. If a leader focuses on the job at hand and continues to communicate, positively and negatively, to the followers how important they are in doing that job, then wonderful things can happen.

I learned on a Navy ship, 90 percent of the wardroom and crew are focused on doing their jobs and toeing the line; 8 percent of the others have to be monitored and provided direction in doing their jobs; and the other

2 percent will always be a problem, requiring more attention and more work than that effective 90 percent. I also learned this is true regardless of gender, or any other group classification.

$$\bullet \ \bullet \ \bullet$$

This is my story from an executive officer's perspective. I wish I could have given more insight into the men and women sailors who made it all happen. *Yosemite* long maintained the reputation as the best destroyer tender on the East Coast if not the entire Navy. The sailors aboard *Yosemite* during the 1983-84 deployment performed beyond the norm. I wish I could tell every one of their stories.

I made a career out of the Navy, just over 22 years of active duty, retiring just shy of 46 years old. My retirement was on the day my second daughter was born. The Navy did not find me attractive for Commanding Officer, my final goal. I met all of the requirements for command at sea, but I was not promotable because of various reasons: broken service, no graduate degree, and no Washington DC tours. The Navy wanted officers who could make an impact in Washington. I had no desire to go to Washington and wanted to spend my career at sea. I had two shore tours, two too many for me (and they were good tours) and not enough for the Navy. I should note had I been on my selection boards, using their screening criteria, I would not have selected me. I am not disappointed, just recognizing my choices and their criteria kept me from command. I had a wonderful Naval Officer career and *Yosemite* was a significant part of that career.

As much as I disliked the term, I was a "Surface Warfare Officer." I, as I was commissioned, considered myself a "line officer." No special designation was needed to distinguish me from the other officer branches. The other branches of the Navy invented their special designations and logos to differentiate them from a line officer who was on surface ships.

The surface community at higher levels, the captains and the flags, did not agree with my view. During my first tour, the designation "Surface Warfare Officer" was created as well as the insignia required to be worn by those who qualified. The qualifications were needed. I never liked having to have a designation other than line officer. The Navy was created with officers who were leaders on ships, officers of the line. That's enough.

My job throughout my quarter of a century of association with the Navy was to do my part to meet the Navy's mission, which was, "To conduct sustained operations at sea in support of national policy." That was pretty much the same for all of the military services, leaving out the "at sea" part.

There is no caveat about who is supposed to perform that mission. The military's job is to provide defense of our Constitution and win wars for our country as well as conduct operations to support national policy. It does not have a place for politics, religion, or sex. The people who are best qualified to meet that mission should be selected for that job, not because of their gender, sexual preference, political positions, or from where they graduated. They should be the folks best fitted to wage war.

The military has morphed into bureaucracies that fight for political advantage and budget dollars. It appears as if it is a platform for social engineering. Many officers position for promotion and become "experts" in specialized fields so they can make rank, follow their military careers with politics, military contracts, or become hired to be those "experts" by news media.

The services have become so competitive against each other, they do not function well together, and they attempt to expand their roles to become more powerful than the other services and the other divisions within their own service. The Army has more boats than the Navy. Each service has aircraft, boats, special forces, and missiles. Duplication is crazy, extremely dysfunctional, and very expensive in spite of the claims backed with statistics suiting the needs of those who promote their agenda.

The last I checked several years ago, the Navy had more admirals than they had ships, aircraft squadrons, and submarines. Without claiming to be an expert, I would suggest this might be just a tad top heavy.

This is not to malign all senior officers. In my time associated with the military, the good senior officers outnumbered the bad. But some of the bad ones were doozies. The evolving Navy and the other branch's systems have driven the changes, not necessarily the people. I experienced a number of outstanding flag officers.

My tour on *Yosemite* was an eye-opener in many ways. I realized having an effective fighting force at sea was secondary for senior officers to make a name for themselves, having their way within their community, and getting a leg up on those they considered their competitors for the next promotion. Most importantly, I discovered my ideas about life as a Navy officer should always be ready to adapt to change for meeting the mission.

The women aboard *Yosemite* were just as good and often better than the men in a comparable job. One of the best officers, if not the best, whoever served under me was LT Noreen Leahy. She was in the second class of women midshipmen to receive their commission from the US Naval Academy. There is no doubt in my mind that had she stayed in she would have been successful and made flag officer. She stayed for one more tour to meet her commitment but became a successful school administrator with a doctorate primarily for two reasons: the way the Navy handled her situation when she became pregnant, and her career options conflicted with her being with her family. It was the Navy's loss.

The female officers and enlisted aboard *Yosemite* not only did their part to meet the ship's mission, but in many ways improved our performance because they were women.

In 1983, the Women at Sea program was in its infancy. The women selected were well aware their performance was critical in determining if women would continue to serve on Navy ships at sea. From an old sailor's vocabulary, they busted their butts to do as good a job as possible. When a woman was put in a work center, she worked effectively and put in long hours to show she belonged. The male sailors saw the way the women performed and became determined to not let the women outwork them. The quality and amount of our production were incredible throughout my 22 months as XO.

The next of my discoveries would be a wonderful thing to research using the SYMLOG Consulting Group's assessment process. SYMLOG, which stands for "Systematic Multiple Level Observation of Groups," was created by Harvard social psychologist Robert Freed Bales through more than fifty years of work. It is the most powerful tool for effectively assessing and improving performance of teams in any form and team leadership. On board *Yosemite* when a woman was assigned to a workgroup, she became that male's workgroup special person. The males worked to make her feel a regular member and were protective of her. The work centers' *esprit de corps* went through the roofs. Almost to a team, our work centers were more cohesive and more effective. There is no doubt in my mind had the work centers, divisions, and departments on *Yosemite* been rated through the SYMLOG system, they would have been assessed to be in the Most Effective Profile (MEP). I believe the ship would also have been in that same profile.

There was another phenomenon created with women aboard I would have never considered as an outcome before I became *Yosemite's* XO. During our six-month plus deployment, *Yosemite* did not have one international incident of any type during port visits. Not one. I had never, ever been on a deployed ship which had no international incidents. There were usually quite a few, not just one. Bar fights, drunks, crimes, and many other bad acts were a common occurrence. Not on *Yosemite's* 1983-84 deployment. Why?

The women did not go to the red light districts or the bars. They went to the beach; they went to the local attractions; they volunteered to go to orphanages, etc., and help paint or otherwise provide succor to children or others in need. Most of the men followed the women. The red light districts and the bars were nearly empty. Navy ship's MWR programs nearly always set up tours for sailors to go see local attractions, historic sites, scenic vistas. Out of the ten other ships I had served, I do not recall any tour program coming close to 20 percent of crew usage. *Yosemite's* tour usage was around 75 percent.

Military service should not be served to get a college degree later. Pay and benefits should match the capability of the one serving and the risk involved. Front line troops and sailors face the fact they may die. That, unfortunately, is part and parcel of being a warrior.

Politics, gender, and all of the other categories our culture chooses to display prejudice should never be part of the equation. If they can do the job, are willing to put their lives on the line, and are the most effective choice to do that job, they should be allowed to serve. Effective fighting forces and effective leadership are required to make that happen, choice of sexual preference, skin color, or other discriminators should not be a consideration in the choice.

I saw an effective fighting force and effective leadership make *Yosemite* a marvel at getting the job done.

Yes, our dangers, except for the threat of Iranian gunboat attack, were minimal as far as life threatening, and *Yosemite's* mission was to provide repair and maintenance services to forward deployed ships. *Yosemite* did such a great job at meeting her mission she received a letter of commendation for being a member of Battle Group Echo, the *USS Ranger* carrier group. I have never heard of a tender or repair ship being considered a member of a battle group, let alone get a letter of commendation for such inclusion.

Leadership was critical. We had great leaders on *Yosemite*. Old sailors, hard-crusted warrant officers and limited duty officers; new junior leaders, male and female, ignored gender to enhance our performance at every turn. And there was the captain. I have often described CAPT Francis J. (Frank) Boyle as a man so much a Naval officer that Navy blue was the color of the blood in his veins. He understood the ship's mission. He was knowledgeable in all aspects of a ship's operation and what it took to get there. And his admonition that "We don't have women on this ship; we don't have men on this ship; we have sailors, and we are going to act and perform like sailors" should be the watchword for every military command.

Spare me the rhetoric about what sex sailors or troops should be; spare me the posturing about morale problems and women's physical differences from men.

Give me the best people for the job.

And oh, how I would like to have "a ship and a star to navigate by" once again.

In conclusion, the below is the text of the Yosemite's "Meritorious Service Citation" for that 1983-84 deployment:

Meritorious Service Citation
   The Secretary of the Navy takes pleasure in commending
   USS Yosemite (AD 19)
   for service as set forth in the following
   CITATION:
   For meritorious service during forward deployment to the United States SEVENTH Fleet from 13 September 1983 to 21 March 1984. During this period, USS YOSEMITE (AD 19) provided fleet repair service for Indian Ocean carrier Battle Groups at Masirah Island expending over 80,000 man-hours of superb repair work for twelve ships. In addition, USS YOSEMITE provided over 70,000 man-hours of invaluable medical, dental, and supply services. The high quality of work, exceptional dedication, and crisp efficiency exhibited by YOSEMITE was most clearly demonstrated during her rapid repairs of USS RANGER's fire damages. The conduct ashore of USS YOSEMITE crewmembers was impeccable and contributed significantly toward cultivating international understanding in the Indian Ocean. By their continuous display

of professionalism, pride, determination, and complete dedication to duty, the officers and enlisted personnel of USS YOSEMITE (AD 19) reflected credit upon themselves and upheld the highest traditions of the United States Naval Service.

//John Lehman//
Secretary of the Navy

Chronology

1983

20 JAN – XO screening board delayed

Early March – XO Selections announced

Early April – Assigned to Yosemite

16 May – Detached from *USS Okinawa (LPH 3)*

13 June – Reported to Pre-XO Training, Destroyer School, Newport, RI

13 July — Leave, missing last week of XO training for going to DC/ Norfolk to learn more about Women at Sea (WAS) program

18 July – Prospective Commanding Officer and Executive Officer (PCO/ PXO) Leadership, Management, and Training (LMET) course, Little Creek, VA

30 July – Wedding followed by honeymoon in San Diego

09 August – Flight to Nashville, picked up car, drove to sister's home on Signal Mountain, TN

10 August – Drive to Mayport, FL

11 August 0830 – Report to *Yosemite*

12 August – Hail and Farewell Party for incoming and outgoing officers, CDR Janek's home

16 August – Relieved CDR Sheffield as XO

30 August – Underway, Sea Trials

31 August – Moor Mayport

02-05 September – Maureen visits Mayport

07 September – Evaporator casualty delays scheduled departure of 8 September

09 September – Underway for Rota

11 September – Hurricane Chantal, Fleet Weather Center orders us to stay east of track

20 September – In port Rota

21 September – Underway for Palma

23 September – In port Palma

27 September – Underway for Augusta Bay, Sicily

28 September – Refuel Augusta Bay; Underway for Port Said

02 October – Arrive Port Said

03 October – Traverse Suez Canal

04 October – Transit Red Sea

06 October – Transit Bab el Mendeb; en Route Diego Garcia

12 October – Crossing the Line (ceremony for crossing the equator)

14 October – Anchor Diego Garcia

14-15 October – Turnover from *USS Cape Cod (AD 43)*, the tender *Yosemite* relieves

21 October – POD Note about garbage barge

24 October – Refuel *Lynde McCormick*

24 October - Underway for refueling at POL pier

25 October – Underway for Masirah

28 October – Boat transfer for female officers, Emily Baker and Sharon Carrasco

30 October – Anchor Masirah

31 October – *Fletcher* TAV/XO note in POD about CFC XO dinner award

04 November – *Fletcher* departs; *Stoddert* TAV

11 November – *Stoddert* departs; *Fife* TAV

11 November Shift anchorage to international waters (before Fife comes alongside)

12 November – Saturday Vertrep with *Camden*

15 November – Belladonna USO show embarks; *Fife* departs; *Horne* TAV

17 November – Awarded Battle E, Engineering E, DC, Fleet Support, and NAV deck seamanship awards

19 November – POD sked Boxing "smoker" with *Horne*

20 November – The infamous day when Belladonna actually came aboard

21 November – *Horne* departs; *McCormick* TAV/VERTREP

22 November – *Camden* TAV

22 November - Belladonna departs

23 November – Battle Group anchors nearby; RADM Arthur COMCARGRU 7 visits *Yosemite*

24 November – *McCormick* departs; *Shields* TAV

24 November - Thanksgiving

25 November – *Camden* departs; *Sample* TAV

26 November – *Sample* departs; *San Jose* TAV

28 November – Command Screening Board

30 November – *Detroit* TAV

06 December – Detroit departs; *Fife* TAV

10 December – Underway for Diego Garcia

16 December – arrive Diego Garcia

20 December – *Tattnall* (DDG 19) TAV

1984

01 January – Assigned to CTU 78.2.3

05 January – Underway for Mombasa

11 January – In port, Mombasa

16 January – Underway for Chismayo

19 January – En route Masirah

24 January – FRS Masirah, Kirk TAV

4 February – Kirk departs; Sterett rough weather anchors, does not come alongside for TAV

6 February – Sterett comes alongside

10 February – Sterett departs, Hammond TAV

14 February – Hammond departs

15 February – Commodore Butcher, CTF 73 spends night aboard

16 February – Turnover with *USS Prairie (AD 15)*

17 February – En route Red Sea

21 February – Chop to Sixth Fleet

22 February – Transited Red Sea

25 February – Transit Suez

26 February – Ops en route Naples

29 February – In port Naples

5   March - En route Rota

08 March – In port Rota

10 March – en route Mayport; CHOP to Second Fleet

21 March – In port Mayport

Introduction for Landlubbers

I found it difficult to write about my Navy and make it understandable for those who have not been on a Navy ship. Therefore, I have chosen to explain as much as I can as an introduction to this glossary of terms.

This is a difficult proposition. Having been on Navy ships for a significant part of my life, what is unfamiliar to many landlubbers is ingrained in me.

• • •

When discussing this book with a friend, I was asked what was the color of the *Yosemite*. I had not thought about this in years because of the old Navy saying "Haze gray and underway." All U.S. Navy ships are painted gray unless they are camouflaged for battle as they were in World War II. All of the Navy ships I was on from 1963 until 1989 were painted with various hues of gray: haze gray for the hull, bulkheads, and other vertical surfaces, deck gray (a darker shade) for exterior decks, and machinery gray for any interior machinery. Most interior surfaces were either shades of grey or white.

• • •

Some folks wanted to know what kind of ships the Navy has. This has changed greatly since my time. The Navy had the Submarine Force, the Aviation Force, and the Surface Force. Submarines and aircraft carriers are still around. The Surface Force consisted of the cruiser and destroyer forces; the amphibious forces, the service forces, and the mine sweeper forces. The types of ships in those groups that are involved in this story are listed in the glossary below.

The *Yosemite* and other destroyer and repair ships were in the service force — submarine tenders were in the submarine force — All of them provided maintenance and repair services as well as medical, dental, and administrative support to the combatants.

Tenders were initially used to provide those services as close to the area of combat operations as possible.

• • •

Life aboard Navy ships was pretty much the same in many ways. There were always three messes: the enlisted mess, the chiefs mess, and the wardroom for officers. On larger ships, some had a first class mess. The enlisted mess was served cafeteria style, the chiefs mess and wardroom normally served family style although on larger ships, those messes might also have cafeteria style dining.

The morning meal was served from 0700 until 0730, sometimes running later to feed the off-going watch. Lunch, the noon mess was served at 1130 and ran until the off-going watch was served. The evening mess was served at 1700. Midnight rations, or "midrats" was served to the oncoming watch around 2315 to allow that watch to have a snack such as soup, sandwiches, evening mess leftovers, or a combination of the three. The off-going watch was also afforded the opportunity to have midrats.

• • •

On Navy ships, the executive officer announces when liberty call, which allows sailors and officers to go ashore, and sets the time for liberty to expire. The quarterdeck does not allow any of the crew off the ship except for business or with special permission to pursue personal matters until liberty call. After liberty expires, personnel who report aboard after that are put on report for being an unauthorized absence, their time late reporting recorded, and they are put on report.

• • •

In the beginning of the U.S. Navy's history, "Commodore" was the title reserved for captains in command of a fleet or squadron. From 1899 until 1982, "Commodore" remained a courtesy title, usually reserved for a senior captain in charge of multiple ships. During that 83-year period, the Navy used two stars and the rank of "Rear Admiral" for the first two levels of flag rank while the other services used one star and "Brigadier General" for the first flag level, and two stars and "Major General" for the second level.

A great deal of grousing about the Navy not having a one star rank came from the other service flag officers. The Navy's lowest flag rank (two star "Rear Admiral") was often misconstrued as a higher rank than their one-star brigadiers, In 1982, the rank of "Commodore" with one star was reintroduced as a rank. But the Navy objected and in late 1983, Rear Admiral, Lower Half, with one star, and Rear Admiral, Upper Half, with two stars, became the Navy's first two levels of flag officers.

Glossary

AAW – Anti-Air Warfare

Acey-Deucy - a term for first and second class petty officers (E5 and E6), usually used to describe the senior petty officer club

Accommodation Ladder - An accommodation ladder is a portable flight of steps down a ship's side

AD - Destroyer Tender

Admin - Administrative Department

ADTAKE - Advise Action Taken, usually addressing some form of communication, correspondence, or submission of a report, which had not been received

AFS - Combat Stores Ship

AO - Fleet Oiler: These are ships that bring fuel oil to the combatant ships and refueling is conducted with the ships side by side underway while the fuel is transferred by hose rigs

AOE - Fast Combat Support Ship - could provide both fuel oil and ammunition

ASUW – Anti-Surface Warfare

ASW - Anti-Submarine Warfare

ASWO - Anti-Submarine Warfare Officer

BIOT - British Indian Ocean Territory

BM - Boatswain's mate - this rating for enlisted sailors who specialize in deck and boat operations and maintenance, among other duties

BOQ - Bachelor Officers Quarters

Bosun's Chair - As used here, the "Bosun's Chair" was a metal seat for carrying personnel between ships using a "hi-line"

Bosun - a short term for Boatswain; the term is used for Warrant Officers and LDO's who specialize in deck and boat operations and maintenance

BUPERS - Bureau of Personnel

BZ - "Bravo Zulu:" a Navy flag signal meaning a job well done, now used in writing and vocally to express the same

CDR - Commander

Note: I have used my own "style" when using Navy ranks and rates. For the shorter titles: Admiral, Captain, Commander, Lieutenant, Ensign, Petty Officer, Seaman, Airman, Fireman, etc. the ranks are spelled out; for the longer titles: Lieutenant Junior Grade, Chief Warrant Officer, Chief Petty Officer, I have either shortened or abbreviated to LTJG, Warrant or CWO, Chief or CPO. For ratings, I have spelled them out, e.g. torpedoman

CFC - Combined Federal Campaign

CG- Guided Missile Cruisers

CHENG - Chief Engineer, a department head on ships, more formally known as the Engineering Officer

Chopped - Acronym for Change of Operational Command

CIC - Combat Information Center: the tactical center nearly always located just aft of the pilot house on older ships. CIC provides processed information from radar, etc. to the Officer Of the Deck (OOD) and the Commanding Officer (CO)

CNO - Chief of Naval Operations

CO - Commanding Officer

COMCRUDESLANT - Commander, Cruiser, Destroyer Force, Atlantic Fleet

COMSEVENTFLT - Commander, Seventh Fleet, the operational commander for U.S. Navy Forces in the Pacific and Indian Oceans

CRUDESLANT - Cruiser, Destroyer Force, Atlantic Fleet

CTF - Commander, Task Force

CV - Aircraft Carrier

DCA - Damage Control Assistant

DD - Destroyer

DDG - Guided Missile Destroyer

Department Head - The organization on a ship starts with the commanding officer, the executive officer, officers in charge of the ship's departments, and divisions within each of those departments

DGAR - an acronym and another name for Diego Garcia

DASH - Drone Anti-Submarine Helicopter, a drone designed to deliver torpedoes against submarines from long distance put into service in 1963 and cancelled in 1969 due to half of the drones were lost, most due to electronic failure; they were also known in the Navy as CRASH and SPLASH. The DASH deck on *Yosemite* allowed the ship to conduct maintenance on the DASH, land and recover the helicopters. On destroyers they also served as a place for the crew to watch movies

DLG - Guided Missile Frigate

DT- Dental Technician

EDO - Engineering Duty Officer

EDF - Enlisted Dining Facility, known by sailors as the "crew's mess," or "mess decks"

ENS - Ensign

Exec - Executive Officer

Fetch - The area in which ocean waves are generated by the wind. Also refers to the length of the fetch area, measured in the direction of the wind. In the case mentioned here, the fetch created waves from a constant wind building the seas due to the monsoons from the Persian Gulf to Somalia, a distance of more than 1500 miles

FF - The acronym for a ship smaller than a destroyer. In earlier days, many had been called destroyer escorts (DE's)

Geedunk - a Navy term for snacks and fast food

Gopher - Someone who is assigned menial but important tasks, like going to get a piece of equipment. "Gopher" for "Go For"

Gundecking - fake or falsify especially by writing up (as a series of official reports) as if meeting requirements but actually without having carried out the required procedures. (Merriam-Webster) Also used when referring to skipping important parts of a task such as not preparing a surface properly before painting

Gunner - a short name for a warrant officer who had been promoted from his enlisted status as a gun expert. Usually a "gunner" had been a "gunner's mate."

Gunnersmate - a Navy enlisted rating for personnel specializing in ordnance

Head - a bathroom on a ship

Helo - Helicopter

Hi-Line - a means for transferring personnel between Navy ships at sea

HMC - Corpsman Chief Petty Officer

"I" Division - "I" was for indoctrination. When new personnel reported aboard, they spent a week or less being indoctrinated in the way the ship operated and what was expected of them as part of the ship's company

LCDR - Lieutenant Commander

LDO - Limited Duty Officer

LHA - General-Purpose Amphibious Assault Ship, also known as Landing Ship, Helicopter, Assault

Line - the Navy term for what landlubbers call rope

LT - Lieutenant

LTJG - Lieutenant, Junior Grade

LLB - Attorney's degree

LPH - Landing Platform, Helicopter

LST - Landing Ship, Tank

MARS - Military Auxiliary Radio System, a system to communicate to family and friends on Navy ships

Mediterranean Moor - a means of mooring to a pier with the fantail tied to the pier and the bow held steady by two crossing anchors

MO - Medical Officer

MSC - Military Sealift Command

MSTS - Military Sea Transport Service (the forerunner to MSC)

NAF - Naval Air Facility

NESEP - Navy Enlisted Scientific Education Program

NRMC - Naval Regional Medical Center

OCS - Officer Candidate School

OOD - Officer of the Deck - the officer in charge of the ship representing the commanding officer

OPS - Operations Department; also operations department head

PACE – Program for Afloat College Education: professors would ride ships on deployment and conduct college courses.

PCO - Prospective Commanding Officer

PXO - Prospective Executive Officer

Orange Force - In U.S. military exercises, the units taking on the role of the opposition forces are labeled the "Orange Force"

PBFT - Planning Board for Training

PFT - Physical Fitness Test

PO - Petty Officer

POL - Petroleum, Oil, and Lubricants: a terminology used for piers where ships could refuel

Port and Starboard - a reference to watch standing sections and duty sections where one half of the involved unit is on for six hours and relieved for six hours by the other half of the unit

Punt - A small boat often used for painting a ship's hull near the water line

RADM - Rear Admiral

Radioing - see "Gundecking."

RAV - Restricted Availability - a period of downtime for a Navy ship to focus on scheduled maintenance and repair, most often with a destroyer tender

R&R - Rest and Relaxation: an area set aside for military personnel to get away from battle fronts and take a break, often with their spouses joining them

RN - Royal Navy

SEPCOR - Separate correspondence

SIMA - Ship Intermediate Maintenance Activity

SINKEX - An exercise where a decommissioned Navy ship is used as a target and sunk by missiles, torpedoes, or gunfire

SRF - Ship Repair Facility

SN -Seaman

SOPA - Senior Officer Present Afloat; the senior Navy Officer on ships within an operating area or port who is the most senior in rank and therefore in command of all of the ships

SORM - Standard Organization and Regulations Manual

SSN- Nuclear submarine

SURFLANT - Surface Forces, Atlantic

SWO - Surface Warfare Officer

TAD - Temporary Additional Duty

TAO - Tactical Action Officer

Note: For the below, the "T-" designates the ships are USNS ships operated by merchant marines, not regular Navy officers and enlisted personnel

T-ATF - Fleet Tugboat: an ocean going tugboat that had been a Navy ship but transferred to the Military Sealift Command and manned by merchant marines

T-AO - Fleet Oiler (Military Sealift Command ships manned by merchant marines)

T-AP - Transport, Auxiliary, Personnel (Military Sealift Command ships manned by merchant marines)

TAR - Training and Administration of Reserves

T-AKR - Fast Logistics Ship, a Military Sealift Command ship manned by the Merchant Marine to provide equipment and supplies to U.S. military forces

TAV - Tender Availability – Normally, a period of two weeks where a ship is limited in its operation and provided maintenance and repair support from a tender.

UNREP - Underway Replenishment: This is where fuel, stores, personnel, mail, etc. are transferred by attaching fuel lines and "Hi Lines" between two ships

US - United States

USNS - United States Naval Ship: the designation for ships controlled by the Military Sealift Command, supporting the Navy, e.g. oilers, cargo ships, fleet tugs and manned by the Merchant Marine

USS - the abbreviation for United States Ship: used before the names of ships in the U.S. Navy

VERTREP - Vertical Replenishment; this is similar to "UNREPS" but the transfers (except for fuel) are accomplished by helicopters to the ship

Wardroom Admin - a hotel room or suite rented for a liberty stop for use by the wardrom officers for taking a break from liberty, or to just get away from the ship

XO - Executive Officer

YNC - Yeoman Chief Petty Officer

Acknowledgements

I have been working on and off on this book for almost 40 years. There are a lot of folks who have helped me complete this book in those years. Undoubtedly, I will omit someone with no intention to slight anyone who has helped me. Please forgive me if I have done so.

The people who have supported me provided not only information about *Yosemite's* 1983-84 deployment but gave me access to supporting information and motivated me to keep working toward completion.

Captain Francis J. Boyle, USN, retired, repeatedly either corrected or corroborated when and how events occurred. He also offered encouragement from start to finish. Ms Noreen Leahy, Ms Emily Baker Black, Ms Sharon Carrasco Friendly, Captain Linda Schlesinger, USNR, retired, and Doctor Frank Kerrigan are other officers from the deployment who not only provided information on where, when, and how certain events occurred, but added new information of which I was unaware. It was a pleasure to lunch several times with Linda, who also provided some of the photos included here. These officers sent me a number of correspondence and recollections that have been included.

Mr. Chris Hyde provided me insights from the crew's perspective and introduced me to a Facebook group, "USS Yosemite A.D-19 I.O. Cruise 83-84." This group provided me valuable information as well as motivation to reach the goal line of completion. This led to frequent communication with Darryl Gunter, who not only provided information I did not previously have but also supplied photos to include in the book.

The Facebook group mentioned above and another group, "*USS Yosemite (AD 19)*" have encouraged me to keep working toward completion.

One of the most challenging aspects of my research was microfiche of the ship's logs during the deployment. I attempted many efforts to obtain readable copies. The Coronado Library gave me access to those files. Mr.

Shaun Briley, Library Director, and Mr. Glenn Risolo, Principal Librarian, and the library staff went beyond the norm to give me access to a state-of-the-art microfiche reader and scanner. The Coronado Library operates the way all libraries should run.

Andrew Maraniss and his father, David Maraniss, both incredible authors, have been supportive and were extremely helpful when I encountered an ethical problem in my narrative. Andrew has been one of my biggest supporters.

Ms Jennifer McCord has been fantastic as my editor. She has been patient in guiding me through numerous versions, correcting my mistakes, making things clearer and more readable. She has also been a partner in this enterprise by pointing me toward the most effective way to publish this book and connect me to the right people to make it happen.

My brother Joe Jewell and his wife Carla Neggers are invaluable in my writing and my life. Joe has been an inspiration for all my writing. Carla, a gifted and successful novelist, has guided me through this entire process with words of wisdom and introduced me to Jennifer McCord, my editor.

Walker Hicks, who created my website and has maintained it over more than a decade, has been my main man in multi-media graphics. He is the photographer of my current headshot and been a source of knowledge and support.

Eleanor, Alan, and Maren Hicks (no relation to Walker) put me on point. After years of my procrastination and working on other projects, Eleanor told her father I should write this book. She, Alan, and Maren have been my biggest supporters in my writing efforts. They are also the best friends I could possibly have.

My daughters, Ms. Blythe Jewell and Ms Sarah Jewell both provided editing support. Blythe, who is an author and superb editor, gave me some suggestions that were invaluable in making my memoir as good as it could be.

Finally, there is this woman whom I cannot praise enough. Ms Maureen Boggs Jewell is my wife. Her marrying me made my assignment as *Yosemite's* Executive Officer as good as it gets. Maureen was a line editor for the manuscript. She caught and corrected many errors.

I might have cobbled some version of this without whom I acknowledge here, but it would not have happened had it not been for Maureen.

Finally, I thank Samuel James Jewell Gander. Everything I write now is, in some manner, for Sam, my grandson (I should note his middle two names are in honor of my father, not me).

About the Author

Jim Jewell served for twenty-two years in the Navy. In the Navy, he served on ten ships. In his two shore tours, he was a NROTC Instructor at Texas A&M and the Director of Leadership and Management Training for the West Coast and Pacific Rim, as well as lead facilitator for the Command Excellence Seminar for Senior Officers.

He also has been a sportswriter and editor, a news correspondent, a weekly newspaper columnist, Director of Safety, Business Development Manager, organizational development consultant, disk jockey, Mister Mom, and grave digger.

He currently writes posts on his own website, *www.jimjewell.com* and previously published a book of poetry, *A Pocket of Resistance: Selected Poems*.

He is married and lives in California. He has two daughters and a grandson.

www.ingramcontent.com/pod-product-compliance
Lightning Source LLC
Chambersburg PA
CBHW060520160726
47991CB00001B/118